Lisa Heinzerling

Priceless

On Knowing the Price of Everything and the Value of Nothing

FRANK ACKERMAN AND LISA HEINZERLING

THE NEW PRESS

NEW YORK
LONDON

Published in the United States by The New Press, New York, 2004
Distributed by W. W. Norton & Company, Inc., New York

LIBRARY OF CONGRESS CATALOGING-IN-PUBLICATION DATA

Ackerman, Frank.
Priceless : on knowing the price of everything and the value of nothing /
Frank Ackerman and Lisa Heinzerling.
p.   cm.
Includes bibliographical references and index.
ISBN 1-56584-850-0
1. Environmental economics.   2. Product safety.   3. Business ethics.
4. Consumer protection.   5. Commercial policy.   6. United States—
Economic policy.   I. Heinzerling, Lisa.   II. Title.
HC79.E5A27   2004
330—dc22   2003061446

The New Press was established in 1990 as a not-for-profit alternative to the large,
commercial publishing houses currently dominating the book publishing industry.
The New Press operates in the public interest rather than for private gain, and is
committed to publishing, in innovative ways, works of educational, cultural, and
community value that are often deemed insufficiently profitable.

The New Press, 38 Greene Street, 4th floor, New York, NY 10013
www.thenewpress.com

In the United Kingdom: 6 Salem Road, London W2 4BU

Composition by dix!

Printed in the United States of America

2   4   6   8   10   9   7   5   3   1

To the people who matter the most
in our private and public lives:
Robin and Janet, Mariah and Lucas,
Becky, Bob, and everyone fighting for health
and environmental protection in hard times

Contents

Priceless

1

Prices Without Values

Right up to the day they died, Russian immigrants Mariya Diment and Liya Murkes loved to take long walks together along the oceanfront near the senior residence where they lived in Santa Monica. One summer day in the year 2000, Cheryl Chadwick, reportedly talking on a cell phone while driving her Mercedes-Benz, plowed into Diment and Murkes while they were strolling, killing them both.

What happened to Mariya Diment and Liya Murkes is not unusual, and almost certainly will become less so; as many as 1,000 people a year now die in car accidents caused by what some are calling "phoneslaughter." Researchers have found that people who are talking on cellular phones while driving are four times more likely to get into car accidents than people who are not—about the same as the increased risk from driving after several drinks (around the legal threshold for drunk driving in most states).[1] Ten years ago, only 10 million people worldwide had ever even used a cell phone; by now, cell phone users number a billion and counting.[2] The vast majority of Americans with cell phones talk on them while driving.[3]

Most states, and many cities and towns, are deciding

whether to do something to prevent these accidents. Some places have banned cell phone use while driving. Others have used laws already on the books—even homicide laws—to try to get at the problem.

Some of the country's most influential economists, how-ever—based on research conducted with the help of generous funding from wireless providers—have concluded these re-strictions are a bad idea.[4] Why? Because the people who are talking while driving are willing to pay a lot to talk on the phone—more than many people who face deadly risks are willing to pay to avoid the risk of being killed. What these re-searchers have done is compare the price of phone calls made while driving with the "price" of deadly risks. Since risk is not, like cell phones and calling plans, directly bought and sold in the marketplace, economists have tried to find places where it is sold *indirectly*. They have focused mainly on risky workplaces, where extra wages are, in theory, required to con-vince workers to accept increased risks of death. In compar-ing levels of wages and risk, economists have estimated that groups of workers doing dangerous jobs are paid, on average, a total of about $5–6 million more, per work-related death. By comparing the price of cell phone use with this "price" of risky work, economists have concluded that banning cell phone use in cars makes no economic sense.

The technique of translating lives into dollars is complex, but the bottom line of the cell phone studies is simple to state: the Cheryl Chadwicks of the world can go on talking into their cell phones while driving their Mercedes-Benzes, even though it means that quite a few of the Mariya Diments and Liya Murkeses of the world end up in the morgue. All based, amazingly enough, on the price of someone else's phone call.

. . .

It was "a colorless liquid of sweetish odor, very poisonous if absorbed through the skin, resulting in lead poisoning almost immediately." In 1922, Pierre du Pont, the head of General Motors (GM), used these words in a letter to his brother Irenee, the head of Du Pont Chemical, describing the leaded gasoline a GM scientist had just developed to prevent auto engine "knocking." For the next fifty years, the makers of leaded gasoline would deny this basic fact about lead: it is a poison. When faced with the warnings of public health authorities about the potentially dire effects of millions of automobiles spewing lead into the atmosphere, the leaded gas industry had a simple response: prove it.[5]

The trouble was, it was hard to prove that the day-to-day, low-level exposures to lead caused by leaded gasoline hurt people. The kinds of health effects we now know come from leaded gasoline—reduced learning capacity, neurological disorders, and high blood pressure—are so common that it is difficult to say which portion of these effects is due to lead and which to other causes. Thus, although the U.S. government suspected the risks of adding lead to gasoline from the very beginning, it would not seriously try to regulate leaded gasoline until lead had been pouring from almost every automobile in the country for half a century.

With the passage of the federal Clean Air Act in 1970, the era of leaded gas finally began to draw to a close. The Act directed the federal Environmental Protection Agency (EPA) to set pollution limits based on public health. Although EPA could not put exact numbers on the health effects caused by lead, it thought the existing scientific evidence was strong enough to justify strict limits on lead in gas. Of particular concern to the agency were the terrible effects lead could have on the cognitive and neurological development of children.

After a hard-fought court battle in which the leaded gasoline industry argued that EPA should not be allowed to regulate unless it could prove leaded gasoline had actually harmed identifiable people in the past, EPA's new restrictions on leaded gasoline were upheld. The court's ultimate decision in the case is considered a landmark in U.S. environmental law because it established that EPA could act in a precautionary fashion rather than wait for scientific certainty about the harmfulness of a substance before acting. EPA set its initial standards for lead based on the goal of protecting virtually all children from lead exposures that would harm their health and cognitive development.

In the 1980s, EPA decided to phase out lead in gasoline entirely. In coming to this decision, however, the agency not only looked at the public health effects of leaded gasoline; it also tried to determine how much these health improvements were worth in dollars. In justifying additional policies to reduce lead poisoning of children, EPA returned to the issue several times in the 1990s. The agency's analyses have considered the costs of medical care for lead poisoning, the costs of remedial education for children whose cognitive development had been impaired by lead, and the children's expected loss of future income due to their lowered IQs. In deceptively simple terms, EPA has asked how much an IQ point is worth to an individual. Published estimates have ranged as high as $8,346.[6]

Now, analysts—including economist Randall Lutter, of the American Enterprise Institute—are busily working to show that EPA got it wrong when it looked at the economics of banning leaded gasoline almost two decades ago.[7] Rather than assessing the "worth" of children's health by considering lost income or the costs of remedial education, Lutter thinks EPA should have relied on what parents spent pursuing one particular treatment known as chelation therapy—a standard treatment for very high levels of lead poisoning, but less common and less clearly effective for chronic, low-level exposures.[8] Most of the costs associated with this treatment reflect the time parents spent taking their children to the doctor— most often, in fact, the costs consist of the value that economists have assigned to the time of mothers who stay home with their children. Since the value of this time, and the cost of the treatment, are not very high, these analysts say EPA has overvalued the health of the children affected by exposures to lead and, as a consequence, has overreacted to the exposures themselves. Using the chelation yardstick, an IQ point is worth as little as $1,100—a fraction of the previous value. On this view, the appropriate level of spending on lead removal would be only a fraction of the amount that EPA endorses.

Almost one-third of the land in the United States is owned by the federal government. The national forest system—one part of the public lands—was created at the turn of the twentieth century with a view toward using forest resources to achieve their greatest benefit through time—a view promoted by the first head of the Forest Service, Gifford Pinchot, and one that has contemporary resonance in the concept of "sustainable development." Over time, however, the national forests came to be used more in the service of timber companies and related interests, for short-term gain, than in the service of broader interests, for long-term stability. Throughout much of the twentieth century, the national forest system was characterized, and ravaged, by policies such as below-cost timber sales, in which the national forests were auctioned off to private interests for less than the government spent preparing the forests for sale.

At the turn of the twenty-first century, the U.S. Forest Service proposed taking the remaining roadless areas of the national forests—among the most pristine and, by definition, least traveled, places in the country—and setting them aside, off-limits to roads and the timber interests that would use the roads to take the trees. Hundreds of thousands of citizens applauded the idea, and wrote to the Forest Service expressing their enthusiasm. It would be one of the largest single decisions preserving wilderness—affecting some 60 million acres in all—in the history of the United States, perhaps in the history of the world. The "roadless area" policy would, the Forest Service announced, protect not only the trees themselves but the watersheds, flora, and fauna dependent on them—not to mention the burgeoning ecotourism industry.

Timber interests immediately challenged the new policy in court. When, at about the same time, the Bush administration came into office, it did nothing to defend the policy. Usually known for its aggressive and effective defense of government initiatives and prerogatives, the Justice Department in this case simply sat on its hands and let the environmental groups answer the lawsuit alone. Perhaps even more remarkable, however, was the government's official tallying of the costs and benefits of this historic policy.

In a 2002 report to Congress, the Office of Management and Budget (OMB) announced that the new forest initiative would cost about $184 million and produce benefits of only $219,000 a year.[9] This lopsidedly negative result made forest protection look, in narrow economic terms, like one of the least defensible regulatory ideas of the previous year. So little, indeed, did OMB think of the forest initiative that the office put the policy on its infamous "hit list" of regulatory policies to be reconsidered by the agencies that had dreamed them up.[10]

How did a rule protecting 60 million acres of publicly owned lands, containing fragile and precious sources of water, wildlife, and plant species, come to look so bad in economic terms? The answer is simple: just ignore most of the good things one wants to protect forests *for*—both the good things that could comfortably be stated in dollar terms (such as the economic value of a forest for tourism) and the good things that money cannot buy (such as the knowledge that pristine forests are being protected in perpetuity). What did the tiny annual benefit of $219,000 reflect in this case? The savings from not building roads. Every park and forest that we protect "saves money" in this sense: imagine the cost of the asphalt that would have been required to pave the entire area. But is the avoided cost of exploiting nature—as OMB assumed— the only benefit of protecting it?

At the start of the twenty-first century, the clock is starting to run backward as laws and regulations protecting health, safety, and the natural environment—some of the proudest accomplishments of the past thirty years—are now under attack.

The attackers do not explicitly advocate pollution, illness, and natural degradation; instead, they call for more "economic analysis." And the stories of "phoneslaughter," lead poisoning, and forest despoliation show where their kind of analysis all too often leads.

The new trend toward economic critique of health and environmental protection has caught on in every branch of the federal government—within the White House, in Congress, and even in the courts. Environmental advocates, decision makers, and citizens concerned about the environment often find themselves on the defensive, without an effective response to the arcane arguments and imposing data offered to show why, when it comes to protective regulation, less is better.

Our opening examples of this kind of economics in practice are not isolated or unusual; in fact, they are just the tip of the iceberg. Rules limiting arsenic in drinking water, air emissions from factories and power plants, snowmobiles in national parks, new development in pristine areas, and pollution in our rivers, lakes, and streams, all have been or may be weakened or even eliminated based on the same kind of counterintuitive economics.

The basic problem with narrow economic analysis of health and environmental protection is that human life, health, and nature cannot be described meaningfully in monetary terms; they are priceless. When the question is whether to allow one person to hurt another, or to destroy a natural resource; when a life or a landscape cannot be replaced; when harms stretch out over decades or even generations; when outcomes are uncertain; when risks are shared or resources are used in common; when the people "buying" harms have no relationship with the people actually harmed—then we are in the realm of the priceless, where market values tell us little about the social values at stake.

There are hard questions to be answered about protection of human health and the environment, and there are many useful insights about these questions from the field of economics. But there is no reason to think that the right answers will emerge from the strange process of assigning dollar values to human life, human health, and nature itself, and then crunching the numbers. Indeed, in pursuing this approach, formal cost-benefit analysis often hurts more than it helps: it muddies rather than clarifies fundamental clashes about values. By proceeding as if its assumptions are scientific and by speaking a language all its own, economic analysis too easily conceals the basic human questions that lie at its heart and excludes the voices of people untrained in the field. Again and again, economic theory gives us opaque and technical reasons to do the obviously wrong thing. Obscuring the fundamental issues with talk of wage premiums and protest votes (topics that we'll meet in later chapters), cost-benefit analysis promotes a deregulatory agenda under the cover of scientific objectivity.

To say that life, health, and nature are priceless is not to say that we should spend an infinite amount of money to protect them. Rather, it is to say that translating life, health, and nature into dollars is not a fruitful way of deciding how much protection to give to them. A different way of thinking and deciding about them is required.

The most common justification for the new mode of economic screening of regulations is that even a rich society can't afford to do everything. There are tradeoffs between different policy options, the argument goes, so it is important to pick the most cost-effective ones. Our response is twofold. First, resources are of course ultimately limited, but there is no evidence that we have approached the limits of what is possible (or desirable) in health and environmental protection. For instance, the fuel efficiency of automobiles is ultimately limited by physical laws, and cannot keep improving forever. But we are so far from the ultimate constraint that it is irrelevant to the practical challenge of improving fuel efficiency today.

Also, widely quoted evidence of absurdly expensive regulations is, as we explain in Chapter 3, mistaken on numerous grounds, and does not deserve to be taken seriously. In fact, only a minority of the costs of regulation show up in the federal budget. For federal expenditures, the limiting factor is not our society's limited resources in any absolute sense, but rather the mania for tax cut after tax cut, especially for those at the top who are most able to pay. However, most of the costs of regulation are borne not by the government but by the regulated industries themselves. There is no evidence that these corporate burdens are, or are about to be, unaffordable. Despite frequent rhetorical claims to the contrary, virtually no job losses can be traced to environmental regulations.[11] On average, 999 out of every 1,000 major layoffs are *not* due to environmental policies.[12]

The second part of our response is that, even if some kind of screening of regulations is needed, the current methods are incoherent, as we will explain in the following chapters. Cost-benefit analysis of health and environmental protection rests on simplistic, implausible hypotheses about the prices that would prevail if priceless values were to show up next to the lettuce on the supermarket shelf. A different method of analysis and comparison is needed to separate good policy proposals from bad ones, a method that does not pretend that a mathematical formula can solve our problems for us.

In this book, we offer an attitude rather than an algorithm. We reject the atomistic analysis offered by contemporary economists, in which a problem is severed into its component parts, examined by experts, and reconstructed in a way that leaves most of the important parts on the cutting room floor. In its place, we advocate a more holistic analysis, one that replaces the reductive approach of cost-benefit analysis with a broader and more integrative perspective. We also urge precaution in the face of scientific uncertainty and fairness in the treatment of the current and future generations. Above all, perhaps, we aim to restore a sense of moral urgency to the protection of life, health, and the environment—the kind of moral urgency today reserved mostly for questions concerning the military.

The kind of economic thinking featured in our opening anecdotes is ascendant in public-policy circles today. If the advocates of free market economic theory get their way, the simplistic use of economics will become even more prominent; in fact, it will become *the* way of making critical policy decisions.

How have we come to this point?

The answer is a blend of political philosophy and economic research. Throughout this book we will criticize the role of economic analysis and theory as it has been applied to health and environmental policy. Cloaked in the language of scientific objectivity, economic arguments have repeatedly played a partisan role. It is time to look underneath the cloak, beginning with the theories behind the new approach to public policy. When free market economists dream of a better world, what does it look like? Chapter 2 explores those dreams and their frequent collisions with reality.

2

Myths and Markets

We offer a blueprint for auctioning off all public lands over 20 to 40 years. . . . The owner of the surface rights to the Grand Canyon, whether it was the Nature Conservancy or Atlantic Richfield, would have an incentive to seek donations or charge visitor fees, or both, to manage the scenic resources of the Grand Canyon. . . . Slant drilling from outside the park might be negotiated, where feasible, and timber cutting might be permitted.

—Terry Anderson, et al.[1]

As George W. Bush was pursuing the Republican nomination for the 2000 presidential election, Bush adviser Terry Anderson was offering a modest proposal to sell off all 628 million acres of public land nationwide. Unique, famous parks and natural wonders, up to and including the Grand Canyon, were included. As a bonus, surface and subsurface rights could be sold separately for even greater market value. This unprecedented disposal of public assets was said to be necessary because everyone "knows" that the federal government does a terrible job taking care of public lands. "Both environmental quality and economic efficiency would be enhanced by private rather than public ownership."[2]

Although it sounds extreme, Anderson's proposal to sell

the national parks rests on some simple ideas about economics that are gaining increasingly wide acceptance today: in the crudest terms, it is claimed that the government always does things wrong, while the private market reliably does things right; in seemingly more sophisticated terms, it is suggested that economic efficiency is the best measure of the wisdom of all public policy. The logical result of these ideas is a call for sweeping changes in existing institutions. If markets and private businesses inevitably do a better job than Washington bureaucrats, why not sell the Grand Canyon to an oil company?

This new conventional wisdom about government, markets, and efficiency starts with a simple but unrealistic view about how markets work, a view shared by conservative ideologues and "objective policy analysts" alike. After describing this widely held but misguided perspective, we'll turn first to those who have taken the simplest ideas about markets to the strangest extremes; then to two popular policies, privatization and deregulation, that rest on naive faith in markets; and finally to the most sophisticated and reasonable-sounding theories about efficiency—which turn out to be just as crazy as any of the others.

Dreams of Optimality

The simple economic ideas that figure so prominently in today's public policy discussions flow from an abstract academic vision of the marketplace—a vision that is scarcely recognizable as a portrait of a modern market economy. Surprisingly, political debates seem to turn on a chapter straight out of a college textbook—and not the liveliest one on campus, either.

For those who have avoided or forgotten the textbook, economic theory maintains that competitive markets lead to "optimal" results; that is, they are as efficient as possible. In the imaginary, idealized market economy, competition among buyers ensures that every resource ends up in its highest valued use; competition among employers implies that every worker finds the highest paid available job. Whatever you're looking for, you can have it your way.

Better yet, you can have it for exactly the cost of producing it in the most efficient possible manner. The price of a car necessarily includes the full cost of producing the steel, aluminum, plastics, and other materials in the car, because the automaker had to pay those costs to its suppliers. But in the ideal world, competition ensures that you are not charged any more than the bare minimum of costs for the capital, labor, and materials used in production.

This story about the benefits of competition offers an interesting insight, though hardly a universal explanation of economic life. Nor is it particularly new; it can be traced back at least to Adam Smith, who wrote more than 200 years ago. Smith originated, almost in passing, the metaphor of the market as an invisible hand, coordinating private producers to meet consumer demand. In the centuries since Smith, this image has repeatedly been adopted by conservatives who see any government policy as an unnecessary and inefficient interference with the market. Launched again with great fanfare in the latter part of the twentieth century as a new political insight, it may be the oldest new idea in public life.

Markets that perfectly fit the textbook description would indeed be efficient, for the reasons that economists have explained. But that perfection is impossible to achieve; real markets do not even come close. Take away any one or more of the standard assumptions, and the efficiency of the unregulated market vanishes. When markets fall short of perfection, as inevitably happens, economic theory cannot prove that competition is always efficient, or that government intervention will always make things worse.

Monopoly power, for example, interferes with the efficiency of markets; Microsoft's dominance in the market for operating systems not only keeps the price of Windows high, but has also allowed the company to push aside competition in other areas, such as the market for Web browsers. Lack of information also undermines efficiency; recent immigrants with limited knowledge of English may not be able to find the highest paid jobs for which they are qualified. No one, in fact, could ever possess the total knowledge of the market that is assumed in traditional economic theory. In 2001, the Nobel Prize in economics was awarded to three economists (of whom Joseph Stiglitz is the best known) for their analyses of the problems of limited information. Their conclusions are quite at odds with the standard competitive model. The catalog of flaws in the idealized picture of competitive markets goes on and on; to name another example, the theory presumes that we all fit the unrealistic and unattractive portrait of *homo economicus,* who is narrowly concerned with his own individual material well-being and nothing else.

Health and environmental problems present yet another form of market failure. Even idealized markets can be efficient only if everything of value has a price. The price of a new car

includes the cost of the steel used in the car, because the automaker had to buy it from a steel company. Does the price of
a car also include the cost of protecting workers' health in the
auto plant where it was made, and the cost of preventing pollution from the iron mine that supplied the raw material for
the car? Only if the auto company or steel company is forced
to pay those costs by union contracts or government regulations. It is not that companies want to pollute; no one actually
likes pollution, or wants to create more of it. But avoiding
pollution can be troublesome and expensive, and many people and firms won't go to this trouble and expense unless they
are required to do so.

It is not personal desires for pollution, but rather imper-
sonal market forces and opportunities, that create threats to
health and nature. A competitive market economy allows and
encourages all manner of individual initiatives. One way to
succeed in the market is to find a profitable activity that no
one else is engaged in. Since countless people and businesses
are continually searching for market opportunities, *anything
profitable that is not prohibited by law is likely to occur.* When laws
allowed slavery, the United States had an active market in
human beings. In countries that permit child labor, children
make toys for other children. And when laws allow damage to
human health and the natural environment, the result is dirty
air and foul water. Cleaner, safer production processes are, unfortunately, often more expensive than the quick and dirty alternatives.

The problem goes even deeper. The efficiency of the market results, in theory, from the efforts of firms competing to
sell exactly the goods and services that consumers are willing
to pay for. It is possible to talk about the efficient balance be-

tween cars and clothing; consumer spending on these goods provides guidance about how much of each to produce. But what would be the efficient balance between producing cars and preventing cancer? Or between making clothing and mitigating climate change? For the market to answer these questions, consumers would have to buy, and producers would have to sell, prevention of cancer and mitigation of climate change. The market, in other words, would need prices for preventing the loss of life due to cancer and for protecting the environment for future generations.

As we will show throughout this book, the market has no answer, *because there are no such prices.* Life and nature are priceless. This does not mean that we can or should spend limitless amounts on protecting human lives and the environment, but it does mean that there is no natural or useful way to measure these values in dollars; we need a better way of thinking and deciding about them. There are resource constraints and painful choices in health and environmental policy, but the market cannot make our choices for us.

Fringes of the Free Market

The flaws and failures of the market are invisible, however, in the eyes of the true believers. For some, turning things over to the private sector is not a remedy for a specific problem but a way of life—a philosophy that, in the environmental setting, has come to be called "free market environmentalism."

Terry Anderson has used his position as an adviser to the Bush administration to bring this kind of thinking to the fore. Once upon a time his idea of selling off all federal lands would have been considered lunacy and qualified him for instant dismissal, as someone impossibly far out on the fringes of national debate. But leading up to the 2000 presidential election, candidate George W. Bush met with Anderson and his friends to discuss "free market environmentalism." When he became president, Bush chose two of Anderson's allies to run the Department of the Interior: Gale Norton, who became Secretary of the Interior, and Lynn Scarlett, one of Norton's top deputies, both met with candidate Bush, and Anderson lobbied vigorously and successfully for the Bush administration to appoint Norton.[3]

In Anderson's free market world, you can have as much environmental protection as you are willing to pay for. If you pay enough to the people who own nature, they will agree to stop destroying it. Does this raise troubling questions about the distribution of income and ownership of natural resources? Not a problem, as seen by free market environmentalists: members of environmental groups often have high incomes, so they could pay for a lot of environmental protection if they wanted to.[4]

Despite Anderson's repeated statements that he is developing new, more effective ways to protect the environment, he returns again and again to questionable factoids and rationalizations for what others might call rapacious business behavior. For Anderson and his co-author, Donald Leal, the clear-cutting of forests a hundred years ago—including illegal logging on public lands—made good economic sense, even in cases where the land has not recovered since then.[5] They cast recycling as a fraud that fills warehouses with untold tons of unwanted newspapers—a notion that will come as a surprise to the many recycled-paper mills around the country.[6] And climate change, for Anderson and Leal, is still a controversial new hypothesis, despite the consensus of the world's leading scientists.[7] Free market environmentalism thus blends devout faith in the free market with deep skepticism about science— at least any science that finds a connection between environmental harm and economic activity. As we will see in Chapter 5, this kind of skepticism exists not just on the fringes of the free market, but at the core of current critiques of health and environmental protection.

Paying the Polluters

The same kind of extreme thinking has infected the legal system, as the deregulatory fever has spread to numerous laws designed to control harms caused by private markets. In this setting, it has not been enough to argue that regulation is a bad idea; deregulatory advocates have gone further and also argued that if the government does happen to make the mistake of regulating, it ought to pay for the privilege. In an ambitious but not yet entirely successful initiative, some conservatives have concocted ominous new interpretations of an obscure constitutional provision—the so-called "takings" clause—in the name of making the case against health and environmental regulations. These pro-business advocates argue that virtually any government action that reduces the value of a piece of private property—including, say, a law designed to protect the environment—is illegitimate: it is a "taking" that must be accompanied by payment to the owner.

The idea of "takings" derives from a clause in the Fifth Amendment to the U.S. Constitution, which prohibits the government from taking private property for public use without just compensation. Originally this applied only to literal expropriation or seizure of property. Then, in the 1920s, the Supreme Court applied the "takings clause" more broadly, to apply to some types of restrictions on the use of property. Ruling in favor of a coal company, the Court overturned a Pennsylvania law that banned coal mining practices that caused buildings to cave in (a danger that arose because coal companies often owned subsurface mining rights without owning the real estate on the surface). The Court held that owners of subsurface rights were allowed, literally, to undermine surface dwellings; Pennsylvania's law prohibiting such mining practices was declared an unconstitutional "taking" of company property.

Despite this precedent, takings played little role in our legal framework until the 1980s. At that point, conservative legal scholars and private lawyers launched a campaign to breathe new life into takings doctrine. They argued that many advances in environmental protection represented a "taking" of property rights, again based on limitations on the use of private property rather than actual seizure by the government.

In one important case, decided by the Supreme Court in 1992, a developer named David Lucas successfully sued South Carolina for placing limits on beachfront building—limits that effectively meant he could not build a house on either of two lots he had bought for development purposes. In theory, of course, any government body may adopt legislation without fear of invalidation under the takings clause—as long as it is willing to pay. Thus, South Carolina may pass coastal development laws so long as it pays developers of high-end real estate, like Mr. Lucas, for their beachfront lots. Most governments, especially the local governments that engage in many of the land-use decisions subject to the takings clause, do not have this kind of cash.

New theories of the takings clause, aimed at making environmental protection and other kinds of regulation prohibitively expensive, have struck terror in government agencies. But to date, the regulatory critics' bark has been worse than their bite; actual payouts to property owners have been rare—in part because the courts have surrounded the takings clause with all sorts of procedural hurdles, making it quite difficult to present a successful claim under this provision.

This all may change. A strong form of the takings principle, without the same procedural hurdles, was written into the North American Free Trade Agreement (NAFTA), adopted in 1994 by the United States, Canada, and Mexico. Similar language is being proposed for inclusion in many future trade agreements. NAFTA contains a sleeper provision, Chapter 11, permitting one country's companies to sue for compensation when another country's government engages in conduct that is "tantamount to expropriation." This provision threatens to undo—by making it grossly expensive—any environmental regulation that reduces the value of foreign investments in Canada, Mexico, and the United States.

In one early case, a small California-based company called Metalclad bought a landfill in the state of San Luis Potosí in Mexico and planned to turn it into a hazardous-waste disposal site. The company obtained permits from the national and state governments, but the municipal government at the site vetoed the project on the basis of the health and environmental damages that it was likely to cause. Although Metalclad had invested no more than $4 million in the project, it won a judgment of some $16 million against Mexico's national government for the loss of future income it could have earned from its planned waste-disposal business, plus interest.

Some informal accounts suggest that U.S. business interests insisted on NAFTA's Chapter 11 to protect their investments in Mexico from imagined threats of expropriation. However, the treaty applies evenhandedly to all three NAFTA countries; both Canada and the U.S. have also faced expensive Chapter 11 claims. In another case, a Canadian company is seeking almost $1 billion in damages from the U.S. on account of a California law that prohibited the use of a chemical called methyl tertiary butyl ether (MTBE) in fuel. MTBE is used to boost the oxygen content of gasoline in order to reduce smog from cars, and was promoted by 1990 amendments to the federal Clean Air Act that were designed to cut smog levels nationwide. Unfortunately, MTBE also rapidly and thoroughly contaminates water supplies; a relatively short time after MTBE use increased in California, many of California's water supplies were found to be contaminated with MTBE. California banned MTBE in fuel, and the United States was rewarded with a NAFTA suit under Chapter 11.

The takings clause of the U.S. Constitution and Chapter 11 of NAFTA threaten to turn one of the basic principles of modern environmentalism—"make the polluter pay"—on its head. In one jurisdiction after another, governments are being forced to ask whether they can afford to pay polluters and developers to refrain from conduct that harms commonly held resources. Too often, the answer will be "no."

The vision behind the "takings" movement, of self-regulated property and markets prospering without government, is an impossible fantasy. In reality, there is no escape from government intervention. Market activity fundamentally depends on laws and regulations, without which it would immediately fail. In Russia, the collapse of the Soviet Union was followed by the abrupt introduction of markets and capitalist enterprises, at first with little institutional and legal support. In the early years of post-Communist Russia, bankers often hired gangsters to kill their business rivals—a perfectly logical way to increase a bank's market share, if increasing market share is all that matters. A survivable, let alone sustainable, market economy requires rules that guide competition in acceptable directions—for instance, a legal system that allows banks to compete by offering customers better interest rates, or free toasters for new accounts, but not by killing other bankers. The market does not write its own ground rules; it cannot function properly unless society creates and enforces the rules within which competition is allowed. The extent and shape of those rules is naturally a subject of ongoing debate.

Pushing for Privatization

> The market is rational; the government's dumb.
> —Former House Majority Leader Dick Armey[8]

The simplest ideas about the market have spread far beyond the fringes of debate. It is not only the "free market environmentalists" and takings enthusiasts, but also mainstream politicians of both parties who rely on the abstract vision of the marketplace, with its virtues remembered and its flaws forgotten. But the underlying theory is rarely discussed in any detail. Rather, it has been so widely accepted that it has passed into the conventional wisdom of American politics, reduced to ideas, like Dick Armey's aphorism, that are simple enough to fit on bumper stickers. Two important policy initiatives, privatization and deregulation, flow directly from the simple idea that the market always knows best.

If government is the problem, then the solution must be to privatize its functions whenever possible. Instead of leaving jobs in the hands of well-paid public employees protected by civil service, many government functions can be turned over to the private sector. Private firms will compete to win government contracts; if a firm charges more than its competitors, it will be underbid when the contract comes up for renewal. If privatization works as planned, the efficiency of the competitive market will sweep out the dusty corridors of government bureaucracy.

In a thoughtful review of the subject, Columbia University economist Elliot Sclar points out a number of obstacles to achieving the hoped-for efficiency gains when government services are privatized.[9] Some of the favorite areas for outsourcing and privatization are standardized blue-collar jobs such as janitorial services and garbage collection, where costs are easy to measure and compare. Here, the price of services depends predominantly on labor costs; privatization saves money primarily by driving down wages. This can end up being less of a bargain than it appears at first glance.

The United States has gone further in the direction of privatization of blue-collar services than most other high-income countries. In Europe, for example, airport security is provided by government employees who are paid a living wage, receive considerable training, and typically stay on the job long enough to develop real skills. In the U.S. before the

September 11 disaster, airports were guarded by private security firms that competed to hold down costs. In order to keep
costs low, they usually employed workers at or just above the
minimum wage, with minimal training and extremely rapid
job turnover. There is no question that this made the cost of
airport security lower in the U.S. than in Europe. That is the
point of privatization, the holy grail of the quest for efficiency. Yet, as it turns out, cost minimization is not the only
objective that matters. Sometimes it is also important to pay
enough to do the job right, every time. Experience with airport security has tragically shown that, in a crunch, better
results may be achieved by European-style public employment at wages high enough to retain skilled workers than by
American-style privatization and high-turnover, minimum-
wage jobs. In systems where even small errors can lead to
catastrophe, the market's fixation on short-term profit maximization may end up being no bargain at all.

Many other services performed by government agencies
are more complex, so that, as Sclar demonstrates, a meaningful comparison of public versus private costs can be elusive. In
the early 1990s, when William Weld, the pro-business gover-
nor of Massachusetts, set out to find state programs that could
be privatized, state highway maintenance was high on his list.
An initial experiment in private highway maintenance was
hastily declared a cost-saving success; later analysis by the state
auditor found the private contractor was significantly more
expensive than the public agency that had formerly done the
job. Moreover, despite detailed lists of requirements, important areas of ambiguity remained in defining the job to be
done by the contractor, with some tasks done poorly or not at
all, or still performed by public employees despite privatiza-

tion. However, on the basis of the announced success of the initial experiment, highway maintenance was privatized throughout the state.

When privatized services are as complex as statewide highway maintenance, only a few firms are big enough and specialized enough to perform them; the Massachusetts contract was won by a major highway construction firm. As a result, competitive pressure on costs is minimal. It is no surprise, therefore, that cost comparisons of public versus private services are, according to Sclar, ambiguous, with no clear advantage either way in the provision of large, complex services.

Driving for Deregulation

If the market is always rational and the government is always dumb, then private industries should also be deregulated—or so goes the second half of the conservative argument. If government regulation is needlessly burdensome and bureaucratic—raising costs by excessive intervention in the market—then the answer must be deregulation, rolling back those silly old rules and letting markets be markets. The result is sure to be lower costs for all. Just ask California's electricity consumers.

Once upon a time, in the 1980s and earlier, electricity was subject to detailed regulation by state agencies in California and elsewhere. Electric utilities were granted legal monopolies over their service territories, in exchange for rules that limited them to the rate of profit that a competitive industry would earn, and required them to prove to state regulators that they had found the lowest-cost way to deliver electricity to their customers. The results of this system varied widely, depending on the technical skill and political will of the state regulatory agencies. In general, utility regulation provided stable supplies of electricity at prices that were not exorbitant. At its best, regulation exerted strong pressure on utilities to cut costs and to make environmental improvements.[10]

On the other hand, *deregulated* markets, as California unintentionally demonstrated, can make electricity much more expensive and less dependable than it was under old-school regulation. California's deregulation of electricity provided new opportunities for fraud, deliberate manipulation of the market, and massive overcharging of consumers. Ultimately it also contributed to the supersized bankruptcy of Enron, a company that had once claimed it was promoting efficiency by brokering sales of electricity and natural gas.

The idea that regulation was inefficient and that deregulation could lower costs swept through the electricity industry in the 1990s—although in many states the traditional regulatory system survived, in whole or in part. Some states took the plunge and experimented with new ideas: California's deregulation law, for example, passed in 1996, sought to create competition by separating electricity production from distribution.[11] The same old utilities would still distribute electricity to their customers, but separate firms would produce most of the electricity. At the time, the state had excess generating capacity; the hope was that electricity producers would compete by lowering the price they charged to the utilities.

After 1996, new investors entered the state's electricity industry—but primarily to buy existing plants (and perhaps to corner the market, in anticipation of big profits from future scarcity); almost no one built any new ones. Meanwhile, the

California economy grew rapidly, as did its use of electricity. Soon the state's excess generating capacity had disappeared, but the utilities were no longer required by government regulation to build new plants to meet the growing demand, as they were back in the regulatory era. In 2000, rapid economic growth coincided with a drought that lowered the generation of hydroelectric power and an unusually hot summer that increased the use of air-conditioning. As a result, California hovered on the brink of an absolute physical scarcity of electricity, with a few months of rolling blackouts imposed as an emergency method of rationing. Several neighboring states had experienced even faster growth and similar weather problems, so they had no surplus power to spare.

Wholesale prices skyrocketed in the spring of 2000 and stayed high for about a year. Some of the new investors, such as Enron, quickly figured out how to beat the system, using the unfamiliar rules of the new wholesale electricity market and their role as middlemen—literally, power brokers—at a time of shortage to create and exploit temporary monopoly positions. (This would clearly have been illegal under the old, "inefficient" regulatory system; some aspects of industry practices may have been illegal even under deregulation.) The wholesale price of electricity, which had been below $0.04 per kilowatt-hour (kwh) in 1998, jumped to a monthly average of over $0.25 per kwh in late 2000, with exorbitantly higher rates for peak hours. Under the terms of the deregulation, the utilities had to buy power at the market price, which was suddenly much higher than the maximum price they were allowed to charge their customers, They lost an estimated $12 billion to $14 billion, and the largest utility in the state, Pacific Gas and Electric, declared bankruptcy.

The crisis was resolved only when the state government stepped in and took over buying power for the utilities, abolishing most of the market mechanisms created in 1996. That, together with improvement in the weather and worsening of the economy, led to the rapid decline of prices back to normal levels. Deregulation did not replace old utilities with more efficient new businesses: Enron, the largest of the firms that had prospered from and helped to create the California energy crisis, itself collapsed in late 2001, just months after California electricity rates returned to normal.

Enron is remembered today for its elaborate, colorful, and pervasive accounting frauds that deceived lenders, investors, and regulators throughout the 1990s, and for its meteoric descent from the nation's seventh-largest corporation into bankruptcy, destroying its workers' retirement savings along with their jobs. But Enron's original line of business, the source of its earlier, equally meteoric rise from obscurity, was its manipulation of newly deregulated energy markets in California and elsewhere. And Enron was not alone—it was only the biggest and brashest of a new breed of corporate hustlers, trading on temporary monopoly positions, public ignorance, and outright deception. Contrary to the new conventional wisdom, there were almost no real consumer savings to be gained from deregulated, Enron-style wholesale power trades, since regulated utilities already traded power whenever it was profitable. According to Richard Rosen, an electric utility analyst at the Tellus Institute, "New wholesale traders like Enron could have reduced our national average electric rates by perhaps 1 percent, if that."[12]

The cities of Los Angeles and Sacramento, along with several smaller communities, had never gotten around to privatizing their municipally owned public utilities, and hence were sheltered from the worst impacts of the state's deregulation. They continued to generate their own electricity and were spared from the disruption and losses of the California electricity crisis. Like the European airports with high-priced public security systems, the California cities with municipal utilities benefited immensely from what was once derided as inefficiency.

Electing Efficiency

A subtler, more sophisticated form of faith in the free market appeals to many people who might be appalled at Terry Anderson and the "takings" enthusiasts, people who might even agree that some cases of privatization and deregulation have been ill-advised. The most sensible critics of regulation admit that some regulation is inevitable, maybe even wise; they just want to be sure that it is efficient. Getting as much as possible from our limited resources is treated as the unquestioned goal of public policy.

Efficiency, to an economist, means getting the most output for the least input, sometimes phrased as "avoiding waste." In the theorist's perfectly competitive economy, nothing of any productive value would ever sit idle, and no one would be paid less (or more) than her maximum potential earnings. Notice, however, that nothing is said about what determines everyone's potential earnings; if some people have forgotten to acquire marketable skills, or neglected to inherit capital, that is simply too bad for them. Furthermore, efficiency means putting everyone to work providing the most of whatever customers are able and willing to buy, whether it is luxury yachts or city buses; a society can be very unequal and, at the same time, very efficient in producing baubles bought by the rich.

As a result, it is not obvious that efficiency is in everyone's interest, or that it would always win a popular vote, if it were subject to a referendum. Starting from a very efficient, very unequal society, many people, even a majority, could be made better off by moving to a more egalitarian but less efficient state of affairs. Economists, seeking to justify the pursuit of efficiency as a social goal despite this objection, have seized on an esoteric concept called "Pareto optimality." Although its political meaning is not immediately obvious from the abstract definition, Pareto optimality has come to serve as a technical alternative to democratic decision making in the hands of economists today.

Vilfredo Pareto was an aristocratic Italian sociologist, who was active at the end of the nineteenth century and the beginning of the twentieth. He had an abiding disdain for the masses and for democracy, an attitude that permeates his extensive writings. His best-known contribution to economics is the criterion for optimality that bears his name. Surely society must prefer, Pareto said, to move from one state of affairs to another, from A to B, if at least one person prefers B to A, while no one prefers A to B. In this case, B is said to be "Pareto-superior" to A. If there is no other state of affairs that is Pareto-superior to B, then B is said to be "Pareto-optimal." If, for example, society could not move to state of affairs C (or any other state) without making one person—and it only has to be one person—worse off than he was in B, then B is Pareto-optimal. An efficient economy is always Pareto-optimal. In fact, economists often say that efficiency is desirable *because* it is Pareto-optimal.

This is not a very informative standard for public policy purposes; contrary to the usual meaning of the word, many different states of the world are optimal in Pareto's terms. However, economists maintain, as Pareto himself did, that Pareto-optimality is the most that can be said about society's preferences without taking partisan sides in the debates of the day. If no one's income goes down, and someone's income goes up, society must be better off. This is seen as the strongest possible objective judgment about public policy.

The influence of Pareto's antidemocratic leanings is implicitly felt here, since Pareto optimality could also be viewed as the most that can be said about society's preferences without doing anything as distasteful as asking the masses about their opinions, or letting them vote. This perspective was not lost on Pareto's students, some of whom found him quite an inspiring teacher. As one of them said,

> I looked forward to every one [of Pareto's lectures]. For here was a teacher who was outlining the fundamental economic philosophy of the future.[13]

The student who wrote these words was Benito Mussolini, who became the Fascist ruler of Italy and Hitler's ally in World War II. In the first year after he seized power, Mussolini made his beloved professor Pareto an honorary member of the Italian Senate.

Pareto's connection to Fascism is not usually mentioned in economics textbooks. However, a more practical problem with Pareto's work arises as soon as it confronts reality: even though many different states of the world are Pareto-optimal, Pareto's criterion for *changing* social conditions is so restrictive that it almost never condones alterations in the status quo. Real-world problems generally involve solutions, each of which would create some winners and some losers relative to the existing state of affairs. That is, the solutions are not Pareto-superior to the status quo because someone will end up being worse off as a result of them. This point highlights the antidemocratic bias of the Pareto criterion: it gives, in effect, a veto power to any one member of society who might be hurt by a change that will improve the lot of many other people. A decision that makes Bill Gates worse off is, in Pareto's world, no good, even if everyone else is made better off by it.

To escape the restrictiveness of the Pareto criterion, while still cloaking their work in the aura of objectivity surrounding Pareto's test, economists have developed the even more exotic standard of "*potential* Pareto improvement." Potential Pareto improvements are identified by a compensation test, known as the Kaldor-Hicks Test, after the two economists who introduced the idea in the 1930s. If a decision increases the dollar value of net benefits (i.e., benefits minus costs) to society, the winners will gain more than enough to compensate the losers for their losses. If the winners compensate the losers, then everyone is better off, and the new state of affairs would be Pareto-superior to the old. However, even if the losers are not compensated, the new situation is a *potential* Pareto improvement, and that's turned out to be good enough for modern fans of efficiency.

Amartya Sen, a Nobel Prize–winning economist, has observed that "potential Pareto improvement" is of no real value as a decision rule. If winners do compensate losers, then everyone is actually better off, and the new outcome *is*

Pareto-superior, not just *potentially* Pareto-superior. But if winners do not compensate losers, then it is possible, for instance, that a decision has made the rich richer and the poor poorer. In this case, Sen argues, the *potential* for improvement in Pareto's terms—the fact that compensation *could* have been paid so that the poor didn't become poorer—does not justify the *reality* of increased poverty.

Undaunted by this critique, advocates of potential Pareto improvement use this theory to rationalize "cost-benefit analysis," the favored tool for judging efficiency. Thus the cost-benefit goal is to maximize the dollar value of net benefits, while paying no attention to who wins and who loses. All that is required is a finding that compensation of the losers *could* occur because the winners' gains are so large. Compensation does occur, of course, only if the winners choose to be generous; but all too often, they do not. Questions of fairness (which we will take up in Chapter 6) are dismissed from the cost-benefit equation from the start.

Costs, Benefits, and Biases

Despite its inegalitarian premises, cost-benefit analysis presents itself as the soul of rationality, an impartial, objective standard for making good decisions. Of course some environmental programs and regulations make sense, the analysts say; it's just that we have to figure out which ones are sensible, and which are not. Who could object to a careful comparison of the pros and cons of public policies?

Yet cost-benefit analysis has become a powerful weapon in the hands of vocal opponents of regulation. This is no coincidence. There are, in fact, built-in biases in cost-benefit methods. The problem is not only that those who start from an antienvironmental perspective have often used cost-benefit analysis to support their preconceptions. Even when the methods are applied in good faith by neutral or environmentally inclined investigators, we will see that the results tilt strongly toward endorsement of business as usual, and rejection of health and environmental protection. This is not obvious from the description of the methods and objectives of cost-benefit analysis, which sounds noble and nonpartisan.

Cost-benefit analysis tries to set an economic standard for measuring the success of government projects and programs. In other words, cost-benefit analysis seeks to perform, for public policy, a calculation that happens routinely in the private sector. In evaluating a proposed new initiative, how do we know if it is worth doing or not? The answer is much simpler in business than in government.

Private businesses, striving only to make money, will produce something only if they believe that someone is willing to buy it. That is, the profit motive reliably steers firms toward producing things for which the expected benefits to consumers, measured by consumer willingness to pay for them, are greater than the costs of production. It is technologically possible to produce men's business suits in brightly colored polka dots. Successful producers suspect that few people are willing to pay for such products, and usually stick to minor variations on suits in somber, traditional hues. If some firm *did* happen to produce a polka-dot business suit, no one would be forced to buy it; the producer would bear the entire loss resulting from the unsold suits.

Government, in the view of many critics, is in constant danger of requiring the production of polka-dot suits—and making people pay for them. Policies, regulations, and public spending do not face the test of the marketplace; there are no consumers who can withhold their dollars from the government until it produces regulations dressed in navy blue and charcoal gray. There is no single quantitative objective for the public sector comparable to profit maximization for businesses. Even with the best of intentions, critics suggest, government regulations and programs can easily go astray for lack of an objective standard by which to judge whether they are meeting citizens' needs.

Cost-benefit analysis sets out to do for government what the market does for business: add up the benefits of a public policy and compare them to the costs. But there is no ledger that presents the costs and benefits of public undertakings to every member of society. Cost-benefit analyses have to create that ledger, a task that often turns into a multiyear, multimillion-dollar research effort. Calculations of costs and benefits involve challenging questions of very different varieties. We begin with the costs.

Many public policies impose measurable economic costs. For example, the government may require a certain kind of pollution-control equipment, which businesses must pay for. Even if a regulation only sets a ceiling on emissions, it results in costs that can be at least roughly estimated through research into available technologies and business strategies for compliance.

Although the calculation should be straightforward, in practice there is a tendency to overestimate the costs of regulations in advance of their implementation.[14] Massachusetts Institute of Technology researcher Nicholas Ashford argues that compliance costs typically drop after a regulation is im-

plemented, for three reasons: pollution–control technology
gets cheaper as industry produces more of it; over time,
managers learn how to comply with regulations more cost-
effectively; and regulations encourage innovation, which can
dramatically reduce the cost of compliance.[15] Confirming
this perspective, a study by the Office of Technology Assessment of occupational safety and health regulations found
many cases in which actual compliance costs were lower than
anyone had expected. For example, the Occupational Safety
and Health Administration (OSHA) 1974 standard for vinyl
chloride, a known human carcinogen, lowered the permissible workplace exposure from 500 parts per million (ppm) to 1
ppm. Industry predicted total economic catastrophe, and
OSHA's own consultants predicted compliance costs would
reach $1 billion. The actual costs were about a quarter of a
billion dollars, as industry quickly developed a new control
technology that improved the production process as well as
lowered worker exposures.[16]

Similar patterns show up in other regulations. One study
found that costs estimated in advance of regulation were
more than twice actual compliance costs in eleven out of
twelve cases.[17] Another study found that advance cost estimates were more than 25 percent higher than actual costs for
fourteen out of twenty-eight regulations; advance estimates
were more than 25 percent too low in only three of the
twenty-eight cases.[18] Before the 1990 Clean Air Act Amendments took effect, industry had anticipated that the cost of
sulfur reduction under the amendments would be $1,500 per
ton. In 2000, the actual cost was under $150 per ton.

In a related vein, many companies have begun to discover
that environmental protection can actually be good for busi-

ness. Increased energy efficiency, profitable products made from waste, and decreased use of raw materials are just a few of the cost-saving and profit-making results of turning more corporate attention to environmentally protective business practices.[19] Harvard Business School analyst Michael Porter maintains that carefully crafted, moderately demanding regulations can inspire business to create profitable, environmentally friendly innovations.[20] Cost-benefit analyses typically do not take such money-saving possibilities into account in evaluating the costs of regulation. Indeed, prominent conservative policy analysts, such as Robert Hahn of the American Enterprise Institute, have expressed great skepticism that the government could discover cost savings where the market had not[21]—much like the old joke about the economist who refuses to pick up the twenty-dollar bill in the street on the theory that if it were real, someone else would have picked it up already.

Despite these problems, the cost side is the easy part of cost-benefit analysis. In principle, one could correct for the potential sources of bias in estimating the costs of regulations and other public policies. No such correction is possible in assessing the benefits of regulation, because the benefits are, literally, priceless. Herein lies the fatal flaw of cost-benefit analysis: to compare costs and benefits in its rigid framework, they must be expressed in common units. Cancer deaths avoided, wilderness and whales saved, illnesses and anxieties prevented—all these and many other benefits must be reduced to dollar values to ensure that we are spending just enough on them, but not too much. As we will explain in the chapters that follow, most of what we think is important about human life, health, and the environment is lost in this translation. By monetizing the things we hold most dear, economic analysis ends up cheapening and belittling them.

In comparing monetized benefits to monetized costs, and making this comparison the criterion for judging public policies protecting people and the environment, the analysis also stacks the deck against such policies. In practice, most cost-benefit analyses could more accurately be described as "complete cost–incomplete benefit" studies. Most or all of the costs are readily determined market prices, but many important benefits cannot be meaningfully quantified or priced, and are therefore implicitly given a value of zero. Thus, despite the common claims that cost-benefit analysis is philosophically and politically impartial, its very methodology systematically disfavors protections of goods that, like health and environmental protection, are priceless.

Perhaps recognizing the likely political unpopularity of a method that requires translation of lives, health, and nature into dollars, many policy analysts have started to take a different tack in arguing for cost-benefit analysis. They do not just say that they want to create economic efficiency—after all, few people go to the polls or pull the voting lever in pursuit of efficiency. They say, instead, that what they're after is the same as what environmentalists are after: saving more lives, protecting more health, preserving more natural resources. The government, they say, often issues rules that are insanely expensive, all out of proportion to their benefits—a problem that could be solved by the use of cost-benefit analysis to screen proposed regulations and shifting money to more efficient uses. Thus much of the case *for* cost-benefit analysis depends on the case *against* current regulation. The stories supporting the case against regulation come next.

3

The Unicorns of Deregulation

The case against health, safety, and environmental protection rests on a handful of widely circulated stories, told by just a handful of storytellers. The stories enter the public's consciousness as they are credulously spread by editorial writers, newspaper reporters, and others, but the original storytellers themselves are little known and rarely noticed. It's worth taking a moment to ask who they are, and where they came from.

Richard Belzer, Robert Crandall, John Graham, Wendy Gramm, Robert Hahn, Thomas Hopkins, Robert Litan, Randall Lutter, John Morrall, and W. Kip Viscusi are not exactly household names. But they have had an influence on attitudes toward protective regulation that is out of all proportion to their name recognition and their size as a group. These analysts and their institutional homes—places like the AEI-Brookings Joint Center for Regulatory Studies, the Mercatus Center, the Harvard Center for Risk Analysis, the Cato Institute, and the Competitive Enterprise Institute—are responsible for generating the critical pieces of "antiregulatory" data and analysis, upon which the second Bush administration bases its ardently pro-industry stance. Not coincidentally, the

donor lists of organizations like the Mercatus Center, an institute at George Mason University devoted to celebrating the
free market, and the Harvard Center for Risk Analysis read
like a Who's Who of American industry.

Several of the analysts named above are alumni of a small,
now defunct government agency, the Council on Wage and
Price Stability (COWPS), created in 1974 to study and to try
to control the effect of inflation on the U.S. economy.
COWPS quickly enlarged its role to include cost-benefit
analyses of health, safety, and environmental regulations, reasoning that regulations which did not pass the test of economic efficiency would inevitably have an unacceptable
impact on inflation. COWPS (followed by its successor in the
Carter administration, the Regulatory Analysis Review
Group, or RARG) presided over both the first major efforts
at deregulation in this country, beginning with deregulation
of the airlines, and the first major efforts to evaluate regulations according to the criterion of economic efficiency.

In 1981, the Reagan administration reassigned the job of
regulatory oversight to a new and obscure office within the
White House's Office of Management and Budget (OMB)—
the Office of Information and Regulatory Affairs (OIRA).
OMB's OIRA is, by Executive Order, responsible for reviewing all major federal agency rules from the perspective of
cost-benefit analysis. Thus OMB is the perfect place to insti-
tutionalize an antiregulatory stance within the federal government. The Clinton administration made little use of
OMB's cost-benefit judgments in practice, but did not reduce
OMB's formal authority over other agencies' rules. In contrast, the Reagan, Bush I, and Bush II administrations have
embraced OMB's ability to roll back progressive regulations.

Meanwhile, the cadre of COWPS alums at right-wing think tanks, working to create the intellectual underpinnings for conservative environmental policy, have put into circulation three different myths that recent Republican administrations have used as cornerstones of antiregulatory policy. Despite the popularity of these myths, the studies on which they rest are full of problems and are based on extensive misinterpretation of the economic and environmental evidence.

The first mythical story is about the huge and inconsistent costs of regulations. We spend, we are told, $72 billion to save a single person from dying from exposure to formaldehyde.[1] We spend $99 billion to reduce chloroform exposures enough to save a single year of one person's life.[2] These costs have been cited again and again by economists at the AEI-Brookings Joint Center for Regulatory Studies, the Mercatus Center, the Harvard Center for Risk Analysis, and OMB itself, as evidence of the need for more intensive economic analysis and regulatory "reform." The tale of staggering regulatory costs has been repeated so often that it is now taken for granted as established fact.

The political meaning of this "fact" is spelled out in two newer stories, which have rapidly become popular in Washington. First, reallocation of resources from expensive regulations to cheaper ones could supposedly save lives and/or money; in the most popular form of this story, we could save 60,000 more lives every year if we regulated more intelligently.[3] Second, regulations in general are so expensive that they are killing people, by taking money away from other life-saving expenditures. A typical claim is that EPA's standards for soot and smog, set during the Clinton administration, will actually *kill* 27,000 people every year because they cost so much money.[4]

These arguments and their ominous statistics are widely circulated and widely accepted in the academic and popular literature on risk regulation. They have also become ubiquitous in political debates on environmental law. Scarcely a congressional hearing on this subject occurs in which these kinds of figures do not figure prominently. These accounts have surfaced, among other places, in Bjorn Lomborg's popular but problematic denunciation of environmentalism, *The Skeptical Environmentalist*.[5]

Yet, for all their wide circulation and widespread acceptance, these stories deserve no credence. They are myths rather than serious research findings, as flimsy as the case for basing public policy on the price of a phone call or dismissing the dangers of lead. But because they retain such a tenacious hold on the political imagination, and because the economic analysis we criticize in this book derives a large part of its support from these stories, we offer a brief guide to what's wrong with the three antiregulatory stories.[6] The first story, about the allegedly huge costs of some regulations, is the oldest and most widely accepted, and requires the most detailed rebuttal.

Regulatory Costs of Mythic Proportions

One does not have to read very far into the literature on risk regulation before running across huge tables listing the costs per life saved of various federal regulations. The numbers on such tables are fantastic: according to these lists, we are often spending hundreds of millions, and sometimes billions, of

THE UNICORNS OF DEREGULATION

dollars for every life we save. Numbers like these have contributed to the fashionable idea that more attention to such
numbers will promote greater objectivity in risk regulation.
The trouble is that the numbers themselves are flawed reflections of a deep bias against regulation.

The first and most famous of the studies on costs per life
saved was published in 1986 by John Morrall, a longtime
economist at the Office of Management and Budget, first at
COWPS and now at OIRA. A table in this study, reproduced
in part as Table 3.1, purports to show the costs per life saved of
various risk-reducing federal regulations. According to the
table, these costs vary from a low of $100,000 per life saved to
a high of $72 billion. One-third of the regulations on the
original list reportedly cost over $100 million for every life
they save.

As the table shows, the regulations that fare best in
Morrall's analysis—that is, the ones that cost the least per
human life saved—are safety regulations designed to prevent
deaths from accidents. These include rules relating to such
things as fire extinguishers on airplanes and safety devices
for space heaters. The regulations that fare worst—indeed, all
of the regulations in the costly right-hand side of Table 3.1—
are regulations designed to limit exposures to hazardous
substances, such as arsenic, asbestos, benzene, and formaldehyde.

A second, now almost equally famous study on life-saving
costs essentially replicated John Morrall's results. In research
supervised by John Graham, the former director of Harvard's
Center for Risk Analysis and now head of OIRA, graduate
student Tammy O. Tengs and several co-authors★ analyzed
the costs of 587 life-saving interventions.[7]

Table 3.1

The Costs of Various Risk-Reducing Regulations per Life Saved

Regulation	Costs per Life Saved ($1,000's)	Regulation	Costs per Life Saved ($1,000's)
Steering Column Protection (NHTSA)	$100	Asbestos (OSHA)	$7,400
Oil & Gas Well Service	100	Benzene (OSHA)	17,100
Unvented Space Heaters (CPSC)	100	Arsenic/Glass Plant (EPA)	19,200
Cabin Fire Protection (FAA)	200	Ethylene Oxide (OSHA)	25,600
Passive Restraints/Belts (NHTSA)	300	Arsenic/Copper Smelter (EPA)	26,500
Fuel System Integrity	300	Uranium Mill Tailings (EPA)	27,600
Underground Construction (OSHA)	300	Acrylonitrile (OSHA)	37,600
Trihalomethanes (EPA)	300	Uranium Mill Tailings/ Active (EPA)	53,000
Alcohol & Drug Control (FRA)	500	Coke Ovens (OSHA)	61,800
Servicing Wheel Rims (OSHA)	500	Asbestos (OSHA)	89,300
Seat Cushion Flammability (FAA)	600	Arsenic (OSHA)	92,500
Floor Emergency Lighting (FAA)	700	Asbestos (EPA)	104,200
Crane-Suspended Platforms (OSHA)	900	DES (Cattlefeed) (FDA)	132,000
Children's Sleepwear Flammability (CPSC)	1,300	Arsenic/Glass Manufacturing (EPA)	142,000
Side Doors (NHTSA)	1,300	Benzene/Storage (EPA)	202,000
Concrete & Masonry Construction	1,400	Radionuclides/DOE Facilities (EPA)	210,000
Hazard Communication (OSHA)	1,800	Radionuclides/Elemental Phosphorous (EPA)	270,000
Grain Dust (OSHA)	2,800	Acrylonitrile (OSHA)	308,000
Benzene/Fugitive Emissions (EPA)	2,800	Benzene/Ethylbenzenol Styrene (EPA)	483,000
Radionuclides/Uranium Mines (EPA)	6,900	Arsenic/Low-Arsenic Copper (EPA)	764,000
		Benzene/Maleic Anhydride (EPA)	820,000
		Land Disposal (EPA)	3,500,000
		EDB (OSHA)	15,600,000
		Formaldehyde (OSHA)	72,000,000

Source: John F. Morrall III, "A Review of the Record," *Regulation,* November–December 1986.
Note: Some hazards, such as arsenic and asbestos, are regulated in more than one industry or application.

As with John Morrall before them, Tengs and Graham found that cost-effectiveness ranged widely across interventions. Also like Morrall, Tengs and Graham found that controlling toxins was often the most expensive way to save human lives. They found that the costs of toxin control to regulated industries reached as high as an incredible *$99 billion for every year of life saved.* Tengs and Graham's estimates of costs have, like Morrall's estimates, figured prominently in critiques of environmental law. Table 3.2 reproduces one portion of Tengs and Graham's results, reporting the costs of controlling pollution at paper mills.

Unfortunately, these studies on regulatory costs contain three major flaws:

- They are full of regulations that were never adopted and, in some cases, never even proposed.
- They ignore risks and benefits other than human life and death.
- They play a statistical trick with future deaths that devalues the lives of the elderly, and is dismissive of long-term risks to everyone.

Regulations That Aren't

The first big problem with these studies is that they include many life-saving interventions that have never been implemented by any agency; indeed, they include many interventions that have never even been *proposed* by any agency. Fully

---

* For brevity, we will refer only to the lead and senior authors, Tengs and Graham.

Table 3.2
Alleged Costs per Life-Year Saved by
Pollution Control at Paper Mills

Intervention	Cost/Life–Year
Chloroform emission standard at 17 low–cost pulp mills	≤$0
Chloroform private well emission standard at 7 paper–grade sulfite mills	$25,000
Chloroform private well emission standard at 7 pulp mills	$620,000
Chloroform reduction by replacing hypochlorite with chlorine dioxide at 1 mill	$990,000
Dioxin emission standard of 5 lbs/air–dried ton at pulp mills	$4,500,000
Dioxin emission standard of 3 (vs. 5) lbs/air–dried ton at paper mills	$7,500,000
Chloroform emission standard of 0.001 (vs. 0.01) risk level at pulp mills	$7,700,000
Chloroform reduction by replacing hypochlorite with chlorine dioxide at 70 mills	$8,700,000
Chloroform reduction at 70 (vs. 33 worst) pulp and paper mills	$15,000,000
Chloroform reduction at 33 worst pulp and paper mills	$57,000,000
Chloroform private well emission standard at 48 pulp mills	$99,000,000,000

Source: Tengs, *et al.,* "Five-Hundred Life-Saving Interventions and Their Cost-Effectiveness," 15 Risk Analysis 369 (1995). As we explain in the text, none of these interventions was ever proposed by a regulatory agency, let alone adopted.

half of the regulations on John Morrall's list that cost more than $5 million per life saved were never implemented by any regulatory agency. Many of them were rejected for the very reason that their benefits were not deemed to justify their costs. For example, Morrall lists three benzene emission control rules that EPA briefly considered in 1984; EPA promptly rejected these rules on the grounds that they were too expensive, and achieved too little reduction in risk to be worthwhile.

Thus, no one ever spent the $202 million, $483 million, or

$820 million per life saved on benzene regulation that is re-
ported in Table 3.1, and no government agency ever proposed spending these amounts, precisely because they were so
expensive. Nevertheless, bizarrely, these non-rules are used by
regulatory critics such as Kip Viscusi at Harvard and John
Graham of OMB as proof of the wastefulness of government
actions. To be sure, in his original article, Morrall noted that
these rules had been rejected. But this is a subtlety that has
largely been missed in subsequent uses of the table.

The gulf between reported costs and actual programs is
even greater in Tengs and Graham's study. While Morrall included some measures that had been proposed but never en-
acted under existing programs, Tengs and Graham included
hypothetical, never-proposed programs as well. Their only
criterion for the inclusion of a life-saving intervention was
the availability of quantitative estimates of the intervention's
costs and benefits. The result is, predictably, the same as with
Morrall. Although nine of the ten most expensive life-saving
interventions in the Tengs and Graham study involved toxin
control, not one of these nine interventions ever became law.
Similarly, no regulatory agency ever proposed *any one* of the
Tengs-Graham paper mill interventions listed in Table 3.2.
Tengs and Graham's infamous $99 billion-per-life-year rule
never happened.

Thus the studies by Morrall, and by Tengs and Graham,
demonstrate conclusively that it is possible to describe a collection of nonregulations that would have been expensive,
had they ever been adopted. To interpret this "analysis" as describing the real-world performance of any actual regulatory
agency is deeply misleading. Despite the subtle concessions of
the researchers that their cost estimates include measures that

were not implemented, it is easy enough to take away from these studies the impression that they describe the systematic workings, and failures, of current regulation. Amazingly, John Graham himself has drawn this erroneous lesson from his own research, in testimony before the U.S. Senate.[8] Imagine how confused his readers must be.

Regulations That Aren't About Death

A second problem with reports like those by Morrall, Graham, and Tengs is that they imply that the only important benefit of health and environmental protection is to prevent human deaths. Thus the reports ignore many other significant benefits of health and environmental programs.[9] Most obviously, they ignore *nonfatal* harms to human health and also harms to ecosystems, two concerns that often lie at the core of regulatory programs. Consider the case of formaldehyde regulation: at a purported $72 billion per life saved, it is the most expensive item on Morrall's list. OSHA's decision to regulate formaldehyde was based on the large number of health effects caused by this chemical. Prolonged exposure to formaldehyde can cause skin problems; respiratory problems, including asthma; and eye problems, up to and including blindness in extreme cases. It is also a probable human carcinogen—but most of the people harmed by formaldehyde do not get cancer from it. To get to Morrall's $72 billion number, you have to minimize the substantial benefits of formaldehyde regulation in reducing non-fatal health problems,[10] and imagine that it was proposed primarily as a way of preventing cancer. Workplace regulation of formaldehyde is not a bad answer, but it is largely answering a different question.

Another reason the formaldehyde rule fared so poorly on Morrall's table is that Morrall dramatically reduced the regulatory agency's estimates of the number of cancer cases that would be averted by the rule. In fact, he did the same thing with respect to quite a few rules on his list. His explanation: the agencies' risk assessments just seemed implausibly gloomy.[11] As we'll see in Chapter 5, this skepticism about and manipulation of scientific results—often to the point where a risk vanishes entirely—has become a common feature of cost-benefit analysis. Because, as we will show throughout this book, the economic critique of environmental policy is so fundamentally flawed, it is easier for the critics to start from the premise that there actually are no underlying environmental problems at all.

Deaths That Aren't About to Happen

The final problem with these studies involves their treatment of policies that are designed to avoid deaths or other harms *in the future*. The future is particularly important in evaluating regulation of toxins. Often the only quantified benefit of toxic-substances control is the prevention of cancer. Since cancer has a long latency period, today's new regulation may have benefits in the form of avoided cancer deaths some decades from now. Morrall, and Tengs and Graham, "discount" those future deaths over the latency period, treating them as less significant than deaths today. Discounting is a technique normally applied to short-run financial decisions; if, for example, you are given a choice between receiving $100 today and $200 ten years from now, you'll need some way to weigh the ten-year delay against the greater eventual payoff. This is what discounting does. As we will explain in Chapter 8, discounting becomes problematical, and systematically undervalues the future, when applied to long-run decisions involving health and environmental benefits—decisions that are fundamentally different from short-run market calculations. Ignoring all such concerns, Morrall, and Tengs and Graham, used discounting to value the lives of those who, without regulation, would have died at some point in the future, in effect making those lives worth only a small fraction of a life today. In Morrall's study, for example, whereas the OSHA rule limiting arsenic exposures in the workplace would prevent an estimated 11.7 *future* cancer cases per year, Morrall calculates that this is equivalent to only 0.35 *current* cases prevented per year.

Tengs and Graham, focusing on life-years saved by regulations, add another, equally suspect, approach to future health benefits. By counting life-years instead of lives, Tengs and Graham assume that it is better to save more rather than fewer life-years. Put simply, this means that, in their view, a measure that saves the lives of the elderly is not as good as one saving the lives of the middle-aged; likewise, a measure saving the lives of the middle-aged is not as good as one saving the lives of the young.[12]

Killing older people who have shorter remaining life expectancies is, in most moral or legal systems, just as serious a crime as killing the young. The stealth rejection of this principle of equality through Tengs and Graham's dubious arithmetic of risk analysis threatens to create a startling change in our approach to life and death.

These numerous flaws have not prevented the widespread acceptance of these studies of the allegedly astronomical costs of risk regulation. Indeed, despite their flaws, such studies have served as the foundation for a second research "finding," purportedly showing how many more lives we could save if we did things differently. The second myth arising from anti-regulatory research stars two of the same investigators, Tengs and Graham.

A Statistical Murder Mystery

If you could save 60,000 lives every year at no cost, would you do it? This enticing question is the implicit punch line of an additional study by Tengs and Graham, building upon their Five-Hundred Life-Saving Interventions study. The second study sets out "to assess the opportunity costs of our present pattern of social investments in life-saving."[13] What, they ask, do we give up in addressing life-threatening risks the way we now do?

The later study (we'll call it the Opportunity Costs study) considered 185 policy interventions, all the ones included in their earlier work for which the data were national in scope.[14] Of the 185 measures, 90 were toxin-control measures that were under the jurisdiction of the EPA (or would have been, if they had ever been proposed, which many were not).[15]

In this study, Tengs and Graham found that if our resources were directed to the most cost-effective of the interventions they considered, we could either save 60,000 more lives every year with the same amount of money, or save the same number of lives we do now while cutting costs by $31 billion. Never mind the fact that most of the 60,000 lives reflect complex hypotheses about changing medical priorities, not government regulations. Nonetheless, Graham provocatively calls the current state of affairs "statistical murder": we are, he suggests, literally killing people because our life-saving priorities are so misguided.

Many observers have agreed, citing the Opportunity Costs study as if it proves that government regulation does indeed cause the "statistical murder" of 60,000 Americans every year. Congress has been frequently told, by representatives of AEI-Brookings, the Mercatus Center, and other antiregulatory think tanks, that Tengs and Graham's research shows that a rearrangement of regulatory priorities would save 60,000 lives per year.[16] John Graham himself, testifying in favor of Newt Gingrich's "Contract with America" and other legislation, has repeatedly asserted that his research demonstrates that federal regulation is in serious need of reform.[17] A group of economists (including Graham) urged the Supreme Court to interpret the Clean Air Act to require cost-benefit analysis of national air quality standards; they premised their argument on the perceived failings of current health, safety, and environmental regulation. Citing Tengs and Graham's study, they asserted:

> Both the direct benefits and costs of environmental, health, and safety regulations are substantial—estimated to be several hundred billion dollars annually. If these resources were better allocated with the objective of reducing human health risk, scholars have predicted that tens of thousands more lives could be saved each year.[18]

Yet the startling, sound-bite conclusions about the cost-ineffectiveness of current health and environmental regulation do not follow from Tengs and Graham's research. Tengs and Graham have failed to identify a huge body of overly expensive health and environmental regulations that are actually in effect, and have proposed only trivial opportunities to enact cheaper life-saving rules.

Of the ninety environmental measures included in Tengs and Graham's second study, fully seventy-nine were *never implemented*.[19] Once again, Tengs and Graham have succeeded mainly in proving that there are a lot of potential regulations out there that *would* be wasteful, if they were ever set in motion; what they haven't shown is that the regulations we actually have are foolish.

Equally important, some of the cost-effective regulations have already been fully implemented, leaving no room for further improvement. For example, one of the measures that fares best in Tengs and Graham's work is the phasedown of lead in gasoline, a regulation that in their view produced economic *savings* rather than imposing costs. But we did this one already—there is, thankfully, no more lead in gasoline. This is not a regulation that we can have "more" of; we cannot keep banning lead in gasoline, over and over again, in order to produce more low-cost, life-saving results. The same is true for many of their lowest-cost regulations.

We cannot save lives by moving imaginary funds from expensive regulations that were never even proposed, to cheap regulations that are already completely implemented and therefore need no further funding. The 60,000 lives Tengs and Graham offer to save by diluting environmental protections are mythological creatures, the unicorns of deregulation.

Is Richer Safer?

A final story alleges that regulation designed to save lives can actually kill people by making them poorer. The claim is that the cost of regulation may itself increase risk by lowering personal income. For example, a study of the impacts of revised national air quality standards asserted that as many as 27,000 additional people would actually die as a result of regulatory expenditures associated with the standards, as compared with the 15,000 or so people whose lives the regulations were predicted to save.[20] In short, "richer is safer," a provocative argument based on a simple two-part syllogism: wealth creates health, and regulation destroys wealth.[21]

Unlike the first two antiregulatory stories, the "richer is safer" claim does not rest on intricate research. Rather, the claim that wealth creates health is a hunch about the economy and public health—or, more specifically, a series of hunches leading to different numerical estimates.

In the first study of its kind, Ralph Keeney, an engineer and expert in systems analysis at the University of Southern California, simply observed the statistical relationship between income and life expectancy. He then offered a set of "illustrative" examples of the effects of regulation, assuming that because the cost of regulations makes people poorer, regulations also decrease life expectancy. Specifically, he estimated that one fatality will result from every $3 million to $7.5 million of regulatory expense (his higher figure has been more widely quoted).[22] Alternatively, Kip Viscusi has asserted that people are willing to spend about $5 million to save a life, and that people tend to spend about 10 percent of any increase in income on risk-reducing measures. Thus, he concluded, if society lost $50 million of income to regulatory costs, it would lose $5 million of risk reduction, and hence lose one life.[23] Finally, Viscusi's more recent work, co-authored with John Morrall and Randall Lutter, adds the observation that poorer people not only spend less on risk reduction, but also engage in more dangerous behavior in the first place—for instance, they are more likely to smoke. With this added twist, Viscusi and his co-authors now estimate that the loss of just $15 million to regulatory expenditures will make us poor enough to induce one more fatality.[24]

In any of these variants, both parts of the "richer is safer" syllogism are suspect. Does wealth directly create health? There are numerous reasons to doubt that changes in life expectancy automatically result from small changes in income.[25] Keeney's first study of the issue acknowledged that there was a strong relationship between income and health only at incomes below $20,000—a qualification that he has since forgotten. Moreover, all of the "richer is safer" calculations assume that deaths will be strictly proportional to nationwide total income losses, no matter how small the loss for each household. Since there are more than 100 million households in the U.S., an annual average income loss of *seven cents* per household (due to any cause) amounts to a total of more than $7 million nationwide, and thus should cause one death according to Keeney. To reach Viscusi's original $50 million figure, the highest cost for a fatality in this guessing game, each household would have to lose fifty cents a year, or a penny a week—an amount unlikely to change either behavior regarding risk, or life expectancy. If everyone looks under the sofa

cushions and finds a lost penny every week, will a life be saved
as a result?

Even more absurd is the second leg of the "richer is safer"
argument, the notion that regulation always destroys wealth.
Government-bashing has become so fashionable that one can
now apparently assume without comment that money spent
on regulation simply vanishes into a hole—it creates no jobs,
no business, no productive gains whatsoever. In fact, environmental protection is big business in this country, employing
people who make and install the complicated, expensive
pollution-control technologies, inspect and measure environmental compliance, fill out forms documenting environmental performance, file lawsuits to enforce regulations, and so
on. The people in those jobs are not poorer as a result of regulation. Yet the claim of a relationship between regulatory expenditures and mortality is completely dependent on the
assumption that "we" are worse off as a result of regulation.
This, in the end, is the weakest link: the critics prove that environmental regulation is bad for us only by first assuming
that we do not benefit from it.

To uncover the hidden bias in the "richer is safer" studies,
one need look no further than the limited use to which they
have been put. Every large program, whether it has an educational, military, environmental, or other purpose, imposes
costs on some people and creates jobs and incomes for others.
There is no other way to accomplish things big enough to
matter. If the "richer is safer" crowd were really serious about
their argument, you would expect them to be concerned
about the big-ticket items in the federal budget. Using
Keeney's $7.5 million per life estimate, the budget for na-

tional defense in a typical year will kill about 50,000 American citizens. Yet no one—not Keeney, nor Viscusi, nor anyone else who has criticized environmental law for making people poorer—has suggested that the military or public schools or, in fact, any program that does not save lives should be scrutinized for their indirectly lethal effects.

There are real, ongoing debates about the usefulness and effectiveness of our current approaches to education, national defense, environmental protection, and other public programs. But the argument that the main problem is that a program makes us poorer is a sure sign of a hidden judgment that the program is undesirable on other grounds.

Washington's Urban Legends

Rules that cost billions for every life saved, missed opportunities to save tens of thousands of lives, regulations that kill more people than they save: these are the stories that have captured the imagination of regulatory critics and their gullible publicists. The stories are the supermarket tabloid sensations of Washington policy debate, the regulatory equivalent of reports that alligators can be found in New York City's sewer system, or that Elvis is alive somewhere in America. The wonder is not that someone invented the stories; the wonder is how widely they have come to be believed. Belief in them, however, is critical to the cost-benefit project.

Translating lives, health, and nature into dollars and cents is an alien activity, which seems awkward, indeed immoral, to most noneconomists. The stories we have described function as a warm-up act for the real show; they prepare the audience for the bizarre spectacle to come, in which the things we might want money *for*—a long life, good health, serene and unspoiled surroundings—are transformed into money itself. In the next chapter, we turn to the strange process of valuing human lives in monetary terms.

4

The $6.1 Million Question

How much is one human life worth? According to the Environmental Protection Agency, $6.1 million.

Whether this is precisely the correct answer—whether, indeed, the question has a meaningful answer—cost-benefit analysis demands some such number. The most significant benefits of environmental protection are often the deaths prevented by regulation. To decide whether the benefits of regulation are larger or smaller than the costs, it is essential to assign a dollar value to lives saved.

Putting a price on human life makes most people uncomfortable. It is clearly unacceptable to virtually all religions and moral philosophies. Nonetheless, the quantitative valuation of life has become central to recent analyses of public policies, forcing us to pay some attention to the details of this troubling calculation, and to the troubled theories on which it rests.

The estimate of $6.1 million per life was developed in 2000 in order to evaluate the benefits of removing arsenic from drinking water. As we will see, there is an established but debatable rationale for the belief that $6.1 million is the right number. The debate matters because the value of life is easily the single most important number in the economics of health and environmental protection, frequently accounting for the great majority of the benefits in cost-benefit studies. In two major EPA studies, more than 90 percent of the monetized benefits of removing arsenic from drinking water, and more than 80 percent of the benefits of the first 20 years of the Clean Air Act, consisted of avoided deaths.[1]

Since life-saving benefits loom so large in regulatory analysis, the exact value of a life is of critical importance. With arsenic in drinking water limited to 10 parts per billion (ppb), the regulatory standard that was ultimately adopted, the estimated dollar value of health benefits is almost equal to the costs of arsenic removal. This conclusion stands or falls on the value of a life. Raise the value of a life to $12 million, and the same cost-benefit analysis could justify even 3 ppb, the most protective, and most expensive, standard considered by EPA. Cut the value of a life to $3 million, and the analysis would swing all the way in the other direction, with costs overwhelming monetary benefits even at a lax 20 ppb standard.

Traditional Values

Monetizing life did not begin with cost-benefit analysis, and debate about the practice extends far beyond the economics profession. In varying forms, the monetary valuation of life, and the accompanying moral dilemmas, are as old as Beowulf and as new as September 11.

Aethelbert I, the first Christian king of Anglo-Saxon England, issued his "dooms," or legal code, in A.D. 601–604.[2] Aethelbert's dooms included the principle of "wergild," the monetary compensation that the killer had to pay to the family of a murder victim. Wergild varied with the victim's status: e.g., it was much more expensive to kill a prince than a peasant. In an era that had not yet established a criminal justice system, payment of wergild was thought to be a superior alternative to the long, bloody feuds that could otherwise result from a killing. Wergild was an established custom in medieval Norse, Germanic, and Russian societies, and plays an important part in *Beowulf*, the Old English epic poem written sometime before A.D. 1000.

A second tradition emerged in the medieval Catholic Church, and was widely accepted in Western Europe by the twelfth century. Aggressively seeking expanded sources of revenue, the church sold indulgences, or pardons, for all manner of crimes up to and including murder. That is, the church was willing to accept cash in lieu of the burdensome and time-consuming penance that would otherwise have been required. The price depended on the wealth of the person seeking the pardon, as well as on the nature of the sin. By the fourteenth century, the sale of indulgences had come to seem disreputable to many: one of the pilgrims portrayed by Chaucer in his *Canterbury Tales* was The Pardoner, who made his living selling tawdry relics and pardons of dubious authenticity to credulous peasants. Anger at such abuses grew stronger as time went on; Martin Luther's challenge to church authorities in 1517 over the sale of indulgences was one of the sparks that ignited the Protestant Reformation, while the Catholic Church itself abolished the practice in 1562.[3]

A third tradition, all too well known, was slavery. A market that established a price for human beings was one of the underpinnings of American economic development, and remained an integral part of Southern agriculture until the end of the Civil War. Ownership of slaves sometimes included the right to kill them; the purchase of a slave was, indeed, the purchase of a life.[4] Once again, there was a price list: since prices for slaves depended on their expected economic value, it was no surprise that younger, stronger, and healthier people were worth more.

These glimpses of history seem alien and remote, looking back into a world that is thankfully no longer with us. The modern American legal system does not draw directly on the traditions of wergild, indulgences, or slavery. Yet the courts routinely assign prices to human lives, particularly in lawsuits seeking compensation for the wrongful death of loved ones. Younger and healthier victims again tend to be worth more, as payments depend in part on the loss of expected future income. However, awards in these lawsuits vary capriciously from one jurisdiction to another, and often attach great weight to trivial aspects of the victim's life. For example, insurance adjusters have found that legal judgments are usually much larger for people who enjoyed outdoor recreation than for those who stayed home reading or watching television.[5]

After the terrorist attacks of September 11, 2001, the Federal Victim Compensation Fund was established to provide compensation to the families of the deceased. Elaborate formulas were developed to calculate the payments that would be made from the fund.[6] To begin with, one uniform sum was allocated for each deceased individual's pain and suffering, plus a uniform additional award for a spouse and each dependent, if any. An additional payment was based on the loss of expected earnings, depending on age, family status, and income at the time of death. The total projected payment for a poor, elderly, single, and childless victim was a small fraction of that for a young, high-income victim with a spouse and children. The goal was not to achieve equity, but to discourage the families from suing the airlines or the government for compensation. Therefore the payment schedule was based, in part, on a guess about how much the families of different victims might have won in court. Even in the twenty-first century the government offers wergild to the families of the dead, hoping to prevent a long legal feud.

Victims of other disasters have received much less—and, in some cases, have protested the inequity. No government compensation was offered for those who died in the Oklahoma City bombing of 1995, the worst terrorist attack in the U.S. before 2001. Responding to questions about differences in the treatment of victims of different attacks, one Congressman said, "Well, a lot of things in life are not fair, and this may turn out to be one of them. Some unlucky victims are more unlucky than others."[7] Some of the Oklahoma City victims' families are suing for compensation, offended by the unfairness of their lesser recognition.

The valuations from death settlements, whether established by federal agencies in the aftermath of disaster or in individual court cases, may not be directly comparable to cost-benefit analysis of public policy. Death settlements are, in large part, personal and retrospective, providing compensation to relatives of someone who has already died. The legal system as presently constituted really has nothing but money to offer by way of redressing a harm already done. To refuse, in this setting, to ascribe a monetary value to the harm of death would be, perversely, to add insult to injury. Twelve days after the attack on the World Trade Center, the worst U.S. mining disaster in twenty years occurred in Brookwood, Alabama,

killing thirteen miners. The mine owner offered less than
$100,000 per family in compensation, leading most of the
families to refuse the offer and sue for more. "It's not about
the money," said Linda Mobley, the widow of one of the miners. "I don't want this to happen to anyone else's husband. I
want the company to make things safer. But money is the
only thing you are allowed to sue for."[8]

Laws protecting health and the environment, in contrast, are
social and prospective, expressing society's commitment to
preventing deaths and other harms that have not yet happened.
To refuse, prospectively, to protect someone from harm caused
by another person is to grant a kind of license to harm—a license that can be purchased for a finite cost. The values of life
for retrospective/compensatory and prospective/preventative
purposes could be very different numbers—if, that is, both of
these values are in fact numbers.

Life, Risk, and Ethics

What does it mean to say that the value of a life is $6.1 mil-
lion? There are two very different ways in which that statement can be interpreted, giving rise to two distinct sets of
problems. First, there are underlying ethical and philosophical
questions about whether any such number exists. The decision to proceed with valuation, for cost-benefit analysis or
other purposes, is in effect a decision to set aside these problems or to pretend they have been resolved. Yet the debates
about the conceptual questions remain pressing and contentious. Second, if such a number does exist, calculation of
the number involves puzzling problems of economic analysis.
The controversies surrounding the calculation lead back, in

the end, to the fundamental questions about the meaning and plausibility of any dollar estimate for the value of a life.[9]

How can lives be translated into dollars? We do not ordinarily act as if money is involved when lives are at stake. A missing child, or a person trapped in a collapsed or burning building, is cause for calling in the rescue squad and for making immediate, heroic efforts to save the person. This is our society at its best; we would not be nobler if we stopped to do an economic analysis and ponder the precise numerical value of the life at risk before deciding to proceed. Human life is the ultimate example of a value that is not a commodity, and does not have a price. In an age that has left wergild, indulgences, and slavery behind, you cannot buy the right to kill someone for $6.1 million, or for any other price.

Most systems of ethical and religious belief maintain that every life is sacred. A common inference is that the value of life must therefore be infinite. That statement, however, leads to paradoxes of its own: if life has an infinite value, should all available resources be spent on risk-reducing or life-saving measures? A more careful restatement of the ethical objection is that there is no "price" for life because its value is immeasurable.[10]

The standard economic response is that a value like $6.1 million is not a price on an individual's life or death. Rather, it is a way of expressing the value of small risks of death, which, when aggregated to produce one death, can be called a "statistical life"; for example, the value of one statistical life is one million times the value of a one in a million risk. If people are willing to pay $6.10 to avoid a one in a million increase in the risk of death, then the value of a "statistical life" is $6.1 million.

It is true that risk (or "statistical life") and life itself are distinct concepts, but both are involved in many questions of health and safety. Regulations often reduce risk for a large number of people, and avoid actual death for a much smaller number. A complete cost-benefit analysis should include valuation of both of these benefits. In practice, however, analysts often ignore the distinction between valuing risk and valuing life, and act as if they have produced a valuation of life itself.[11]

To clarify the distinction, imagine that the producers of "reality" television come up with a new show called *You Bet Your Life.* The show's contestants each agree to undergo 100 exotic and dangerous events apiece, each of which has a 1 in 100 risk of death. It turns out that the odds are that 4 out of every 11 contestants will survive, and 7 will die.[12] The survivors each experience the loss of a statistical life, since they suffer 100 separate $\frac{1}{100}$ risks of death. The losers have a rather different, and worse, experience.

Economists have calculated only the value of a statistical life, not the value of life itself: numbers like $6.1 million attempt to measure what happens to the contestants who survive but not those who die. Yet, just as in the imaginary television show, loss of statistical life for some and loss of life itself for others frequently have the same causes. In an economy that makes widespread, routine use of toxic chemicals, we are all involuntary participants in a form of *You Bet Your Life,* albeit with somewhat better odds than the imaginary version. A complete measure of the damage done by toxic chemicals cannot stop with a value for the risk to everyone who is exposed; it must also value the costs to the smaller number who actually die as a result of that exposure.

But what is the dollar value of an actual life or death? If the value of life itself were based on the compensation required in exchange for it, the price would be infinite, for, as the philosopher John Broome has pointed out, "no finite amount of money could compensate a person for the loss of his life, simply because money is no good to him when he is dead."[13] In the discussion of risk and the value of a statistical life, the paradox of monetizing the immeasurable value of human life has not been resolved; it has only been glossed over.

Another problem with the standard approach to valuation of life is that it asks individuals (either directly through surveys, or indirectly through observing wage and job choices, as explained in the next section) only about their attitudes toward risks to themselves. A recurring theme in literature, religion, and cultural tradition suggests that our deepest and best sentiments involve valuing someone *else's* life more highly than our own: think of parents' devotion to their children, soldiers' commitment to those whom they are protecting, lovers' concern for each other. Most ethical and spiritual beliefs call on us to value the lives of others—not only those closest to us, but also those whom we have never met.

In valuing nature, as we will see in Chapter 7, economists often ask about existence values: how much is the existence of a wilderness area or endangered species worth to you, even if you will never personally experience it? If this question makes sense for bald eagles and national parks, it must be at least as important when applied to safe drinking water and working conditions for other people. How much is it worth to you to prevent a death of an unknown person far away? Or, more pointedly, how much is it worth to you to ensure that you are not complicit in the death of such a person? The answer cannot be deduced solely from your attitudes toward risks to yourself. We are not aware of any attempts to quantify the existence value of another person's life; but we are sure that, if the value of life is a number in the first place, then there is a substantial existence value to the life of a stranger, let alone a relative or friend.

Less profound, but equally dubious, is the assumption that there is a single value for all equal risks to life, such as $6.10 for a one in a million risk. That is, the process of valuation assumes that there is a single thing called "risk," with a price that applies to it regardless of context. Yet despite the finality of death, there is no reason to think that all deaths are equivalent and interchangeable. Nor are all one-in-a-million risks of death directly comparable with one another.

For example, the death rate is about the same—just over one in two million—from a day of downhill skiing, from a day of working in the construction industry, or from drinking about twenty liters of water containing fifty parts per billion of arsenic, the old regulatory limit that was in effect until 2001.[14] This does not mean that society's responsibility to reduce risks is the same in each case.

Most people view risks imposed by others, without an individual's consent, as more troubling and more worthy of government intervention than risks that an individual knowingly accepts. On that basis, the highest priority among our three examples is to reduce drinking water contamination, a hazard to which no one has consented. The acceptance of a risky occupation such as construction is at best quasi-voluntary—it involves somewhat more individual discretion than the "choice" of public drinking water supplies, but many people go to work under great economic pressure, with little information about occupational hazards. In contrast, the choice of

risky recreational pursuits such as skiing is entirely discre-
tionary; obviously safer alternatives are readily available. Safety
regulation is thus more urgent on construction sites than on
ski slopes, despite the equality of the probability of harm.[15] We
will return to these issues in Chapter 6.

There are other ways in which equal risks of death may
not look equally bad. For example, the circumstances preceding death are important: sudden, painless death in pleasant
circumstances is different from agonizing, slow deterioration
surrounded by medical technology. One economist who has
explored these issues, E. J. Mishan, argues that there is no
meaning to the value of a statistical life divorced from the particular policy that increases or decreases risk.[16] That is, even
for an ultimate value such as life and death, the social context
is decisive in our evaluation of risks.

It is useful, where possible, to collect quantitative information about the lives saved and health improved through public policy, but it is confusing and even pointless to express
those lives in terms of their dollar "equivalents." This conclusion is only strengthened by a closer look at the source of
those dollar figures.

Young, Rich, and Valuable

The value of lives saved by forward-looking public policy
could be based on expected future earnings, as in wrongful
death settlements. This approach has been tried in the past,
but has fallen out of favor as its drawbacks have been recognized. A future earnings standard is highly unequal; it makes
some people appear more valuable than others, because they
will earn more in the rest of their lifetimes. Is it then more

"efficient" to spend more on protecting the health of those with higher expected earnings? A price list with different values for different lives is difficult to reconcile with ideals of democracy and equal treatment under the law, let alone the sacredness of every human being.

One of the worst results of a future earnings standard is that it implies that the lives of retired people are worth nothing—or perhaps less than nothing, since they consume scarce goods and services without earning or producing any marketed goods themselves. If society's values were all about money, there might appear to be a net social benefit to something that kills a lot of older, retired people—such as tobacco.

Several years ago, states were in the middle of their litigation against tobacco companies, seeking to recoup the medical expenditures they had incurred as a result of smoking. At that time, W. Kip Viscusi, a professor of law and economics at Harvard Law School (and a COWPS alumnus—see Chapter 3), undertook research concluding that states, in fact, *saved* money as the result of smoking by their citizens. Why? Because smokers die early, saving their states the trouble and expense of providing nursing home care and other services associated with an aging population. According to Viscusi, the financial benefit to the states of their citizens' premature deaths was so great that, if some of his results were "taken at face value," then "cigarette smoking should be subsidized rather than taxed."[17]

Amazingly, this cynical conclusion has not been swept into the dustbin where it belongs but instead has been revived by the tobacco industry itself. The tobacco company Philip Morris commissioned the well-known consulting group Arthur D. Little to examine the financial outcomes, for the Czech Republic, of smoking among Czech citizens. Arthur D. Little found that smoking was a financial boon for the government—because, again, it causes citizens to die earlier and thus reduced government expenditure on pensions, housing, and health care.[18]

A valuation of life based on expected future earnings will depend on wealth as well as age. After all, the rich have higher expected earnings, and they are also able and willing to pay more for risk reduction. An actual "price list" with different values for rich and poor lives made a brief and embarrassing appearance in the discussion of global climate change in 1995. Every few years, the Intergovernmental Panel on Climate Change (IPCC) publishes a massive assessment of the current state of knowledge on climate change, with thousands of experts from around the world contributing to chapters in their areas of specialization. For the 1995 report, the economists writing about costs and benefits of greenhouse gas reduction decided to assign monetary values to the lives that would be lost to global warming. A careful reading of the fine print revealed that they were valuing lives in rich countries at $1,500,000, in middle-income countries at $300,000, and in the lowest-income countries at $100,000.[19]

A furor naturally ensued when these figures were publicized, shortly before the report was completed. The IPCC was created by a United Nations–sponsored conference, and reports its findings to the governments of the world—many of whom were livid at discovering their citizens being valued at ¹⁄₁₅ of a European or North American life. Despite widespread criticism, the economists insisted that there was not enough time before the publication deadline to change the numbers. The final 1995 report relies on the unequal values of rich and poor lives, surrounded with last-minute verbal qualifications and suggestions of alternative perspectives. The next IPCC report, published in 2001, recommends the use of a worldwide average value of a life, and mentions a possible value of $1 million.[20]

As the IPCC realized, grave moral and political problems can be avoided by using a single value of life for the entire population under consideration—the world for global issues, or the nation for U.S. policies. However, key federal decision makers are moving in exactly the opposite direction, making ever more intricate distinctions about the value of different lives that are at risk. The Office of Information and Regulatory Affairs within the Office of Management and Budget has even tried to evaluate the benefits of regulation not by looking at the number of lives saved, but by the number of *years of life* saved (as the head of the office, John Graham, did in his research with Tengs, described in Chapter 3).[21] On this criterion, a rule saving the life of a seventy-five-year-old is not nearly as worthwhile as a rule saving the life of a forty-year-old. Indeed, in 2002, OMB—for the first time ever—put its official stamp of approval on this conclusion when it estimated that people age seventy and older were worth about sixty-three cents on the dollar compared to younger people.[22]

At first blush, the life-year approach has a reasonable sound. Surely it must be more important to cherish and protect the young. Many parents, faced with the "who goes in the lifeboat?" type of disaster scenario, would put their children ahead of themselves. But the implications of valuation of life-years are troubling; the idea of setting standards based on life-years does not survive closer scrutiny. When ethical and religious thinkers talk about the equal value of every life, they do not mention life-*years*. The legal penalties for killing someone do not depend on the victim's age. Moreover, when OMB devalues the lives of the elderly relative to the young and, as a consequence, undermines the case for a particular rule, it does not go searching for new rules that might protect the young. The money that would have been spent protecting the elderly doesn't go to protecting the young; it just stays in the pockets of the people who are endangering the lives of the elderly.

Whereas the calculation of the value of a statistical life is disturbing enough, the value of a *life-year* is no more meaningful or well-understood, and in practice it leads to even stranger epicycles of statistical inference, as we will explain in Chapter 8. There is no easy escape through talking about life-years; valuing life is still a disconcerting process. For those who want to assign a numerical value to life without raising intractable issues of fairness, the challenge is to produce an estimate, such as $6.1 million for the U.S., that applies to society as a whole. The story gets confusing at this point, because there is no correct answer.

Behind the Numbers

The $6.1 million figure widely used in policy circles comes from so-called "wage-risk" studies. These studies try to infer the value of a life from the extra wage, or wage premium, paid for risky jobs. This is by far the most popular method for deriving a value for a statistical life. If two jobs are similar in many respects but differ in the risk of death, a higher wage is often required to attract workers to the more dangerous job. The wage difference between the two jobs could be thought of as the amount of compensation that workers demand in exchange for accepting the additional risk. (In real life almost no one has ever thought this way about taking a job; but in economic theory, ordinary people are endlessly and effortlessly engaged in complex calculations.) Once we know the "price" of risk in the workplace, it is easy to compute the value that workers apparently place on a statistical life. If the entire population places the same value on risk, independent of its social context, then the workplace value of a statistical life can be applied to other risks of any variety.

If this strikes you as implausible and misleading, you have correctly anticipated the conclusion of the next few pages. However, wage-risk calculations are widely accepted and often employed in analyzing and shaping public policy. For that reason, it is worth spelling out the flaws in the wage-risk logic.

Here is how the calculation works. Hypothetically, suppose that a job with a 1 in 10,000 annual risk of death (a typical risk for male blue-collar workers) paid 30 cents per hour, or $600 per year, more than a similar but completely safe, risk-free job (most white-collar jobs, for example, involve virtually no risk of death on the job). Then workers who took the risky job would be accepting $600 compensation for a 1 in 10,000 chance of death, implying that they valued a statistical life at $600 × 10,000 = $6 million.

As in this example, it is possible to take the data on wages and risk, do the math, and come up with a wage-risk estimate. But several debatable steps are required in order to interpret that number as society's true value of a statistical life, suitable for use in cost-benefit analyses unrelated to job risks. Limitations at each step suggest that society's actual valuation of risk—if there is such a thing—is higher than wage-risk estimates would imply.

Wage-risk analysis assumes not only that there is a well-defined value of a statistical life, but also that workers' job choices accurately reveal that value. This means that workers must know exactly how risky their choices are. In reality, of course, workers do not always understand the dangers they face at work. Hispanic workers in the U.S. now die on the job at a higher rate than whites or blacks. Among other reasons, workers with limited knowledge of English sometimes misunderstand written or spoken safety warnings. "If someone yells, 'Watch out,' you don't necessarily act as fast if it's not your native language," says AFL–CIO educator James Platner.[23] If workers are uninformed about job risk, they will not demand appropriate compensation for risky work.

If workers' choices are to tell us the value of risks, workers must be free to choose among jobs at varying levels of risk; this, too, is a standard assumption in theory. However, the workers who end up employed in risky occupations may lack the skills or mobility needed to find alternatives. Some of the most dangerous jobs are in forestry, mining, fishing, and agriculture, industries that are often located in remote areas with few other employers. Alaska is the state with the highest rate of death on the job, followed by Wyoming, Montana, Idaho, West Virginia, and Mississippi.[24] Also, minority workers may end up in undesirable, risky jobs as a result of discrimination. If workers are stuck in high-risk occupations due to geography or prejudice, statistical estimates of wage payments for risk will be too low; workers who were truly free to choose would demand more for accepting risk—or they might choose a safer line of work.

If workers are well-informed and able to switch occupations, a process of self-selection will occur: those who are most willing to accept dangerous challenges will take the risky jobs, and those most concerned about safety will work elsewhere. Those workers who are most afraid of heights don't end up working as roofers (one of the most dangerous jobs in construction); they presumably don't even apply for the job. Their valuation of the risk of climbing around on roofs is much greater than the wages paid for the job. Society's average valuation of risks should reflect the choices made by those who would never dream of doing dangerous work, as well as by those who do accept the job at the going wage. Correction for this bias would clearly raise the value of a statistical life above the wage premium that is actually paid for risky work.

It is not only risk-averse workers who are left out of wage-based calculations of the value of risk. Many people are not in the paid workforce; their attitudes toward risk may not be the same as those of workers. Those outside the workforce include people who are particularly vulnerable to environmental hazards, such as children, pregnant and nursing women, the disabled, and the elderly. Health and environmental regulations are often of greatest benefit to these vulnerable, non-working parts of the population, but the value of a life based on wage risks reflects only the behavior of workers who take dangerous jobs. Inclusion of these other groups again seems likely to raise the value of a statistical life above the wage-risk estimates.

One large part of the population is virtually invisible in wage-risk calculations, namely women. As academic studies and common stereotypes both agree, women are much more risk-averse than men.[25] This shows up in employment patterns: most of the workers in the riskiest jobs are male. In the

1990s, men accounted for only about half of the paid labor force, but almost all fatalities on the job. As a result, a calculation of the overall wage premium for risky work primarily reflects what it takes to get men into the most dangerous jobs.

A recent wage-risk study, using data from 1996–98, estimates the value of a statistical life separately for different groups of workers. Among blue-collar and service workers, the value of a statistical life is $2.6 million for men and $13 million for women. Among unionized blue-collar and service workers, the value climbs to $6.1 million for men and $42.3 million for women.[26] Union membership apparently gives workers the power to demand better compensation for risk; nonunion workers might want the same, higher-risk premiums, but could be unable to bargain successfully for that level of pay for dangerous work.

Using all of these numbers, what standard should be adopted to represent the value of risk to society? The male and female figures could be averaged, but these figures apply only to blue-collar workers. Many white-collar workers presumably could have taken risky jobs, but did not; does that mean that they are at least as risk-averse as blue-collar women? The same question applies to people who are not in the paid labor force. If white-collar workers and all nonworkers are at least as risk-averse as blue-collar women, then the great majority of the population has a value of a statistical life of at least $13 million—or perhaps $42 million, if unionized workers are the only ones in a position to express society's true preferences.

The same study that considered women's risk preferences also looked at racial differences, but for black workers it was unable to find any statistically significant wage premium for risky work. That is, black workers doing dangerous jobs are not consistently paid more for the risks they face at work. Yet who would suggest that this means they value risks to their lives at zero? The obvious fact of racial discrimination can easily explain the lack of a wage premium for risk among black workers, while the textbook model of well-informed job choice cannot.

A final observation about the study we have been discussing is that it reveals the incredibly narrow wage differences on which the entire pyramid of analysis rests. The average female blue-collar worker faces risks on her job that merit a wage increase of a mere 7 cents per hour over completely safe, risk-free work. For her male counterpart, the comparable risk-based wage increase for the average job is only 13 cents per hour over risk-free work. For unionized blue-collar workers (who, surprisingly, face slightly higher risks of death on the job than their nonunion counterparts), the average job pays 32 cents per hour more than risk-free work for men, and 34 cents per hour for women. The expected wage premium is larger for more dangerous occupations, but reaches as much as a dollar an hour only in a handful of the absolutely riskiest jobs.[27] From pennies per hour added to paychecks, the value of life is divined. And with that value, judgment is passed on the merits of life-saving health and environmental regulations for the nation as a whole.

The leading alternative to wage-risk analysis is "contingent valuation," a specialized kind of public opinion poll that will be examined more fully in later discussions of health and nature, where it plays a more central role. For valuation of life, polling a cross-section of the population about what dollar values they place on risks of dying seems like a curious and problematical enterprise. One attempt by well-known environmental economists involved such a complicated questionnaire that the researchers had to pay the participants to spend several hours filling it out at a computer center.[28] Thus the study was in danger of selecting for people who are not very busy, and who respond well to small monetary incentives— not necessarily a representative cross-section of society when it comes to valuing risk.

Contingent valuation surveys elicit only hypothetical evaluations of risks in contrived, artificial scenarios. Unlike wage-risk analyses, surveys do not reflect actual decisions made when real lives or real money are at stake. However, the federal Office of Management and Budget, apparently determined to leave no methodology unturned in its pursuit of lower values for benefits, has used contingent valuation estimates in evaluating regulatory policy, which lowers the standard value of a statistical life from $6.1 million to $3.7 million.[29]

The Washington Consensus

The value of $6.1 million per life, developed in 2000 for EPA's cost-benefit analysis of arsenic standards for drinking water, was not the first such estimate. Between 1988 and 1999, federal agencies adopted monetary values for life at least fifteen times in the course of evaluating regulations, as summarized in Table 4.1.[30] Some of the values adopted in 1996, and all of the ones thereafter (below the line in Table 4.1) were between $4.8 million and $5.8 million. Adjusted for inflation, these figures are in close agreement with the more recent estimate of $6.1 million. It appears that a consensus (a fragile one, it is turning out) emerged in Washington in the late 1990s that the value of a life is around $5–6 million.

The estimates of $5–6 million emerge from the work of the same economist who wrote about the benefits of smoking for states' treasuries. W. Kip Viscusi has authored or co-authored a number of studies of the value of a life, and has written several influential reviews of the available literature on the subject.[31] In the 1990s he estimated the value of a statistical life at around $5 million in 1990 dollars. An EPA re-analysis of Viscusi's data produced the more precise estimate of $4.8 million, also in 1990 dollars.[32] This value, adjusted for a decade of moderate inflation, crept up to $6.1 million in 1999 dollars in the arsenic study. In other words, in the late 1990s, regulators seemed to treat the EPA–Viscusi estimate as an established empirical constant, needing adjustment only for inflation.

Viscusi's literature reviews encompass the majority of the available U.S. work on the subject. The estimates he cites are extremely diverse, ranging from about $900,000 to more than $21 million in today's dollars.[33] Averages of these disparate values have been used to arrive at figures such as $4.8 million, $5 million, or (adjusted for inflation) $6.1 million. In his most recent review, adding just a few newer studies, Viscusi suggests a slightly higher value: $7 million per statistical life.[34]

The individual estimates cited by Viscusi—the basis for the average valuations of a statistical life—are very old: even in his latest (2003) survey, only three of the thirty estimates were published after 1991, and only one uses labor market data collected as recently as 1985.[35] The data underlying his surveys largely describe the labor market of the 1970s and the early 1980s.

Table 4.1
Valuations of Life in Regulation

Agency	Subject of Regulation	Year	Value (million $)
EPA	Protection of stratospheric ozone	1988	3.0
FAA	Establishment of airport radar	1990	1.5
FDA	Food labeling regulations	1991	3.0
Dept. of Agriculture	National school lunch/ school breakfast program	1994	1.5, 3.0
Dept. of Agriculture	Pathogen reduction in food inspection	1996	1.6
FDA	Restriction of tobacco sales to minors	1996	2.5
FAA	Flight simulator use in pilot training	1996	2.7
FAA	License requirements for aircraft launch	1996	3.0
FDA	Manufacturing standards for medical devices	1996	5.0
EPA	Children's exposure to lead paint	1996	5.5
EPA	Ambient air quality standards: particulate matter	1997	4.8
EPA	Ambient air quality standards: ozone	1997	4.8
FDA	Mammography standards	1997	5.0
EPA	Disinfectants and by-products in drinking water	1998	5.6
EPA	Radon in drinking water	1999	5.8

Source: Matthew D. Adler and Eric A. Posner, "Implementing Cost-Benefit Analysis When Preferences Are Distorted," *Journal of Legal Studies* 29, no. 2, part 2 (June 2000), 1,146.

Viscusi's data were carefully adjusted for inflation to arrive at the recent EPA estimate of $6.1 million for a statistical life, but were not adjusted to reflect any other changes in job markets or attitudes about risk that have occurred in the last twenty-five years. Yet many significant changes occur in society over periods of time that long. If incomes rise, will there be a corresponding change in attitudes toward risk, and an increase in the wage premium required to attract workers to dangerous jobs? Some economists think so.[36] If they are right, the $6.1 million value should be adjusted upward for income changes since the 1970s. One study developed estimates of the value of life for each census year from 1940 through 1980, and found that the value of life increased 1.5 to 1.7 times as fast as income per capita. If the same relationship continued to hold after 1980, that study implies a value of life in 2000 of $8.5–12.1 million.[37]

Is Life Getting Cheaper?

If attitudes toward risk and job choices had stayed constant since 1976, the $5–7 million average value, adjusted upward for income growth, might still be appropriate. If the historical relationship seen in the data for 1940–80 continued to apply today, one would expect more recent studies of the value of a statistical life to produce estimates around $8–12 million. For the most part, though, that is not the case. A few newer studies have found much lower values, around $2–4 million.[38] As this research gains wider attention from regulatory critics, there will be increasing pressure to lower the value of a life for regulatory purposes—implying a devaluation of health and environmental protection in general.

Why should the estimated value of a life be lower than it used to be? Workers are still dying in noticeable numbers. There were 5,915 fatalities on the job in the United States in the year 2000, and more than 6,000 a year in the 1990s, caused by a broad range of hazards. Fishing boats are lost at sea, with or without perfect storms. Airplanes crash, killing their pilots; despite the media images of the occasional big accident, small planes account for many more workers' deaths than scheduled airlines. Miners are trapped underground. Loggers, farmworkers, and construction workers die in workplace accidents. Traffic accidents kill truck drivers, taxi drivers, and others. Homicides, usually connected with robberies, kill taxi drivers, retail clerks, and others. A handful of the most dangerous industries and occupations are highlighted in Table 4.2.

However, risks of death on the job are, fortunately, declining in every major occupation; the overall death rate today (per 100,000 workers) is less than half the rate in 1976.[39] Regulations adopted by OSHA, EPA, and other agencies have played a part in this dramatic improvement. In addition, some (not all) of the most dangerous industries, including agriculture, fishing, mining, and logging, employ a declining proportion of the labor force.

It is not only dangerous conditions and occupations that have declined. Male blue-collar workers—who fill virtually all the high-risk jobs—have faced worsening job opportunities since the 1970s, as overall industrial employment has fallen.[40] If people are desperate for work, employers do not have to pay as much to attract them to dangerous jobs. Hispanic workers, whose numbers have grown rapidly, are filling some of the most risky jobs in construction and elsewhere, as shown by their high death rate on the job. Immigration status and language barriers may stop many Hispanic workers from asking for or getting higher pay for more dangerous work.

In dangerous industries where employment is declining, such as agriculture and fishing, workers of any ethnicity are typically in no position to demand wage premiums for risk. On the other hand, in several dangerous industries that have

Table 4.2
Fatal Injuries on the Job

	Number of Fatalities	Rate per 100,000 Workers
All Workers (1997)	6,238	4.8

High-Risk Industries (1997)

Mining	158	25
Agriculture, forestry, fishing	831	24
Construction	1,107	14
Transportation, utilities	1,008	13

High-Risk Occupations (1997)

Timber cutters	121	129
Fishers	60	123
Water transportation	49	94
Aircraft pilots	100	83
Extractive (mining, oil & gas)	75	52
Construction laborers	333	41
Taxi drivers	100	40
Truck drivers	862	28
Farm workers	616	27.5
Roofers	55	27.5
All women workers (1994)	521	0.9

High-Risk Women's Occupations (1994)

Taxi drivers	6	24
Construction laborers	6	19
Truck drivers	20	16
Messengers	5	13
News vendors	7	10
Farm workers	12	9

Data on all workers from National Institute of Occupational Safety and Health (NIOSH), *Worker Health Chartbook 2000*, 36–37. Data on women workers from Andrew Knestaut, "Fewer women than men die of work-related injuries," *Compensation and Working Conditions Online,* June 1996 (from Bureau of Labor Statistics), Table 4.

expanded, such as trucking, construction, and air transportation, unions have lost ground and workers are in a weaker bargaining position than they were in the past. Average real wages for truck drivers declined 30 percent between 1977 and 1995, due to the combination of deregulation and the declining power of the Teamsters union; in the same period, average real wages for all manufacturing production workers declined only 8 percent.[41] Thus there was a sharp drop in the wage premium for truck driving relative to other blue-collar jobs, for reasons that had nothing to do with workers' attitudes toward risks.

These are important stories about employment, wages, and workplace risk. However, they have little to do with society's valuation of health and environmental protection in general. Job market conditions have shifted since the 1970s in ways that may have reduced the wage premium for dangerous work, but there is no reason to think that there has been a similar reduction in the benefit of preventing deaths due to pollution. Yet that would be the implication for cost-benefit analyses if regulatory agencies use newer wage-risk evidence to justify a lower valuation of life.

Private Markets and Social Values

To see how inappropriate estimates of the value of a life can give a decision maker seemingly precise and technical reasons for doing the obviously wrong thing, one need look no further than Ford's unhappy experience with the Pinto and its exploding gas tank.

The Ford Pinto, one of the best-selling cars of the 1970s, had a defective gas tank with an unfortunate tendency to burst into flames in rear-end collisions, even at moderate speeds. Crash tests of prototypes in 1969–70, and of Pintos produced in 1971 and 1972, had demonstrated the severity of the problem, yet Ford delayed fixing it, apparently aware that it was saving money by postponing the needed redesign.[42] The story has grown in the retelling, and there is no definitive proof that Ford did a cost-benefit analysis that rejected the re-design that would have fixed this problem. But the truth is not much better.

In the mid-1970s, at exactly the time when Ford should have been fixing the Pinto, the company was instead lobbying against a proposed federal regulation about fuel tank safety in crashes—a regulation that eventually forced them to make the Pinto safer. As part of the lobbying effort, Ford prepared a cost-benefit analysis of one part of the regulation, concerning fuel tank safety in rollover accidents. Other provisions of the regulation dealt with rear-end collisions, the more common source of Pinto explosions. According to Ford's engineers, it would cost $11 per car, or a total of $137 million per year for the industry as a whole, to meet the rollover standard, while avoiding an estimated 180 deaths per year, along with an equal number of serious burn injuries and a few thousand wrecked cars.[43]

Ford's cost-benefit analysis valued those lives at a mere $200,000 apiece. That number was calculated by the National Highway and Traffic Safety Administration (NHTSA) at the request of the auto industry, based mainly on lost wages, plus medical and legal costs and a small amount for pain and suf-fering. At $200,000 per head, 180 deaths are "worth" only $36 million, not nearly enough to "justify" a $137 million ex-penditure. A value of about $750,000 per life is needed to make the benefits equal the cost in this exercise. The accuracy of these calculations has been questioned—for instance, cheaper options may have been available for achieving gas tank safety—but that is not the point. The numbers presented here are the facts as Ford perceived them at the time; as Ford saw it, it was just not worth it to spend an extra $11 per car to fix the gas tank.★

Despite Ford's lobbying, the gas tank safety regulation was adopted, taking effect for the 1977 model year. Ford responded by immediately, and inexpensively, making the 1977 Pinto safer. (It did not cost anything like the much-advertised $137 million, a number that, as we have seen, was Ford's estimate of the cost to the entire auto industry to fix a slightly different problem.) However, despite the safety of the newer Pintos, the damage had been done. It became all too apparent that Ford had knowingly produced a dangerous car from 1971 through 1976, leading to hundreds, perhaps thousands, of easily preventable deaths. As the company lost a disastrous series of lawsuits, recalled all 1971–76 Pintos for retrofits, and finally discontinued the model in 1980, the executives might have reflected that society's implicit value of a statistical life was quite a bit higher than they had been led to believe.

★ These numbers are in 1972 dollars; to correct for inflation since then, they should be multiplied by 4.4 to convert them to 2003 dollars. Thus the cost per car would be a bit more than $44 in 2003 dollars, while the value of a life at which costs equal benefits would be about $3.3 million.

Modern Indulgences

Mechanical application of $6.1 million, or any other value, as a standard of efficiency comes close to selling indulgences once again: is a corporation or public agency that endangers us pardoned for its sins once it has spent $6.1 million per statistical life on risk reduction? New, lower values would only sell society's pardons more cheaply.

Cost-benefit analysis as practiced today assumes that the value of a statistical life is known from the outset, or can be found through objective research, while the policy decision— whether to fix the gas tank—is unclear. But sometimes the correct policy choice can be found by putting yourself in the consumer's shoes: given a choice between a car with the exploding gas tank feature, and a car with a safer gas tank for a few dollars more, which would you buy? The answer does not depend on economists' latest estimates of the value of a life. Reliance on an intricately calculated, "one size fits all" price per life is not the way that reasonable people do, or should, make important decisions about priceless values.

5

An Ounce of Prevention

Fans of murder mysteries know that arsenic is a deadly poison. The villain slips a little bit of it into someone's food or drink, and the deed is done. In real life, people do die of arsenic poisoning, but the culprit is not the butler, or those nice old ladies in *Arsenic and Old Lace;* in most cases, it is the hard facts of geology that are to blame. Rocks in some parts of the world contain small quantities of arsenic, a substance that naturally (or unnaturally, from mining-waste runoff) finds its way into water supplies. Death and disease can result from drinking water containing amounts of arsenic measured in parts per billion (ppb)—though exactly how many ppb are dangerous has been the subject of heated controversy.

Readers of earlier chapters may be able to guess the broad outlines of what comes next, although there are some surprising new plot twists along the way. Technologies are available for removing arsenic from water, at a moderate cost; in exchange for these costs, society obtains the priceless benefits of life and health. Formal cost-benefit analysis of arsenic regulation therefore requires monetary prices for health as well as life. The dollar value of health, like the value of life, turns out to rest on intricate, implausible hypotheses that ignore much of what we know about the actual problem at hand.

In this chapter we also highlight the role that science plays in cost-benefit analysis. Before putting a price on the benefits of regulation, one must obviously have something to price—a human life, a case of illness—that would be avoided by regulation. This is where science comes in. Quantifying human health risks turns out to be just as complicated and controversial as monetizing them. And experience unfortunately shows that the science used in cost-benefit analysis can be manipulated to ensure results that work against regulation. The technical concepts involved, such as risk thresholds and dose-response relationships, have intimidated many observers, but they are important to understand: abuse of these concepts can make the real benefits of regulation magically seem to disappear.

Arsenic, Then and Now

In 1942, the United States decided to limit arsenic in drinking water to 50 ppb. Calls for a stricter standard date back at least to 1962, when the Public Health Service recommended that drinking water should contain no more than 10 ppb. On three occasions in the last thirty years, Congress directed the Environmental Protection Agency (EPA) to update the 50 ppb standard. Finally EPA commissioned an elaborate cost-benefit analysis of possible arsenic regulations, completed in 2000, and announced a new standard of 10 ppb (the standard recommmended by the World Health Organization and adopted by many European countries) in January 2001. The incoming Bush administration promptly withdrew this standard—only to accept it again after eight months of further review and debate.

The new arsenic rule was one of the first U.S. regulations to be set on the basis of a formal cost-benefit analysis. As usual, the cost side of the analysis looks quite different, and much less controversial, than the benefits. Engineers identified and estimated costs for more than a dozen technologies for removing arsenic from drinking water; the choice of technologies depends on the size of the water system, the concentration of arsenic, and other factors. Only time will tell whether the costs were overestimated in advance, as has so often happened in the past. For now, few if any critics have disputed the estimated costs for arsenic removal.

The benefits of arsenic removal consist of avoided deaths and diseases. The avoided deaths were priced at $6.1 million apiece, for all the strange reasons explained in Chapter 4. But bladder cancer, the best-documented ill effect of arsenic, is fatal only about one-fourth of the time. Therefore a price tag is also needed for the experience of those who suffer and survive. What is the dollar value of a nonfatal case of bladder cancer? EPA's answer, explained below, is every bit as absurd as the question.

Similar questions arise in the analysis of other measures to promote public health: without a dollar value for the avoided illnesses and injuries, how can we tell if the benefits of a regulation exceed the costs? Discussion of the economics of the health care system raises a closely related question: without a quantitative measure of medical outcomes, how can we tell if a new medical procedure or device is worth its cost?

Questions like these have led to numerous attempts to assign monetary values to health. There are three leading meth-

ods of valuation,[1] each with its own acronym—and, as we will
see, its own problems. Two of the methods are ambitious in
scope and ambiguous in results: the Willingness to Pay
(WTP) calculations favored by environmental economists,
and the Quality Adjusted Life Years (QALY) approach used
in health economics. A third alternative, the Cost of Illness
(COI) method, is the most humble and most straightforward,
but is clearly incomplete. None of the methods is entirely sat-
isfactory, because health, like life, is priceless—not infinite in
value but, rather, immeasurable in monetary terms.

Shop Till You Drop

Valuation of nonfatal bladder cancers, for the arsenic study, relied on a method that has an intuitive appeal: to find out what
health is worth to people, why not just ask them? Market
prices for ordinary goods and services reflect the amount that
consumers are able and willing to pay. Frequently, though,
there is no market for health problems. So economists often
try to create comparable, artificial prices by conducting public opinion surveys asking the same question—what are you
willing to pay to avoid a health problem? The survey method
is called "contingent valuation," and the data that it produces
are called "willingness to pay" (WTP) estimates. While the
idea sounds simple, implementation of it turns out to be quite
complex.

The story of the bladder cancer estimates for the arsenic
analysis begins, oddly enough, with a study of a different disease in a shopping mall in Greensboro, North Carolina. In the
late 1980s, a survey was conducted to find out how much a
case of chronic bronchitis was "worth." The authors, located

at Duke University and including W. Kip Viscusi, whom we met in the last two chapters, used a marketing firm to conduct the interviews in a Greensboro mall; they had used the same firm for earlier studies at the same mall. They commented about the mall, "This locale has a representative household mix and is used as a test marketing site for many national consumer brands."[2]

In "test marketing" for their "brand," the Duke study team knew they could not just ask people point blank, "How much are you willing to pay to avoid getting chronic bronchitis?" The question would not be likely to produce meaningful answers. The question is about an imaginary payment in a nonexistent market; no one's answer would be based on any experience with such payments. To avoid this problem, the researchers thought they could sneak up on the question, asking it in an indirect way that seemed more likely to elicit society's actual willingness to pay. But this strategy did not eliminate the essential unreality of the question.

In their survey, the Duke researchers first described for shoppers the effects of chronic bronchitis. Next, the interviewers asked a series of questions about which of two imaginary communities the subjects would prefer to live in: Area A had the same cost of living as the subjects' actual residence and a specified risk of getting bronchitis, while Area B had a higher cost of living but a lower risk of bronchitis. The interviewers then changed the exact numbers describing the two communities and asked the question again, repeatedly adjusting the numbers until they reached a point where the subject was equally happy with A and B. At that point the tradeoff between higher risk in A versus higher costs in B was taken, by the researchers, to reflect the value the subject placed on avoiding chronic bronchitis. Two-thirds of the people who were interviewed understood this game and were willing to play it, yielding numerical estimates that the economists could use. (Perhaps shoppers at the Greensboro mall have become accustomed to answering unusual hypothetical questions, given the popularity of the location with economists and market researchers.) For the record, the average value of a case of chronic bronchitis for shoppers in the Greensboro mall was $883,000.[3] EPA used the Duke study as a starting point for valuing chronic bronchitis in its cost-benefit analysis of the Clean Air Act.[4]

Basing public policy on the Greensboro bronchitis value, or other values created in the same manner, raises a host of problems. Most obviously, one can question whether a survey done over a decade ago in one shopping mall in one community accurately reflects national opinion today. Digging deeper into both the original study and EPA's use of it generates less obvious, but equally fundamental problems. The Duke researchers excluded from their results the answers of one-third of the survey participants because the participants failed to play the economists' guessing game correctly, either answering successive questions inconsistently, or consistently giving answers that were judged much too high or much too low. Yet who among us has well-defined, numerically precise preferences about hypothetical tradeoffs between the cost of living and the risk of bronchitis? How many of us might fail the economists' new literacy test for public policy decisions? How many might value our health too much for economists to take seriously? For its part, EPA excluded even more responses, explaining that answers at "the extreme tails" (that is, the lowest and highest values) were "considered unreliable."

After a dizzying array of further statistical manipulations to the Duke results, EPA ended up pulling a much smaller rabbit out of its hat: in EPA's hands, the average value of a case of bronchitis dropped to $260,000.[5]

Now we return to the arsenic analysis. Lacking a dollar value for nonfatal cases of bladder cancer, EPA's arsenic study ignored all the obvious differences between bladder cancer and bronchitis, assumed that the two diseases are equally severe, and declared the bladder cancer value equal to the 1980s Greensboro bronchitis value—carefully corrected for inflation, of course.

This is not, we hope and believe, because anyone thinks that bronchitis and bladder cancer are the same disease. The reason is more mundane: no one had performed an analysis of the cost of bladder cancer, and even the extensive analysis of arsenic regulations did not include enough time and money to do so. Therefore, the investigators used an estimated value for a very different disease. The only explanation offered for this procedure was that it had been done before, and nothing better was available. As one critic said, bronchitis is apparently close enough to bladder cancer for government work.[6]

Use of the bronchitis valuation to represent bladder cancer can charitably be described as grasping at straws. Lacking the time and money for even a moderately thoughtful guesstimate, the economists working on the arsenic study simply picked a number. This is not remotely close to the level of rigor that is seen throughout the natural science, engineering, and public health portions of the arsenic analysis. It is not a failure of will or intellect, but rather the inescapable limitations of time and budget, that lead to reliance on dated, inappropriate, and incomplete information to assign a dollar value to health. That puzzling process appears necessary in order to fill in the gaps on the benefit side of a cost-benefit analysis. Yet even without the inevitable constraints on time and resources, economic analysis would fail to capture the pricelessness of human health.

Reliance on problematic approximations of prices is not needed in real markets. No one pricing the hardware needed to remove arsenic from drinking water had to rely on surveys in a mall in Greensboro over a decade earlier, estimating the price of the wrong piece of equipment. Hardware vendors love to tell you what hardware costs. But who will sell you a cancer-free life? Health, unlike hardware, is not for sale, so you can't ask vendors for a price.

Quality Time

In 1990, the state of Oregon earned a unique place in medical history. Implementing a scheme to ration health care for Medicaid patients, the Oregon Health Services Commission published a comprehensive list of medical treatments, ranked from best to worst. A line was drawn part of the way down the list; the state's plan was that Medicaid would pay only for treatments above the line. Treatments were ranked in terms of cost per Quality Adjusted Life Year (QALY), a new measurement that has been widely discussed in the economics of health care. The Oregon list was the first major use of QALYs in public policy.

QALYs are an attempt to provide a single numerical measure for all forms of health. Assume for now that every possible health status could be ranked on a scale ranging from 0 for death to 100 percent for perfect health. Then a medical treatment that leads to one additional year of perfect health (one year at 100 percent) could be said to have the same value to society as another treatment that yields two additional years of half-perfect health (two years at 50 percent): each produces one *quality-adjusted life-year.* The rankings can be obtained by asking people to assign a number from 0 to 100 to various health states, or by more complicated survey research involving hypothetical gambles and tradeoffs. QALYs offer the advantage of asking people to compare one health status with another, not health status to money. The theory is that health, as measured by QALYs, is equally valuable, however and wherever it is created, so there should be widespread support for the goal of delivering the greatest number of QALYs at the lowest possible cost. However, this theoretical promise does not pan out in practice.

In fact, Oregon's 1990 list was a public relations disaster, met with immediate and overwhelming rejection. It ranked cures for thumb-sucking and treatment of various dental problems as highly cost-effective, ahead of treatments for ectopic pregnancy, cystic fibrosis, and AIDS.[7] No one believed that it was a sensible guide for public policy, and it was quickly withdrawn for revisions. Later versions of the Oregon list reduced the role of QALY-based calculations, and instead relied more and more on judgments by public health officials and other observers. By the time Oregon won federal approval to use the list in running the state's Medicaid program in 1993, all traces of QALYs had been eliminated.[8]

It is possible, as some critics have suggested, that Oregon simply used the wrong formula, or the wrong set of QALY rankings. And it appears that, despite the rhetoric, the adoption of the list has resulted in little or no actual rationing of health care, and only trivial economic savings. Other states have not rushed to follow Oregon's example.[9] But the problem goes deeper than the specific obstacles encountered in Oregon. Even if the numbers and formulas are patched up, QALYs will never provide a good measure of the value of health or a reliable standard for shaping public health policy. A detailed evaluation and critique of QALYs by Erik Nord, a senior researcher at Norway's National Institute of Public Health, points out several flaws in the underlying logic.[10]

The QALY approach assumes that our goal is to maximize total health benefits (the total number of quality-adjusted life years), regardless of how they are distributed. This assumption clashes with widespread beliefs about fairness in medical treatment in at least three ways. First, it ignores the severity of the disease; if more years of improvement can be produced for the same expenditure treating thumb-sucking instead of AIDS, the QALY standard would spend the money on cures for thumb-sucking. Many people, however, feel that we should treat the most serious diseases first, and that AIDS should come before thumb-sucking on the list of health care priorities. In general, the methods used to assign QALY rankings seem to give excessive weight to smaller illnesses. A comparative study found that QALYs give much greater importance to minor complaints, and relatively less importance to death, than other methods of health valuation.[11]

Second, QALY measurements discriminate against the disabled by placing a lower value on their lives. If John is unable to walk and must use a wheelchair, a year of his life is worth less than one QALY, even when he is otherwise healthy, since his experience is adjusted downward for his disability. On the other hand, if Ann is in perfect health, a year of her life is worth one full QALY. If they are both facing the same life-threatening disease, and have the same life expectancy if treated, more QALYs are saved by treating Ann. If resources are scarce and difficult choices must be made, John will lose every time; that is to say, QALY calculations are inherently biased against the disabled—or anyone else with an adverse health condition.

A more equitable approach would offer everyone an equal opportunity to reach his or her own best possible health status, regardless of disability. This is not just a good idea, it's the law: in the first year of the Clinton administration, the federal Department of Health and Human Services objected to the Oregon Medicaid plan because its reliance on QALYs discriminated against the disabled, and threatened to violate the Americans with Disabilities Act.[12]

A third problem is that QALY calculations discriminate on the basis of age: it is generally "worth" less to treat the elderly, because they have so few years left to be saved. QALYs by definition assign an equal value to every person-year, implying that one healthy young person's life is worth more than several of those of older people. This is a radically inequitable standard, which clashes with virtually every major religious and philosophical value system, not to mention the principles of equality embodied in our Constitution and laws. The value of life estimates in Chapter 4 might be said to make life profane—but at least every life is equally so when everyone's life has the same monetary value. In QALY–land the equality of all individuals is gone, replaced by an unfamiliar new standard of equality of all person-years of experience.

Aside from questions of equity and ultimate values, it appears that people do not actually think about health in terms of impacts per person-year. Nord argues that, according to opinion surveys, having a disease for two years is considered worse than having it for one year, but not nearly twice as bad. There is also evidence that the elderly and the sick are just as anxious—and just as willing to pay—to avoid risks as the young and healthy are.[13] Completely lost in the shuffle is the once common, but apparently fast receding, belief that older people are especially valuable because of their greater wisdom and experience.

QALY calculations are relatively new, and it is possible that further development of the method will smooth over some of the roughest spots. If QALYs are to be used, then adjusting the numbers to change the relative weights given to minor versus major diseases, would be an improvement. However, the biases against the disabled and the elderly are intrinsic problems with any version of QALYs. Difficulties also arise from the initial assumption that it is meaningful to put death and minor ailments on the same simple numerical scale. Once this is done, a certain number of headaches become numerically equivalent to losing your life, a notion that is at odds with all ordinary thinking about life and health. Do the people who are interviewed to determine QALY rankings actually understand the numbers game they are playing any better than the Greensboro shoppers who gave us the value of bronchitis?

A Minimal Measure

Some of the costs of illness are naturally expressed in monetary terms. If you suffer from a migraine headache, you will probably produce less at work, either because you stay home or because you are less effective than usual when you stagger through your job. You, or your health plan, may also spend money on medical visits and headache remedies. The costs of lost production and medical treatment have market prices; it is easy to see how to describe them in monetary terms.

In contrast, consider the excruciating pain, the subjective experience of the migraine itself. The pain is central to the story—it is, after all, the reason why a migraine attack is a problem—but it does not have a price; it is not for sale in the market. This is the stumbling block to monetizing health: essential aspects of the experience are not marketed commodities. The simplest method of valuing health, the so-called Cost of Illness (COI) calculation, deals with the problem by intentionally ignoring it. COI estimates include *only* the monetary costs associated with illness, usually meaning losses in economic production plus costs of treatment. The good news is that COI avoids all the tangled philosophical problems of assigning market values to human feelings. That is also the bad news: COI says nothing about what it feels like to be sick, in effect assigning a price of zero to the discomfort, pain, suffering, and disability that can accompany illness and injury.

Recall from Chapter 1 that lead causes neurological deficits in children, who will, as a result, earn less in later years when they enter the workforce. As we've seen, estimates of the monetary cost of lead poisoning—the loss of future earnings, plus the cost of remedial education and medical treatment for extreme cases—have reached more than $8,000 per lost IQ point per child. This is surely an incomplete measure of the social cost of lead poisoning: nothing is included for the change in the child's quality of life and capabilities outside of work, nor for the impact on the parents.

Beyond the obvious incompleteness of COI, its other limitation is the dependence on individual incomes and productivity. Lost production due to illness is a major part of COI, and higher-paid people produce higher-valued output—which seems to mean that their health is more valuable. Judging by COI, it must be worth more to cure the migraines of the rich than the poor, since the rich earn so much when they feel healthy. Similarly, a COI standard might say that it is more important to reduce lead exposure among white boys rather than black girls, because their expected future earnings (which would be diminished by lead poisoning) are so much greater. And it is "worth" very little to cure retired people of anything, since they no longer have earnings that could be lost to illness. Just as the human capital, or future earnings, method turns out to be woefully inadequate and fundamentally inequitable in describing the loss associated with human deaths, so the COI approach is incomplete and inequitable in describing the true costs of illness.

Ergonomic Economics and a Credulous Congress

COI could still be used in a limited form of cost-benefit analysis. If the easily captured monetary benefits of a regulation are larger than the costs, there is a strong argument for the regulation: in this case, the regulation appears desirable, even without considering the benefits of reduced pain, suffering, and disability. Do COI calculations, for all their limitations, receive widespread support in practice? Are regulatory measures readily accepted if their COI benefits exceed their costs? Alas, no. The subtleties and uncertainties of understanding and measuring health are typically overwhelmed by the extraordinarily partisan nature of debate about regulation, destroying any hope of consensus. The debate over ergonomics—the science of designing workplaces to prevent disabling backaches, carpal tunnel syndrome, and other repetitive-motion injuries—provides an unfortunately clear example.

Many workers perform repetitive physical tasks on the job. The same motions are repeated, again and again, in many types of office work and computer use, meatpacking, parcel delivery, assembly line work, truck driving, and hospital and nursing home care. In numerous cases, workers adapt themselves to poorly designed workplaces in ways that make them less efficient, and eventually, in many cases, less healthy as well. More than 600,000 U.S. workers suffer injuries from overexertion or repetition—"musculoskeletal disorders," in the medical parlance—every year, resulting in workers' compensation payments of $15–20 billion. This represents about one-third of all serious occupational injuries or illnesses, and one-third of the total amount spent on workers' compensation. With indirect costs factored in, the COI, or total economic cost of these injuries, may reach $60 billion every year. And this doesn't account for the less tangible human toll exacted by such injuries. In the most extreme cases, workers are disabled by ergonomic injuries, and report that they can no longer perform such simple tasks as doing the laundry, shopping for groceries, or, most poignantly, gathering up their children in their arms.[14]

Many businesses have programs designed to reduce injuries due to overexertion and repetitive motion. What they've found is heartening. Not only are many, perhaps most, such injuries preventable, but they are preventable at low *or even negative net cost.* That is, many companies have found they can protect their workers and save money doing so. (Some members of Washington's think-tank community found this impossible as a matter of principle; they were simply unwilling to take yes for an answer.)[15]

The Occupational Safety and Health Administration (OSHA), an agency within the Department of Labor, is charged with "assur[ing] so far as possible every working man and woman in the Nation safe and healthful working conditions."[16] For over ten years, OSHA kept promising to develop a rule to address workplace ergonomic injuries. During the time OSHA spent studying the issue, more than 6 million workers suffered ergonomic injuries serious enough to require time off from work.

For several years during the 1990s, Congress—through riders attached to appropriations bills, the latest favorite way of sneaking pro-business goodies into law—forbade OSHA from spending any money even to study workplace injuries arising from overexertion and repetition. Finally, when the ban was lifted, OSHA proposed and then, in the last days of the Clinton administration, finalized, a new rule designed to reduce these injuries. OSHA figured that the rule would produce at least $9 billion in easily ascertained benefits while imposing about $4 billion in costs—not a bad ratio, especially given that OSHA tends to overstate the costs of its rules.[17] As a bonus, the rule itself read as though it had been drafted by economists who have been urging greater flexibility in regulation. Rather than forcing employers to adopt specific work practices or to install specific technologies to address workplace injuries, the rule allowed them to achieve injury-reduction in the way they thought best.

Congress, after just ten hours of debate on a regulation ten years in the making, overturned OSHA's rule and told the agency to start over. Many representatives were alarmed by, among other things, the alleged costs of the rule—which might, according to one industry attorney, reach as high as $1 trillion, making the rule the most expensive in the history of the nation.[18] Never mind that OSHA thought the rule would cost $4 billion; so little did members of Congress apparently think of OSHA's ability to estimate costs that a number—the $1 trillion estimate for which no one in the congressional debates could identify the original source—became as authoritative as OSHA's detailed research.

Eugene Scalia, son of Supreme Court Justice Antonin Scalia, was then appointed the lead lawyer in the Department of Labor, where his duties apparently included preventing significant action on ergonomics. The younger Scalia is fond of equating ergonomics with "junk science."[19] Yet the language of cost-benefit comparisons has become so familiar, and its partisan abuses so well-developed, that industry lobbyists were able to dismiss OSHA's hard work on the basis of junk economics.

More than a year after the defeat of the original OSHA ergonomics regulation, the Bush administration offered its own alternative. It imposed no mandatory standards whatsoever, created no obligation to eliminate any hazards, and called on employers to take merely voluntary steps to reduce ergonomic injuries. OSHA's director, John Henshaw, said this was superior to the Clinton approach because it would cost companies less to carry out. If this is the new standard

for protection of health and safety, then it is only the health
and safety of corporate balance sheets that we are still protecting.

Can Cancers Be Counted?

One reason why it was easy for Congress to undo the ergonomics rule was that it was, fundamentally, about pain—
subjective, difficult to verify, but nonetheless very real pain.
Many adverse health conditions have this characteristic: they
can be dismissed, by those who are so inclined, on the
grounds that they are trivial, or perhaps do not even exist.

Economic analysis of health and health-protecting policies
requires a double dose of quantitative precision, not only in
assigning dollar values to each level of health, but also in the
prior step of coming up with numerical measures of health
outcomes. The need for precise numbers creates a bias toward
taking "hard" data on illnesses and injuries, as recorded by experts, more seriously than "soft" data on painful sensations.
Eugene Scalia complained that OSHA's original approach to
ergonomics would have forced companies to respond to
workers' self-reported symptoms such as "tingling" or "fatigue" (which are often the early warning signs of much
worse symptoms to come). While he thinks that "physicians
typically rely on objective criteria to make diagnoses" of conventional diseases, Scalia believes that "ergonomists rely heavily on subjective reports of pain and discomfort in
'diagnosing' musculoskeletal disorders, yet those subjective
reports often will be unreliable. . . ."[20]

To avoid such messy subjectivity, analysis of the health benefits of regulation often narrows its focus to conditions that

experts can quantify. For example, the cost-benefit analysis of the arsenic standard identifies many diseases caused by arsenic but provides numbers for only two types of cancer. The arsenic study is not alone in this respect; quite often, cancer is the only quantified health effect of pollution. Focusing on cancer alone creates the misleading impression that workplace regulation of formaldehyde costs a staggering $72 billion per life saved (see Table 3.1). As we saw in Chapter 3, a major purpose of the regulation is to prevent frequent, painful, but nonfatal effects caused by exposure to formaldehyde; it also prevents a very small, but more easily measured, number of cancer deaths.

Detection of cancer appears to be a simple, well-defined question: do you have a tumor or not? The doctor will tell you the answer, based on "objective" criteria. For research purposes, state cancer registries provide a wealth of data, making information about cancer much more readily available than about other diseases. Yet even in this best case, the image of objectivity and precision can be misleading. Not all tumors are malignant; errors in diagnosis can occur in both directions, as benign tumors may be detected, triggering unnecessary procedures, while more threatening ones may be missed.[21] Additional problems arise in tracing the causal relationships between the cancers we do detect and human activities and substances that we can regulate, such as the release of toxic chemicals into the environment. Here, the critics of regulation are not only challenging the economics of environmental protection; the findings of environmental science are also subject to partisan, often ill-informed, debate. Statistical evidence on toxicity and human health, the scientific foundation of environmental health protection, often receives the same dismissive treatment as "subjective," self-reported pain—and from the same conservative opponents of regulation.

Law and Toxicology

Business lobbies and prominent conservatives have long criticized the science behind EPA's regulations. Here is the Business Roundtable, a lobbying group comprised of CEOs of major corporations, on EPA's science:

> The science capabilities of EPA and other agencies have not kept step with the growing need for good data and rigorous analysis to support decision making. . . . EPA and other agencies do not effectively involve the external scientific community in major risk assessments, implement rigorous peer review programs, or maintain the neutrality of the scientific assessment process.[22]

In order to achieve "neutrality," the Business Roundtable thought it would be a good idea to get the White House more directly involved in managing EPA's scientists. The CEOs have supported "an effective, fully integrated research planning and management process with strong leadership from the White House."[23]

They must be very happy with the Bush White House, which has also made reform of agency science a top priority. Through the Office of Information and Regulatory Affairs at OMB, the Bush administration has begun to assert an unprecedented degree of control over agencies' application of scientific evidence. This office is headed by John Graham, the critic of regulation whom we met in Chapter 3, and is staffed almost entirely by economists, although Graham has also hired a handful of scientists for the first time in the office's history. Despite its limited scientific expertise, Graham's office has waded deeply into the technical aspects of regulation throughout the federal government. Under Graham, it has threatened to make "peer review," the standard for publication in scientific journals, the standard for agency rules as well (which could add years to the research effort needed to justify a new rule); it has presumed to tell EPA how it should conduct scientific research into the health effects of air pollution; and it has issued intrusive, wide-ranging guidelines to federal agencies on how to ensure the quality of the data they disseminate. The package of "reforms" initiated by OIRA threatens to stop many health, safety, and environmental regulations in their tracks.

Likewise, when a controversial new rule is proposed, the right-wing think-tank crowd in Washington goes to work on rewriting the science as well as the economics, to strengthen their "proof" that regulation is always wrong. That's what happened in the case of arsenic regulation. EPA's cost-benefit analysis of the arsenic rule had plenty of problems. As we have noted, it offered numerical estimates for only two of the many diseases caused by arsenic (bladder cancer and lung cancer), and it relied heavily on the problematical $6.1 million valuation of lives saved and the inexcusable equation of bladder cancer with bronchitis. What the study did have, however, was a detailed review of the medical and scientific literature, and a careful calculation of the expected numbers of bladder cancer and lung cancer deaths from drinking water containing arsenic. But as soon as the study was published, a widely cited response, by Jason Burnett and Robert Hahn of the AEI–Brookings Joint Center for Regulatory Studies, attacked EPA's calculation, arguing that the likely number of deaths might be as low as one-fifth of EPA's figure.[24]

The point raised by Burnett and Hahn, though it sounds obscure, comes up repeatedly in attacks on environmental science. We often know the death rate only from very high doses of a toxic material such as arsenic. A few small regions of the world have tragically high levels of naturally occurring arsenic in their drinking water, many times higher than the U.S. regulatory standard would allow. Much of what we know about the harm caused by arsenic comes from studying the health of people in these regions. The debate is about the way in which that information is translated into estimates of the harm from lower levels of arsenic.

Suppose that we knew the death rate only from drinking water containing 500 parts per billion (ppb) of arsenic.* EPA's approach assumes that the impact is proportional to the level of arsenic: with 50 ppb, there would be one-tenth as many deaths as at 500 ppb; with 5 ppb of arsenic in the water, one-hundredth of the original death rate would be expected. The same rule of proportionality is used, no matter how small the exposure. That is, although the effects get smaller as the level of arsenic declines, EPA assumes there is no point at which arsenic ceases causing adverse health effects. On this approach, there is clearly no "threshold" for disease, or completely safe level of arsenic, except zero. In the jargon of the field, this is called a "linear, no-threshold dose-response relationship."

---

* This is a hypothetical round number chosen to simplify the following explanation, not a description of actual data.

Burnett and Hahn object to this assumption because they believe there is a threshold below which arsenic is not harmful, and they also believe that the shape of the dose–response curve above the threshold is nonlinear. If they are right, then as the level of arsenic drops down toward the threshold, the harm caused by arsenic must be falling faster than EPA assumes, and when the threshold is reached, arsenic is harmless.[25] In other words, if there actually is a safe threshold and if the dose–response curve is shaped as Burnett and Hahn believe it is, then EPA's method overstates the death rate from arsenic at low doses. On the other hand, if there actually is no threshold, or a very low one, and if the dose–response curve is linear, then Burnett and Hahn are understating the risks from arsenic. Thus EPA's assumption of a no–threshold, linear relationship is a cautious approach, creating a strong case for environmental protection.

EPA has a long tradition, repeatedly endorsed by scientific reviewers, of assuming that there is no safe threshold for carcinogens, and that there is a linear relationship between exposure and effect, until these assumptions are proved mistaken. However, on the basis of a very casual discussion of the scientific evidence, Burnett and Hahn claimed that there was a threshold for arsenic consumption, that the dose–response curve was nonlinear, and that EPA's scientists were badly mistaken. Legal discussion of the arsenic standard now wanders deep into the scientific arguments for and against the linear dose–response relationship, forcing lawyers and judges who (like Burnett and Hahn) have no training in toxicology to take stands on these technical intricacies.[26] Will "law and economics," the conservative, market-oriented school of legal theory, now be joined by "law and toxicology"?

The technical quarrel over arsenic is not an isolated example. Today, the most vociferous critics of regulation virtually never concede that a scientific risk assessment has been performed adequately by a government agency; rather, they report, almost without exception, that the actual risk of whatever is being regulated is either zero or close to it. The technicalities of the scientific process for assessing risk thus become part of the debate: if, in fact, no one will die because of arsenic or benzene, then no protective regulation is warranted, and it hardly even matters if we get the price right. Likewise, on an even bigger scale, if—as conservative pundit Bjorn Lomborg and others have claimed—none of the environmental problems scientists believe beset the world (climate change, acid rain, etc.) are really problems, then why fret so much about attaching a dollar value to life or health or nature?

The same arguments about linear no-threshold relationships have arisen about standards for radiation exposure. A lot is at stake: a looser standard, allowing higher exposure to radioactivity, would save industry huge amounts of money in the cleanup of contaminated soil around nuclear reactors and weapons facilities, while a tighter, more expensive standard would provide more protection for workers and surrounding communities. EPA favors a tighter standard, while the Nuclear Regulatory Commission favors a looser one.[27] The debate again turns on the question of whether there is a threshold below which radiation is not harmful (supporting a looser standard), or whether it is safer to assume a no-threshold, linear dose-response relationship and maintain a tighter limit.

Radioactivity is one of the best-studied of all health hazards, with evidence of its risks stretching back into the nineteenth century. In 1896, the year after the discovery of X rays, Thomas Edison warned of the dangers of radioactivity. In the same year, Elihu Thomson, a prominent physicist, tested the effects by deliberately exposing his little finger to X rays for long periods of time. The results—including pain, swelling, and blisters—persuaded Thomson of the risks involved.[28] Yet after more than a century of additional experience and research, scientists continue to disagree about the exact health impacts of low doses of radioactivity. The National Council on Radiation Protection and Risks issued a massive report in 2001, entirely devoted to evaluating the assumption of a linear, no-threshold relationship—and recommended sticking with that assumption, finding that "there is not conclusive evidence on which to reject" it.[29]

Delaying the Dioxin Decision

It is tempting to dismiss the partisan debate over the intricacies of arsenic as a problem that will be solved by further research. But the same technical disagreement still lingers over the effects of radiation, after more than a century of intensive study; it may take an impossibly long time for science to resolve all the uncertainties. Moreover, new uncertainties and technical quandaries are appearing all the time, as technology creates countless new synthetic materials and potentially hazardous emissions. The difficulty of providing firm scientific proof of the environmental causes of health problems, suitable for winning in court, has been dramatized in two popular nonfiction movies, *A Civil Action* and *Erin Brockovich*.

Unfortunately, it is often in the interest of industry to highlight the remaining uncertainties and extend the debate about environmental toxins for as long as possible, in order to forestall regulation. Take the long-running scientific debate about dioxin, which many analysts believe to be one of the most potent carcinogens ever discovered. Dioxin contamination was a principal reason for the evacuation in 1980 of Love Canal, in New York, and in 1983 of Times Beach, Missouri. Dioxin is an unwanted by-product of certain kinds of industrial chlorine chemistry (including the chlorine bleaching of paper), and the combustion of chlorine-containing fuels (such as the incineration of polyvinyl chloride, or PVC).

More than a decade ago, at the insistence of industry groups affected by then-existing regulation of dioxin, EPA began to reassess dioxin's risks.[30] EPA eventually produced a draft report concluding that dioxin posed an even greater health hazard than had been previously imagined, and that its hazards extended beyond cancer to other health effects, including effects on the hormonal and reproductive systems. A scientific advisory panel chock-full of industry-connected members criticized EPA for failing to adopt a nonlinear dose-response curve for dioxin—showing again the importance of this arcane issue for environmental regulation. One of the members of this advisory panel was John Graham, then the head of the Harvard Center for Risk Analysis, which received substantial funding from the industries affected by dioxin regulation.[31]

EPA produced a new draft of its dioxin reassessment in the spring of 2000. Once again, in this report, EPA concluded that the risks of dioxin may be distinctly greater than they were thought to be when the reassessment began.[32] A summary of the findings on EPA's Web site says that

> EPA estimates that the amount of dioxin found in the tissues of the general human population . . . closely approaches (within a factor of 10) the levels at which adverse effects might be expected to occur. . . . For cancer, EPA estimates that the risks for the general population based on dioxin exposure may exceed 1 in 1,000 increased chance of experiencing cancer. . . . Actual risks are unlikely to exceed this value and may be substantially less. This range of cancer risk indicates an about 10-fold higher chance than estimated in EPA's earlier (1994) draft of this reassessment.[33]

But the report has not been formally released. The Office of Management and Budget has recommended that the report undergo yet another round of review—this time by the National Academy of Sciences.[34] The dioxin debate, fueled by industry-funded science and kept alive by industry influence, is like a modern-day version of *Bleak House:* it's the regulatory process that just won't end.

Promoting the Precautionary Principle

If technical doubts and partisan debate still surround the effects of arsenic, radiation, and dioxin, there is no hope of waiting for definitive proof and scientific consensus on the effects of all the other health hazards of modern life. Instead, it is essential to act in a precautionary manner as soon as we have reasonable grounds to suspect that there are major risks to health. The proverbial advice "better safe than sorry" has been reborn in recent years as the "precautionary principle," calling for policies to protect health from potential hazards even when definitive proof and measurement of those haz-

ards is not yet available. The Rio Declaration, adopted by the
United Nations Conference on Environment and Development in Rio de Janeiro in 1992, and signed by the first President Bush, states that

> In order to protect the environment, the precautionary ap-
> proach shall be widely applied by States according to their ca-
> pabilities. Where there are threats of serious or irreversible
> damage, lack of full scientific certainty shall not be used as a
> reason for postponing cost-effective measures to prevent en-
> vironmental degradation.[35]

A consensus statement on the precautionary principle by a
group of environmental scientists concludes:

> Scientific studies can tell us something about the costs, risks,
> and benefits of a proposed action, but there will always be
> value judgments that require political decisions. . . . Al-
> though there are some situations in which risks clearly ex-
> ceed benefits no matter whose values are being considered,
> there is usually a large gray area in which science alone can-
> not (and should not) be used to decide policy. . . . When
> there is substantial scientific uncertainty about the risks and
> benefits of a proposed activity, policy decisions should be
> made in a way that errs on the side of caution with respect to
> the environment and the health of the public.[36]

Economists have been slower to endorse the precautionary
principle; the economic literature directly addressing the subject is sparse.[37] But much of what we have already recounted
about the critics' brief against regulation is equally aimed at
rejecting the precautionary principle. The precautionary ap-

proach is hard for the cost-benefit worldview to digest. Pre-cautionary policy making rejects the quantitative formula of cost-benefit analysis, replacing it with a process of reasoning and deliberation that cannot be reduced to an alternative for-mula. As one sympathetic economist says, "Rather than ask-ing how much toxic pollution we can live with, the precautionary principle asks what kind of a world we want to live in, and provides a decision-making framework for getting us there."[38]

Although these descriptions may sound vague and hard to implement, the underlying principle is a crucial one. In spe-cific cases, it is often easy to see how much difference a pre-cautionary approach makes—or would have made. A report from the European Environmental Agency, *Late Lessons from Early Warnings,* documents the high cost of past failures to act on early health warnings.[39] Hundreds of thousands of deaths and painful illnesses could have been avoided if society had responded promptly to the initial evidence of the dangers of asbestos, radiation, benzene, DES, MTBE, and other all-too-familiar hazards to our health.

As Thomas Legge—Britain's former Chief Medical In-spector of Factories—said, "Looking back in the light of pre-sent knowledge, it is impossible not to feel that opportunities for discovery and prevention of asbestos disease were badly missed." Legge made that comment in 1934; the first detailed account of the health hazards of working with asbestos was al-ready old news by then, having been published in Britain in 1898. Insurers refused coverage to asbestos workers, due to their workplace exposure, as early as 1918. Yet use of asbestos continued to expand throughout most of the twentieth cen-tury. The rising tide of asbestos liability claims drove Johns

Manville, the world's largest asbestos company, into bankruptcy in 1982; insurance payments for asbestos claims almost sank Lloyd's of London in the early 1990s. All of those claims were for illnesses contracted decades after the hazards of asbestos had been widely publicized. Still, asbestos was not banned in Europe until 1998, and even then the ban was delayed by a trade protest from Canada, a major asbestos producer. The World Trade Organization finally upheld the European bans in 2001.[40]

Asbestos regulation in the United States has fared even worse. Despite workplace standards limiting asbestos exposures and tort judgments penalizing asbestos companies for failing to warn workers and others of the dangers of asbestos, EPA remained convinced that overall asbestos exposures in the United States were still too high. After studying the issue for ten years and producing an administrative record running 45,000 pages, EPA finally decided in 1989 to ban the production and distribution of asbestos. Three years later, a federal appeals court overturned the ban because it thought EPA hadn't studied the matter carefully enough. Since that legal setback, EPA has never again proposed a ban on asbestos.[41]

Regulating by the Numbers

With health, as with life itself, it simply does not work to replace real policy discussion with artificial number crunching. Interviewing shoppers in shopping malls, asking citizens about "quality-adjusted life-years," assuming that age and disability make lives less worthwhile, generating estimates of medical expenses and lost work days—none of these methods tells us what we need to know about the value of human health. The first two methods, using WTP and QALYs, wind up making us more confused than enlightened, and the last, using the COI, deliberately gives up the effort to value the things we want good health *for,* such as freedom of movement and freedom from pain. When we try to convert health into dollars, as when we try to convert lives into dollars, much of what is important gets lost in the translation.

Even when we try to quantify the illnesses or deaths themselves, quite apart from monetizing them, we run into fundamental problems. Three decades after we started regulating toxic hazards in the environment and workplace, we still have no consensus about which risks are the worst, and how big they are. Maybe there is just too much at stake, economically and otherwise, for consensus to be possible; maybe the science is hard enough that consensus will always lie outside our reach. Whatever the reason, we need a tie-breaking principle for cases of scientific uncertainty. This is the role the precautionary principle plays in the system of risk regulation. The idea is to step in *before* there are "dead bodies"—to step in, in fact, before we can even count how many there might eventually be. We will return to the implementation of the precautionary principle in Chapter 9.

Numbers—of dollars and of dead or unhealthy bodies—are the unifying theme of cost-benefit analysis and its scientific underpinnings. But numbers don't tell us everything. They don't tell us whether chronic bronchitis is indeed like bladder cancer (we suspect it is not); they don't tell us whether it is fair to expose a certain group of people to a lethal risk because other people are willing and able to pay more to avoid it; they don't tell us whether a day of downhill skiing or bungee jumping is just as fit a subject for regulation as a day of exposure to arsenic in drinking water or radiation from nuclear waste handling. For these kinds of answers, we need to turn to something beyond the numbers. The additional, qualitative dimensions of risk, including fairness, are the subject of Chapter 6.

6

Dreadful Events

The four planes piloted by terrorists that slammed into the Twin Towers, the Pentagon, and a field in rural Pennsylvania reshaped American life. Within a year after these terrorist attacks, Congress approved tens of billions of dollars in spending related to the attacks. The entire federal bureaucracy was reshuffled, with tens of thousands of federal employees funneled into a new Department of Homeland Security. The U.S. Capitol was surrounded by barricades. Hundreds of prisoners languished in isolated detention in Guantánamo Bay, Cuba, as a result of alleged ties to terrorism. And our government went to war in Afghanistan, then turned to planning and launching a bigger war with Iraq. Many thousands of people—Afghanis, Americans, Iraqis, Pakistanis, and others—have died in the battles spawned by September 11.

In many different ways, September 11 was indeed an event of monstrous proportions. Yet the official death toll from the terrorist attacks was scarcely 3,000. To put this number in statistical perspective, we could observe that this is far smaller than the number of people who die from ulcers in the U.S. every year.[1] It is smaller than the number who die from viral hepatitis, from nutritional deficiencies, or from anemia. The terrorists' death toll is dwarfed by the yearly toll from emphysema (17,500); suicide (30,500); and motor vehicle accidents (43,500). And it doesn't even come close to the numbers felled each year by diabetes (62,600); cancer (541,500); and heart disease (940,600). Yet viral hepatitis and anemia barely register a blip on the radar screen of public outrage, and even diabetes and heart disease have not caused a large-scale restructuring of American society.

To compare the September 11 death toll to the annual death toll from anemia, or gall bladder disorders, and to express curiosity as to the very different responses to these similar statistics, might persuade many readers that we should have our heads examined. Of course, the readers might respond, September 11 was different from anemia; it was worse. It was worse, even, than the twenty-fold-higher death toll from diabetes. Everyone knows this.

But, as we discuss in this chapter, everyone does not know this. Some people, in fact, think that the way to make decisions about risk is to engage in exactly the sorts of numerical comparisons we have just questioned. And even when people agree that numerically identical risks can justify different responses, they don't always think carefully about *why*. Most of us, when thinking about and responding to risks to life and health, care about more than numerical probabilities of harm. The reasons we care about other things, too, have a lot to do with convictions deeply held and widely shared in American society, including an aversion to catastrophe and an attachment to freedom and fairness.

Killer Bambis

> If most Americans consider industrial waste dumps to pose much greater dangers to themselves than the millions of deer that roam the nation's highways, the reason lies in public discourse, notably the content of the mass media. Whereas the electronic and print media are replete with reports of industrial waste dumps, they seldom pay attention to the traffic injuries and deaths caused by deer herds that have grown fifty-four-fold since the 1940s. . . . [M]any people who consider environmental contamination an omnipresent and devastating danger think of deer as the affectionate, harmless, and vulnerable animals portrayed by Walt Disney's moving fable *Bambi*.
>
> —Timur Kuran and Cass Sunstein[2]

You might be tempted to dismiss the idea that government should be paying more attention to killer deer, and less to hazardous waste dumps, as something out of a *New Yorker* cartoon. But you would be wrong to do this. One of the most pervasive and influential arguments against current health, safety, and environmental policy is the claim that the government has for too long paid too much attention to risks that seem scary—like hazardous-waste dumps—and too little attention to risks that do not—like Bambi—without carefully considering the numerical probabilities of harm posed by each risk. Open any newspaper discussing a newly recognized and greatly feared risk—from shark attacks to West Nile Virus to sniper shootings in the Washington, D.C., suburbs—and you will find "the experts" explaining why, statistically speaking, our fears are unwarranted, even a little crazy.

Just before he was elevated to the United States Supreme Court, Judge Stephen Breyer wrote a book severely criticizing our present system for protecting health, safety, and the environment. (And he is, on most issues, one of the Supreme Court's more *liberal* justices.) He opened his discussion with a table showing the annual risks of dying from various causes. Smoking one pack or more of cigarettes a day topped Breyer's chart; next came skydiving, working as a fireman, being in an auto accident, and having an appendectomy.[3] Most of the risks avoided by health, safety, and environmental regulation would appear at the very bottom of the risk chart. In other words, according to Breyer, they are smaller than many other risks many of us face every day. (Those of us who do not smoke, go skydiving, fight fires, or have appendectomies on a regular basis might feel left out of the high end of Breyer's list. Of course, we might hit one of the millions of deer roaming the nation's highways.)

For Breyer, the apparent minuteness of the risks we regulate compared with the risks we ignore creates a presumptive case against the way our government addresses risks. Breyer was especially critical of environmental laws: rather than spend our money cleaning up hazardous-waste sites posing a relatively small risk of harm, for example, he suggested that we spend our money on programs providing, say, prenatal care and mammograms.

Despite statistics like those cited by Breyer, ordinary citizens who are not trained in the kinds of scientific and statistical methods we discussed in the last chapter tend to be more worried about hazardous-waste dumps than about killer Bambis. They tend to think that nuclear power plants are riskier than X rays,[4] while at the same time, they tend not to worry about quite common hazards such as diabetes and alcoholism.[5] These reactions do not correlate well with the probability of harm calculated by experts in the field of risk assessment. People trained in risk assessment will tell you, for example, that X rays cause more harm to human health in a year than nuclear power plants do. Nevertheless most laypeople fear the latter much more than the former. The result of catering to these fears, say critics like Justice Breyer, White House regulatory czar John Graham, and legal scholar Cass Sunstein, is a skewed regulatory system—one that rings the alarm at the sight of the tiniest amount of toxic waste yet sleeps while thousands fall to diabetes and heart disease. It is a system, John Graham has said, of "paranoia and neglect."[6]

As it happens, some of these same critics think that the scientific methods of risk assessment discussed in the preceding chapter tend to overstate risk by a great amount; this is part of the reason they think the risks we regulate are so tiny.[7] But even if the risks that are regulated are as great as many other experts and government agencies believe them to be, their current human health consequences are nevertheless dwarfed by risks associated with hypertension and diabetes. Thus, even apart from scientific disagreements, there remains a dispute about the kinds of risks that are most worth regulating.

Justice Breyer, along with Graham, Sunstein, and many others, says he wants the government to focus on the risks that kill the most people. To this end, Breyer proposed in his book that decisions about regulating risk be made by a small group of civil servants, trained in science, economics, and administration, and insulated from the political processes.[8] The group's mission would be to rationalize health, safety, and environmental regulation by targeting regulatory resources on programs that would save the most human lives. Breyer envisioned that science—not politics—would be the governing framework of his new regime. In his system, the government would probably decide to pay for vaccinations, prenatal care, and trips to cancer clinics for screening and treatment, rather than requiring cleanup of hazardous-waste dumps or control of toxic air pollution.[9] The government could do so, Breyer thought, only if it were freed from the excesses of public influence on the regulatory process—only if, in other words, ordinary people had little or no role to play in deciding which risks were addressed and which were ignored.[10]

Widely panned as antidemocratic at the time it was published,[11] Breyer's proposal has taken on a whole new life in the Bush administration. By asserting a powerful role for the White House in reviewing agency rules, and by minutely scrutinizing the scientific and economic analysis conducted by agencies in developing rules that protect health, safety, and the environment, the Office of Information and Regulatory Affairs within OMB, led by John Graham, has explicitly embraced Breyer's vision of an elite cadre of civil servants making risk-related policy for the country.[12]

It is hard to deny the rhetorical appeal of reforms billed as efforts to save more lives. When one looks at the reality behind the rhetoric, however, one must be forgiven some skepticism about the actual purposes of this kind of regulatory reform. Consider the following excerpt from a fund-raising letter John Graham wrote while he was the director of the Harvard Center for Risk Analysis:

> The Harvard Center for Risk Analysis was created in August 1989 to promote a reasoned public response to health, safety, and environmental hazards. Currently, America devotes a major share of national resources to minor health risks while neglecting relatively serious health risks. . . . The Center

seeks to participate in a longrun national effort to enhance public discussion about risk. Our strategy is to train young professionals how to think about risk in a balanced way, to target limited technical and human resources at the most important problems, and to participate vigorously in public policy debates about risk. . . . I am requesting $25,000 in financial support in 1992 and 1993 that can help the Center expand its public policy activities. It is important for me to learn more about the risk-related challenges that you face.[13]

The most surprising thing about the letter was its recipient: the Philip Morris Companies. Graham was seeking funding from a tobacco company to help him achieve his stated goal of "advanc[ing] public health by incorporating the principles of risk analysis into training programs, scientific research, and public policy." Smoking is the largest cause of avoidable death in this country; it kills approximately 440,000 Americans every year.[14] Smoking-cessation programs scored extremely well in Graham's studies of the cost-effectiveness of life-saving interventions.[15] Yet Graham clearly thought Philip Morris would find no inconsistency between supporting Graham's organization and its own self-interests. And Philip Morris evidently found no such inconsistency: it promptly sent the Harvard Center for Risk Analysis a check for $25,000.[16] Given the huge number of deaths and illnesses caused by smoking, one might wonder why Philip Morris would want to send money to someone who promoted increased reliance on numerical risk. The mystery is easily explained: while Graham has pushed for more emphasis on numbers, he has pushed just as hard to discredit the risk numbers published by other analysts and relied upon in regulating carcinogens and other harmful substances. Graham wants the experts to be in control, but he wants them to be *his* experts.

Citizens and Experts

Expert risk assessors, as we saw in the last chapter, have a well-established system for evaluating risk to humans. One can, in broad terms, predict what kinds of hazards will be deemed riskiest under their system: hazards that, with a high degree of probability, produce death or serious health effects in large populations of people.

Ordinary citizens also have a quite predictable framework for evaluating risks; it's just different from the experts' system. Decades of research into risk perception have identified a short list of characteristics that help to determine our perceptions of risk. When a hazard is unfamiliar, uncontrollable, involuntary, inequitable, dangerous to future generations, irreversible, man-made, and/or catastrophic, ordinary people are likely to view it as risky. These characteristics work in the other direction when they are reversed; that is, a hazard that is familiar, controllable, voluntary, equitable, dangerous only to the present generation, reversible, natural, and/or diffusely harmful is unlikely to generate much concern in the populace.[17] These dichotomous categories help to explain why an ordinary person might worry about nuclear power even as she makes her way to her doctor's office for an X ray.

Paul Slovic, a psychologist, is one of the leading figures in this field of research. He has found that perceptions of the risk from a particular hazard are closely related to how "dread" and/or "unknown" the hazard is. "Dread" risk is characterized by "a perceived lack of control, dread, catastrophic potential, fatal consequences, and the inequitable distribution of risks and benefits." "Unknown" risk is comprised of hazards thought to be "unobservable, unknown, new, and delayed in their manifestation of harm." Nuclear weapons and nuclear power are at the top of the list of dread risks; chemical technologies score at the high end of unknown risks.[18]

The basic insight from these accounts of risk perception is that ordinary citizens, in judging the riskiness of a substance or activity, take into account quality as well as quantity; they do not assess riskiness solely according to the numerical probability and magnitude of harm, but rely as well on the human setting in which a risk is experienced. As we saw in Chapter 4, the risks of death are numerically equal for a day of downhill skiing, a day of working in construction, and drinking twenty liters of water that just met the old regulatory standard for arsenic. Yet people evaluate these risks quite differently.

Contaminated Communities

Despite the experts' advice, people take their own risk perceptions seriously.[19] Prolonged exposure to dreaded risks frequently leads to deep and widespread anxiety, depression, and distrust. Many environmental risks have the features that create anxiety in ordinary citizens: they are unfamiliar, uncontrollable, involuntary, inequitable, dangerous to future generations, irreversible, man-made, and/or catastrophic. When a dumping ground for hazardous waste is discovered in a residential neighborhood, or a refinery constantly spews toxic pollutants into the air breathed by its neighbors, the affected communities—"contaminated communities," as environmental psychologist Michael Edelstein calls them[20]—often experience a series of reactions that can debilitate both individuals and the communities themselves.

Individuals have reported a wide range of adverse psychological responses to exposures whose harmful physical effects likely will not become manifest for years, perhaps decades. These responses include anxiety and anguish about their future health; depression; and physical conditions linked to their emotional distress, such as fatigue and insomnia, headaches, and stomach problems. Many of these responses have taken place in the context of heightened cancer risk, but a similar set of responses has been reported by people who have been exposed to a risk of other illnesses whose physical effects are not immediately manifest. Where there is no early test available to detect the presence (or absence) of disease in a person exposed to a disease-bearing agent, only time will tell whether the person will become sick. This prolonged uncertainty creates stress. A military veteran exposed to radiation during atomic testing described the awful uncertainty engendered by long-term risk by saying, "the worst would be better than this."[21]

Yale sociologist Kai Erickson has tried to explain why a special anxiety might be reserved for hazards whose physical consequences are remote and insidious:

> Toxic disasters . . . never end. Invisible contaminants remain a part of the surroundings, absorbed into the grain of the landscape, the tissues of the body, and worst of all, the genetic material of the survivors. An all-clear is never sounded. The book of accounts is never closed.[22]

"Chronic disasters" is the name Erickson gives to the cumulative, insidious, and gradual harm that is characteristic of so many environmental problems.[23]

Latent and insidious hazards provoke another kind of psychological response as well. A latent hazard is one that is dormant: a harmful agent, or the beginning of disease itself, is present but invisible. Latency thus creates a sense of *contamination,* of slow and invisible poison. Many people reserve a special dread for this kind of hazard. Kai Erickson's work is illuminating here, too. Toxic substances, he writes,

> invert the process by which disasters normally inflict harm. They do not charge in from outside and batter like a gust of wind or a wall of water. They slink in without warning, do no immediate damage so far as one can tell, and begin their deadly work from within—the very embodiment, it would seem, of stealth and treachery. . . . Toxic poisons provoke a special dread because they contaminate, because they are undetectable and uncanny and so can deceive the body's alarm systems, and because they can become absorbed into the very tissues of the body and crouch there for years, even generations, before doing their deadly work.[24]

In interviews with people who lived near the nuclear reactor at Three Mile Island in Pennsylvania when it experienced the nation's worst nuclear power accident to date, Erickson discovered a widespread sense of the kind of contamination he describes: people feared that radiation from the power plant had infiltrated their bodies, their genes, their houses, yards, and gardens. Simple events, like "grandchildren romping in [one's] backyard," had become laced with dread.[25]

Studies of communities that have lived through exposure

to prolonged and insidious risk have also revealed profound
and adverse effects on the communities themselves, beyond
the individual reactions just described. Within families and
among neighbors, long-lived threats have often produced
schisms and disputes that did not exist before the threatening
exposures occurred. Studies have found that one of the most
dramatic effects of environmental threats is a loss of trust.[26]
This generalized loss of trust in society's institutions extends,
most obviously, to the entities directly responsible for the
threat, but it also reaches the local, state, and federal government entities deemed responsible for reacting to the threat. In
some cases, citizens have lost more faith in the government
than in the polluter. This loss of trust can have severe effects
on citizens' relationship with their government, and on the
functioning of government itself. And once lost, trust is hard
to restore.[27]

The loss of trust experienced as a result of environmental
contamination is connected to the uncertainty surrounding
environmental threats. The government often finds itself in
the position of wanting to say something about the threat,
without having very much it can say. The dilemma is well-
illustrated by the ludicrously uninformative statement by the
U.S. Environmental Protection Agency regarding dioxin exposures in Missouri:

> Dioxin in Missouri may present one of the greatest environ-
> mental problems in the history of the United States. Con-
> versely, it may not.[28]

In the absence of information about the actual physical effects
of pollution—which, with long-term threats, may not be

available for many years, if ever—people are forced to come to their own conclusions about the risks they face. In the absence of good information about insidious threats, people often end up fearing the worst.

The social and psychological reactions we have described have been consistently reported by people who have lived through exposure to prolonged and insidious environmental threats. These include the famous events at Three Mile Island in Pennsylvania; Love Canal, New York; Times Beach, Missouri; and Woburn, Massachusetts. The community reactions are so strikingly similar from place to place, and so intimately tied to the special nature of toxic exposures, that one might say they comprise a kind of syndrome.

The cluster of disparate reactions, and their association with toxic exposures, is captured by the "demoralization scale" developed by Bruce Dohrenwend and his colleagues following the accident at Three Mile Island. The demoralization scale, a measure of "nonspecific stress," includes feelings of sadness, depression, loneliness, and anxiety; nervousness; restlessness; sour stomach; poor appetite; cold sweats; headaches; generalized physical ailments; and feelings of helplessness, hopelessness, uselessness, and failure. Populations exposed to various toxic episodes have been found to score higher on the demoralization scale than many other populations—including even the clients of mental health centers. Demoralization is, in sum, a shorthand way of describing a large part of the cluster of social and psychological responses common to toxic exposures.[29]

To summarize: certain kinds of risk not only frighten people, they also can make people severely anxious, depressed, distrustful, and angry, with correspondingly negative effects

on the communities in which they live. There is no doubt
that these emotional and social reactions are real, and bad, and
that people would be better off without them. One response
is to try to "educate people out of" these reactions by con-
vincing them that their fears are unfounded; another response, which we prefer, is to listen to their stories to see
whether there is some sense in them.

Unlimited Potential

When people worry about risks that are unfamiliar, unknown, and potentially catastrophic, they are expressing, in
part, a distaste for a special kind of uncertainty: one in which
the worst-case harmful potential of a hazard is unknown and
unlimited. When faced with a hard decision, many people
naturally ask: what's the worst that could happen? When this
question is unanswerable, or when the answer is intolerable,
worry sets in. Long intervals between a potentially harmful
event and harm itself only exacerbate the anxiety caused by
uncertainty. The prolonged and uncertain nature of many
modern threats to human health and the environment thus
helps explain why people are especially anxious about such
threats.

The kind of anxiety we are discussing is not limited to
threats caused by environmental exposures. Other kinds of
hazards can exhibit the same alarming and disconcerting uncertainty. Terrorism is an example; indeed, terrorism "works"
through the fear and demoralization caused by uncontrollable
uncertainty. Efforts to offset this fear by attaching necessarily
arbitrary numbers to the probabilities of being harmed by a

terrorist seem, especially in a post–September 11 world, ridiculous.

A case in point is a study done by Robert Hahn of the AEI–Brookings Joint Center for Regulatory Studies. Hahn is one of the most influential of the Washington think tanks' regulatory critics; his analyses of the costs and benefits of federal regulation are consistently cited as authoritative by OMB. He routinely finds that the benefits of regulation are not great enough to justify the costs (as we saw in the arsenic debate in Chapter 5). And it's not just environmental regulation that he finds to be unnecessary.

Shortly after TWA Flight 800 crashed into the ocean off the coast of Long Island in 1996, Hahn tried to assess the costs and benefits of enhanced airport security. He opined that the costs of improved airport security were not worth the benefits. The benefits, he thought, were quite small given that, at the time of his study, only an average of thirty-seven people per year died in terrorist incidents. If that number were increased ten-fold or even one hundred-fold, he said, the benefits of improved airport security still would not exceed the costs. September 11, of course, did increase the terrorist death toll for 2001 by almost one hundred–fold from Hahn's estimate, yet few people would now share his judgment that the costs of improving on pre–September 11 airport security would not have been worth the benefits. Even though the death rate from terrorism in America has, fortunately, not remained nearly as high as in 2001, the uncertainty about future threats remains vivid in everyone's mind. Hahn's gravest mistake lay in imagining that terrorism had a knowable worst-case death toll, when in fact it does not.

When individuals and communities do not know what to expect, when they cannot even expect the worst because the worst is unknown and potentially unlimited, they become fearful, distrustful, and demoralized. Their plight only worsens when the uncertainty is prolonged. From this perspective, citizens' responses to risk are perfectly consistent with the views of regulatory critics like Justice Breyer and John Graham: they want to know "the numbers," they are aching to know them—but the numbers are unknown. In this setting, one must ask who is acting rationally: the person who pretends that unknowable future events can be assigned precise numerical probabilities, or the person who admits that some kinds of events are surrounded by such uncertainty that they outstrip our analytical powers? This uncertainty is a close cousin of the involuntariness and uncontrollability that also make some risks especially scary.

Out of Control

People may be more averse to involuntary hazards than to voluntary ones because they get to choose the hazards to which they are exposed voluntarily. No one makes you take part in a relatively dangerous sport like skiing; you have to decide to show up and buy a lift ticket. Voluntariness implies knowledge and choice;[30] involuntariness implies ignorance or coercion or both. The freedom associated with markets is freedom of choice, and the widespread popularity of free markets should make it unsurprising that people like to choose their health- and life-threatening risks, just as they like to choose their clothes and furniture.

Indeed, the more voluntary a risk appears to be, the less

likely it is to be a target of regulation. Cigarette smoking provides a good example. For decades, cigarette smoking was the quintessential voluntary risk, in both the public imagination and the legal world; cigarette ads extolled the virtues of freedom and independence associated with smokers like the Marlboro Man, and courts of law invariably threw out smokers' legal claims against tobacco companies on the ground that the smokers had voluntarily assumed the risk of disease and even death by the act of smoking.[31]

All this began to change when the secret manipulation of nicotine levels in cigarettes and, at about the same time, the health effects of secondhand smoke emerged in the public consciousness.[32] These events—the deception of smokers and the harm to nonsmokers—paved the way for a sea change in public and legal responses to the risks from smoking. When put within the framework of risk perception that we have been discussing, what really happened was that smoking began to move from the category of a voluntary activity to an activity that was generally more ambiguous and, in some cases—especially secondhand smoke—clearly involuntary.

The controllability of a risk, which also influences citizens' risk perceptions, can be connected to a concern for freedom of choice. With controllable risks, we can decide whether to control the risk or not. We can drive slowly one day, and fast the next. We can eat fatty foods and never exercise, or eat a healthful diet and maintain a good exercise regime. Control is, indeed, very much like freedom itself.

Control, too, works in both directions: just as the perceived uncontrollability of a risk often spurs regulation, the apparent controllability of a risk often discourages regulation. The federal government's decision to ban the pesticide DDT illustrates this point well. In justifying its decision to ban DDT in the early 1970s, one of the first major decisions by the newly created Environmental Protection Agency, the government explained that once unleashed into the environment, DDT could travel long distances, ending up far away from the area in which it was used, and that it accumulated in fat tissue in humans and animals, with consequences that were uncertain but suggested great potential for harm. The pesticide thus bore the hallmarks of a scary hazard: uncertain, involuntary, uncontrollable.

The government then went on to say that banning DDT would not pose a danger to the food supply because substitutes—the organophosphates—were readily available. Unfortunately, although the organophosphates were superior to DDT insofar as they broke down in the environment more readily and thus did not survive in toxic form long enough to travel very far, the organophosphates also created a more serious risk of immediate harm (such as acute pesticide poisoning) than did DDT. Nevertheless, the agency downplayed the acute risk because it thought the risk could be controlled through warnings and proper safety precautions. What EPA did not grapple with was the fact that the people facing these serious acute risks, namely migrant farmworkers, were unlikely to receive adequate warnings and training in practice. Thus, in this case, the *theoretical* controllability of a risk was used to justify a decision to dismiss the importance of that risk.

Another way one might interpret the DDT experience is to say that the government elevated some qualitative features of risk, such as uncertainty and uncontrollability, over another feature that citizens also deem important: fairness. Had the government taken the actual social conditions of migrant farmworkers more seriously, it might not have treated the risks of organophosphates so casually.

Unfair Shares

The perception that risks feel more threatening if they have inequitably distributed consequences implies a concern with fairness. Likewise, citizens' greater concern for risks imposed on future generations has much to do with fairness: in this situation, it is likely that we are imposing a risk on a population that will not enjoy the benefits associated with that risk. Even the greater concern for risks that are catastrophic rather than diffuse—risks that destroy a whole community of people rather than harm one person here and another there—may at some level be about fairness. In such cases it is unlikely that the affected community drew the whole benefit of the risk that undid them. If a nuclear power plant explodes, for example, the people immediately surrounding the plant will be physically hurt, and yet many people farther away also enjoyed the electricity produced by the plant while it was in operation.

Citizens' perceptions of risk also turn in part on the natural or man-made character of the hazard, and this factor, too, seems connected with a concern for justice. Nature's hurricanes and earthquakes cannot be brought to justice in this world; we do not hold anyone responsible for what are sometimes described as "acts of God." But harms created by human hands awaken desires for revenge, for punishment, for justice; we might even say, with Hobbes, that the principal reason for creating a government in the first place is to protect people from physical harm caused by other people. To conclude, with Breyer, Graham, and others, that risks should be judged according to their statistical attributes rather than their human context would be to turn away from the deeply ingrained and commonly held view that the government is here not just to help us to live longer, but to do justice among us.

Concerns about fairness run so deep that they have inspired a large and powerful new wave in environmental law and policy: the environmental justice movement. This movement, as we will see, is quite at odds with the contemporary over-reliance on economic analysis.

Unequal Protection[33]

The environmental justice movement emerged in the 1980s with disputes about the siting of undesirable facilities in communities of color. A protest in North Carolina, at the proposed site of a landfill for polychlorinated biphenyls (PCBs)—highly toxic and persistent chemicals that have been banned in this country and many others—is often cited as the launching point of the movement.[34] This protest inspired several national studies on the siting problem; the studies eventually provided clear statistical evidence that racial minorities were more likely to live near hazardous-waste dumps. In the early years of the movement, there was a lengthy discussion of whether this uneven burden was primarily based on the legacy of racial discrimination or the stark facts of economics. But underlying that debate is the more profound question of why a market economy produces and condones such a marked inequality of hazard.

Siting decisions are only one of the many different ways

that injustice manifests itself in health and environmental policy. For example, government decisions about which polluters to target for enforcement actions and possible financial penalties, and about where and how thoroughly to clean up contaminated sites, have also been shown to be correlated with race and ethnicity—and not in a way that works to the advantage of minorities.

Even the building blocks of health and environmental regulation—the scientific assessments of risk we discussed in Chapter 5—are often infused with assumptions that ignore or intensify racial and ethnic inequality. Assessments of the risk from eating fish contaminated with hazardous chemicals, for example, have often failed to account for the higher fish consumption of certain groups, such as Native Americans. Likewise, studies on pesticide risk often have assumed that the people exposed to pesticides have the body weight and other physiological characteristics of adults, yet many farmworkers bring their children to the fields with them when they work. Assumptions like these have the effect of understating risks to minority racial and ethnic groups, and thus threaten to reduce the health protections afforded these groups.

Likewise, there is increasing concern that the current enthusiasm for market-mimicking regulatory approaches—like pollution trading—has overlooked the potential for injustice in these approaches. A pollution trading program in Southern California, for example, allowed marine terminals to avoid installing expensive new pollution control equipment by buying old, highly polluting cars to get the clunkers off the road; higher pollution at the marine terminals was "traded" for lower pollution from cars.[35] Such systems are supposed to promote efficiency by lowering the total cost of pollution control; in this case, removing old cars from the road is a cheaper way to reduce emissions than controlling air pollution at marine terminals.

Unfortunately, the program did not always reduce pollution from cars; many of the scrapyards where the cars ended up just put the old, dirty engines into other cars that went right back on the roads. And the pollution levels in the mostly Latino, low-income neighborhoods surrounding the marine terminals went sky-high, thanks to emissions from the terminals (because increased pollution at these facilities, in just a few neighborhoods, was supposedly being traded for decreases on the roads throughout a four-county area). Eventually the car-scrapping program was itself scrapped due to these problems. A seemingly sophisticated market mechanism only succeeded in creating inequality and environmental injustice.

There are multiple lessons to be learned from this experience. One is the power of the Enron effect: when a complex new market is introduced, the most profitable short-run strategy, if you understand the market, may be simply to cheat. It will take some time for everyone else to figure out what is going on, and until they do you can make out, literally, like a bandit. Those who like to invent market mechanisms should note the importance of transparency in new institutions, and the essential role of law enforcement.

A deeper lesson is the potential connection between pollution trading and inequality. Even if the California trading system had worked as intended—that is, even if the scrapyards had actually scrapped the dirty old engines—its effect would have been to trade reduced pollution in neighborhoods where the old cars were previously being driven, for increased pollution around the marine terminals. Thus the efficiency achieved by the trading system, consisting of lower total costs for pollution reduction, would have come at the expense of shifting pollution into poorer neighborhoods.

The economists who originally came up with the idea of pollution trading, more than thirty years ago, would not have been surprised to learn that the California trading program created heavily polluted "hot spots"; in fact, they thought something like this might happen, and embraced the idea. In their naive optimism, they thought that local variation in pollution levels would be associated with freedom of choice, not with inequality of power and income. J.H. Dales, a Canadian economist who is often credited with first introducing the idea of pollution trading, concluded that it would be a good idea to allow lots of pollution in some places while allowing very little in others. Polluting an already polluted area was better, Dales thought, than spreading the pollution around so that every place was dirty; "[t]he point is," wrote Dales, "we *all* benefit from variety."[36] If, for example, urban rivers are polluted but rivers in the countryside are kept pristine, the avid angler could enjoy city life yet still drive to a beautiful countryside to fish. Dales referred to his idea, following the lead of economist E. J. Mishan, as the "separate facilities" approach.[37]

But Dales forgot one important fact: *people* might live near each of his separate facilities, and living with pollution around them might harm more than their enjoyment of fishing. When the people who live around the "facilities" we've chosen to keep polluting are disproportionately African American, Hispanic, poor, or otherwise socially disadvantaged, then even the term "separate facilities" has a sinister echo. It was, after all, racially separate facilities on passenger trains that the U.S. Supreme Court endorsed in its infamous nineteenth-century decision in *Plessy v. Ferguson,* with the impossible proviso that the facilities be "separate but equal." The preference for "separate facilities" built into the original case for pollution trading makes it no surprise to learn that trading programs can worsen existing environmental inequalities.

Culture Clash

It is widely agreed, at least in principle, that values like freedom and fairness are important considerations in health, safety, and environmental policy. Yet we have seen that market mechanisms such as pollution trading can work against fairness. The problem is equally severe when it comes to monetization and cost-benefit analysis. Like life and health, the values discussed in this chapter do not come with price tags attached. There is no meaningful way to assign dollar values to risks when the upper limit of potential harm is unknown, when the risk is involuntary, or when the risk is unfairly distributed.

When the upper limit of potential harm is unknown, it is simply not possible to assign a number to the health and environmental benefits obtained by avoiding the harm. The number must either remain blank (in which case it will often be arbitrarily treated as if it were zero) or be based on a hopelessly speculative, perhaps misleadingly reassuring, guess. This is certainly what happened in Robert Hahn's analysis of terrorism threats before September 11: he simply assumed that history was a reliable guide to the future, even in a sphere dominated by—indeed, *defined by*—unpredictable behavior.

In its unpredictability, terrorism closely resembles some of the major, uncertain, potentially unbounded environmental risks, such as climate change, in that reasonable, precautionary policies must be developed based on our current, imperfect understanding of the threats. Waiting for an impossibly precise measurement of the risks—or relying on wildly speculative, low-end predictions about the probability of harm—is a dangerous and short-sighted strategy for climate change, for terrorism, and for other fundamental threats to our future.

Likewise, the special nature of involuntary risks also defies monetization and creates troubles for cost-benefit analysis. The risks that led to the $6.1 million figure for a human life discussed in Chapter 4 are not the same kinds of risks that government often regulates. In the workplace setting involved in deriving that figure, the risks of death on the job are sometimes said to be voluntary; workers choose their jobs, the theory goes, based on their acceptance of a certain risk in return for a certain wage. (As suggested in Chapter 4, the choice of jobs is a somewhat more ambiguous process in reality, perhaps best described as partly or occasionally voluntary.) However, in the environmental setting, risks are not allocated, even in theory, according to market transactions. No one has asked the citizens of Los Angeles whether they will accept money in return for dirty air; they just get the dirty air without being asked.

Some analysts have tried to incorporate the involuntary nature of environmental risks into cost-benefit analysis by proposing a higher dollar value for human life in the environmental setting, based on the claim that people will be willing to pay more to avoid involuntary risks than to avoid voluntary ones.[38] This view misses the fundamental problem with translating involuntary risks to human life and health into dollars.

The philosophical premise of cost-benefit analysis is that a person is the best judge of his or her own welfare. When someone consents to accept an increased risk in exchange for money, the theory says that this choice should be respected for the sake of both freedom and rationality. (Notice, though, that the same cost-benefit analysts don't seem to think that people are very good judges of their own welfare when it comes to perceiving and assessing risks.) Aside from any other problems with this theory, the premise of rational, free choice obviously collapses when it comes to involuntary exchanges, which, by definition, take place without a person's consent. These kinds of exchanges tell us nothing about a person's true willingness to pay for benefits. No one, we suppose, would advocate using the money forked over to robbers or the ransom paid to kidnappers as evidence of the value of life or health.

It is possible, of course, that some voluntary market exchanges could exist with respect to involuntary risks. For example, a person might buy bottled water in order to avoid the risk associated with her contaminated tap water, or she might buy an air filter to mitigate the risk from air pollution in her neighborhood. Thus, it could be argued, involuntary risks pose no special challenge for economic analysis based on "willingness to pay."[39] Such alternatives may not be practical in every case: to avoid climate change, will each person buy an unspoiled individual ecosystem, her own private Idaho?

But even when private expenditures, as for bottled water, could provide technical solutions, there is still a central issue to confront: who should have the right to go about her daily business without seeking permission from the people she affects—the polluter, or the polluted? If the consumer had a right to clean water, then whoever wanted to engage in activities that would contaminate her drinking water would have to seek her permission—and probably pay her—in order to go ahead with those activities. It may well be that a person would demand a much higher amount for her consent to have her drinking water contaminated than she would pay to filter or replace her water, once it was contaminated. She might even, for example, believe that her entitlement to clean water is not something to be bargained away, or she might have a moral aversion to the idea of befouling drinking water for economic profit. In any case, market interactions between polluter and polluted likely would be very different from interactions between the polluted and a neutral third party, such as a bottled water supplier. By forcing even "involuntary" risks—risks not subjected to these kinds of market conversations—into cost-benefit analysis, economists and other analysts have contrived an unrealistic market where none realistically can exist.

Finally, and equally important, cost-benefit analysis also tends to ignore, and therefore to reinforce, patterns of economic and social inequality. Cost-benefit analysis consists of adding up all the costs and benefits of a policy, and comparing the totals. Implicit in this innocuous-sounding procedure is the controversial assumption that it doesn't matter who gets the benefits and who pays the costs. Both benefits and costs are measured simply as dollar totals; those totals are silent on questions of equity and distribution of resources. If pollution trading reduces the total cost of pollution reduction, it increases efficiency as economists define the term, regardless of whether it also makes the dirtiest areas even dirtier. Yet concerns about equity frequently do and should enter into debates over public policy.

It is no coincidence that pollution so often accompanies poverty. Imagine a cost-benefit analysis of siting an undesirable facility, such as a landfill or incinerator. Benefits are often measured by willingness to pay for environmental improvement. Wealthy communities are able and willing to pay more for the benefit of not having the facility in their backyards; thus the net benefits to society as a whole will be maximized by putting the facility in a low-income area. (Wealthy communities do not actually have to pay for the benefit of avoiding the facility; the analysis depends only on the fact that they are *willing* to pay.)

This kind of logic was made (in)famous in a 1991 memo circulated by Lawrence Summers (who later became president of Harvard University) when he was the chief economist at the World Bank. Discussing the migration of "dirty industries" to developing countries, Summers's memo explained:

> The measurements of the costs of health impairing pollution depend on the foregone earnings from increased morbidity and mortality. From this point of view a given amount of health impairing pollution should be done in the country with the lowest cost, which will be the country with the lowest wages. I think the economic logic behind dumping a load of toxic waste in the lowest wage country is impeccable and we should face up to that.[40]

After this memo became public, Brazil's then-Secretary of the Environment José Lutzenburger wrote to Summers:

Your reasoning is perfectly logical but totally insane. . . . Your thoughts [provide] a concrete example of the unbelievable alienation, reductionist thinking, social ruthlessness and the arrogant ignorance of many conventional "economists" concerning the nature of the world we live in. . . . [41]

If decisions were based strictly on cost-benefit analysis and willingness to pay, most environmental burdens would end up being imposed on the countries, communities, and individuals with the least resources. This theoretical pattern bears an uncomfortably close resemblance to reality. Economic theory should not be blamed for existing patterns of environmental injustice; we suspect that pollution is typically dumped on the poor without waiting for formal analysis. Still, cost-benefit analysis rationalizes and reinforces the problem, allowing environmental burdens to flow downhill along the income gradients of an unequal world. It is hard to see this as part of an economically optimal or politically objective method of decision making.

On to the Future

When risks are reduced to numbers alone, funny things happen. Uncertainty collapses into a precise—which is not to say accurate—estimate of future hazards. Inequity is covered up by a market framework that is silent about the distribution of costs and benefits, and silently makes that distribution less equitable. The context of risk, the fairness of burdens and benefits—all these characteristics, which are all-important in real decisions, are priceless. They cannot be forgotten in making effective public policy, but they cannot be remembered with a number.

The risks discussed in this chapter also threaten two other categories of value deeply important to environmental policy: those involving nature and the future. Obviously, these values are linked; the risks to human life and health that we confront today have much to do with the fate of the larger environment, and with the prospects for both humanity and nature in the decades and centuries to come. We turn in the next two chapters to a discussion of how economic analysis also manages to slight both nature and the future.

7

Unnatural Markets

When the *Exxon Valdez* ran aground on the Bligh Reef in March 1989, spilling 11 million gallons of crude oil into the icy blue waters of Alaska's Prince William Sound, a wave of large consequences—environmental, economic, and legal—followed. An estimated 36,000 migratory birds, 100 bald eagles, countless fish, and scores of sea mammals perished. A thousand miles of coastline and 10,000 square miles of water were fouled with oil thick as tar. Three years of intensive cleanup began. And, when it became clear that the disaster involved a drunken captain, antiquated equipment, and a corporate attitude indifferent to all but the bottom line, legal proceedings of all kinds ensued. The captain himself was acquitted of criminal charges, but Exxon found itself at the receiving end of record-breaking legal judgments.

In Washington, the enormous impact of the Exxon Valdez accident created an immediate political consensus about the need to prevent similar spills in the future. The Oil Pollution Act of 1990, which among other things required double hulls on new oil tankers, was passed without a single dissenting vote—long before economists finished their studies of the value of the damages done by the *Exxon Valdez*. Like all of the

environmental laws that are on the books today, the Oil Pollution Act was debated and approved without reliance on formal cost-benefit analysis.

In economics, the *Exxon Valdez* was the ship that launched
a thousand surveys. The accident demonstrated that natural
resource damages could run into the billions of dollars. And
the only way to put a precise numerical price on the largest of
these damages appeared to be through the controversial
"contingent valuation" survey method—the same technique
economists have employed to value bronchitis and other
health problems. Studies of the value of countless aspects of
the natural world have been carried out in the years since
Exxon Valdez. If public policy requires a price for everything
of value, then the surveys are essential; there is no other way to
assign a price to the existence of the natural environment. But
the results do not bear much resemblance to real prices. Although surrounded with an aura of technical precision, the
estimated prices for nature add little to the widely accepted
idea that environmental protection is extremely important.

After the oil spill, there was widespread agreement that
Exxon was liable for substantial damages. There was less
agreement about exactly how much was at stake. What, in
bald financial terms, was the damage to Prince William
Sound, the surrounding waters, the fish, otters, murres and
other seabirds, etc., *worth?* There are two kinds of answers, attempting to measure the different harms done to two groups
of people.

The people most obviously harmed by the spill were the
commercial fishermen and local residents of Prince William
Sound. In 1994, a jury awarded them almost $300 million in

compensatory damages, based on estimates of their actual economic losses.[1] In other words, the economic losses to those who have regular, personal contact with Prince William Sound were estimated at around $300 million. Economists call this a "use value" because it measures the value of the damaged resources to those who make direct personal use of them.

In contrast, most of the people who were outraged by the Exxon Valdez disaster have never been to Prince William Sound, and never expect to be there. In other words, for the great majority of the U.S. population, the "use value" of Prince William Sound and its wildlife is zero. Yet there is still a strong sense of having lost something valuable, of having been harmed by the spill. What is it worth to preserve a piece of Alaska that most of us will never see, in its pristine, oil-free, natural condition? The same question attends the Bush administration's proposal to open parts of the Arctic National Wildlife Reserve to oil drilling. Residents of the other forty-nine states clearly feel it is valuable to avoid oil spills in Alaska, but not for the same reasons as the fishermen in Prince William Sound.

To describe this second category, economists say that there is a "nonuse value" attached to the existence of natural environments, quite apart from any direct use or personal experience of those environments. There are more specific, equally esoteric, terms for various categories of nonuse values. "Existence value" is the value associated with knowing that a special place, a species, or other resource exists, even if one never visits or otherwise uses it in person. "Option value" is the value of knowing one has the opportunity to use a resource in the future. "Bequest value" is the value of being able to pass on natural resources to one's descendants and future generations.

Nonuse values figured prominently in the Exxon Valdez story, explaining why the cost of the oil spill to Exxon did not end with the company's obligations to the local community. Exxon also spent $3 billion on the cleanup of Prince William Sound, and agreed to pay the U.S. and Alaska governments an additional $1 billion to settle claims stemming from the spill. In anticipation of a trial, the governments had hired economists to help them figure out the value of the damages caused by the *Exxon Valdez*. The economists' verdict was that the existence value of Prince William Sound was at least $9 billion, and maybe even more.[2]

To come to this conclusion, researchers designed complicated surveys that asked people—citizens selected randomly from the English-speaking population of the United States—how much in increased taxes they would be willing to pay to put into place controls that would prevent another spill like the Exxon Valdez. The average household in the United States was reportedly willing to spend almost $100 for this purpose, indicating a national total of around $9 billion, or thirty times the use value of the damages to Prince William Sound. When the survey participants were asked how much money they would accept in order to allow another spill to happen, the numbers got even higher; many people said they would refuse to allow such a thing at any price.

In this case, and in many others, a lot is at stake in the calculation of existence values. Was the Exxon Valdez a $300 million accident, as the use values imply? Or was it a $9 billion disaster, as the existence values suggest? The dilemma is that the lower figure ignores the feelings of almost everyone who cared about the event, while the higher number rests on an awkward and imprecise representation of public values.

Valuation of nature may make sense after the fact, in the sadly frequent cases where compensation is needed for damages. Restoration of damages to nature is often impossible; but even in the lucky cases where an ecosystem can eventually be fully restored, its value is diminished throughout the years needed for recovery. In cases of environmental damages, as in wrongful-death cases, society has no way to pay the victims, except with money. The strange technique of contingent valuation was sanctioned in federal law precisely for this purpose.

But the fact that some families may receive, say, $3 million for the wrongful death of a loved one does not mean that we should allow people to kill other people as long as they are willing to pay $3 million for the privilege. The same is true for the wrongful loss of an endangered species, an important wilderness, or a functioning ecosystem. Society may demand compensation after the damage has been done, but this does not establish a price at which future damages should be allowed with impunity.

Indeed, companies that have tried to calibrate the harm they impose based on previous damage awards in legal cases—trying, for example, to avoid safety measures on the grounds that it will be cheaper to pay the legal judgments when people are hurt—have been hit with large punitive damage awards imposed by juries outraged by the companies' cold financial calculations in matters of life and death. This could be called "the Pinto principle," for reasons explained in Chapter 4. Although the pecuniary compensation awarded in such cases—compensation for, say, the lost income of a loved one—may be slight, the punitive damages can be enormous. The idea behind these judgments appears to be that companies ought not to treat human life like just another bookkeeping issue. One can spot a similar idea, as we will see, lurking behind citizens' gigantic responses to contingent valuation surveys concerning natural resources: the responses express moral outrage, and that outrage is real, but this does not mean it has a price.

Surveying Nature

Using statistical tools to get inside people's feelings—I mean, give me a break. I will tell you categorically that there are comparisons that should not be made, and the statistical basis for those comparisons is phony.
                    —Stephen S. Roach, chief economist at Morgan Stanley[3]

Economists have asked, and people have answered, numerous questions about the value of preserving rare, threatened, or endangered species. The answer is invariably that those animals are worth huge amounts of money. On an annual basis, the average household is reportedly willing to pay amounts ranging from $70 to protect the spotted owl that lives in the old-growth forests of the Northwest, down to $6 for the striped shiner, an endangered fish.[4] Since there were 105 million households in the United States as of 2000, that adds up to a total of more than $7 billion a year that the nation is willing to pay for the spotted owl, and more than $600 million a year for the striped shiner. When surveys ask about onetime, rather than annual, willingness to pay, they get even larger responses. The average household would pay $216 to preserve bald eagles, $173 to protect humpback whales, and $67 for gray wolves.[5] Across the whole population, that adds up a staggering $23 billion for bald eagles, $18 billion for humpbacks, and $7 billion for gray wolves.

It is not just the protection of endangered species that elicits such huge estimates. Depending on which study you believe, the median household is willing to pay between $1.60 and $115 per year to prevent a modest worsening of visibility due to air pollution at a major park.[6] Nature in general seems to have an enormous value, according to economists' surveys.

Originally proposed in 1947, the contingent valuation method of estimating these values was first carried out in the 1960s.[7] Its first appearance in the legal system came in the 1980s, as a means of valuing the damages from hazardous waste contamination at Superfund sites. During the Reagan-Bush administrations, the Interior Department—the agency responsible for overseeing restoration of natural resources under Superfund—placed many restrictions on the use of contingent valuation to assess environmental damages. However, these restrictions were largely overturned by a court decision, *Ohio v. Department of Interior*—which coincidentally occurred just months after the oil spill in Prince William Sound.[8]

In the wake of the Exxon Valdez and the *Ohio* decision, contingent valuation, with its potential for attaching multibillion-dollar price tags to nature, suddenly looked much more important. Although the first use of contingent valuation in federal law was to assess damages after a disaster had happened, the Oil Pollution Act of 1990 directed the National Oceanic and Atmospheric Administration (NOAA) to establish standards for damage assessments in future oil spills.

NOAA assembled a panel of distinguished economists, who drafted recommendations for future contingent valuation studies. The NOAA panel recommendations, which were accepted in 1994, are now widely cited, if not always followed, as a standard for contingent valuation on topics ranging far beyond oil spills. Among many other points, the panel endorsed the calculation of nonuse values.

The NOAA panel did not, however, end the debate about the right way to value the environment. Despite the elaborate technical effort devoted to the subject, the entire endeavor of pricing nature remains problematical. What can it mean to assign a dollar value to the survival of a species, to the air we breathe, or to the existence of unspoiled wild places?

A Whale Watch Is Not a Whale

Many of the problems with pricing nature arise only with nonuse values. Although it is easy to assign prices to the *use* of wild places and animals—tour guides and travel agents do so all the time—it is troubling to put a price on the *existence* of a wilderness or an animal species.[9] Measurement of use values may be challenging in practice, but it is feasible in principle. The economic losses suffered by those who work and live in Prince William Sound are naturally expressed in monetary terms, and can be calculated without elaborate surveys of hypothetical values.

Good partial measures of use values can also be obtained from indirect inferences about expenditures and prices. For example, the use value of national parks must be at least as great as the amount that visitors spend on traveling to the parks, and paying admission and other travel-related costs.

Likewise, urban and suburban parks increase the value of nearby properties, reflecting the value of parks to property owners. Boston's massive "Big Dig" construction project is replacing an ugly elevated highway with a tunnel under the center of the city; the official plans call for creating thirty acres of new parks and open space on land formerly occupied by the highway. If the patterns of property values near existing parks continue to hold, the new parks created by the Big Dig will add $250 million to the value of real estate in Boston.[10] The use value of the new parks to nearby property owners must therefore be at least $250 million, to say nothing of the value to others in the community.

Just a few blocks from the Big Dig is Boston Harbor, where many visitors go on whale-watching trips. What is the use value of the humpback whales and other species that can be seen on these trips? The only humans making direct personal "use" of whales, in countries that observe the ban on whaling, are small numbers of researchers studying them and larger number of sightseers on whale-watching boats. Commercial whale watching is a thriving industry that had 3 million customers and revenues of about $160 million nationwide in 1998.[11] But when people are asked what they would be willing to pay to prevent the extinction of humpback whales, the answer, as we have seen, is $173 per household, or *$18 billion* nationwide. In other words, the existence value of humpback whales based on contingent valuation surveys is more than one hundred times as large as commercial whale watch revenues.

Do the prices assigned to nature accurately describe what it is worth? Perhaps for use values, but not for existence values. Suppose you have bought the last available ticket for a whale-watching trip, and someone offers to buy it from you for twice the price you paid. No great moral dilemmas or philosophical issues are involved; if you sell your ticket, you can go another time. A seat on a whale-watching trip is a commodity that has a market price. The price expresses the value of seeing whales, and it is perfectly acceptable to think about buying or selling tickets for the trip.

But a whale watch is not a whale, and the *existence value* of whales is not a meaningful number. Suppose that a crazed antienvironmental billionaire offers to pay $36 billion for the opportunity to catch and kill all the humpback whales in the ocean. Since the existence value of humpback whales has been estimated at $18 billion, the would-be whale killer is offering to buy the existence of the species for twice its price. If whales were commodities and existence values were real prices, this would be a good deal, just like the offer of double payment for your ticket. Yet it is inconceivable that the billionaire's offer would be accepted. Any signs that such an offer was even being considered would produce immediate, outraged protest.

A number like $18 billion is an awkward and incomplete way to describe the immense value that people place on the existence of whales. The exact number contains no useful information: what would change if a new study found that it was actually $16 billion, or $53 billion? The only answer to an offer to buy the whales—regardless of the amount offered—is "We didn't really mean it about the price. Actually, they are not for sale." In short, the ban on whaling is not based on a cost-benefit analysis, but on a widely shared ethical judgment. That judgment is not clarified, nor made more precise, by performing a contrived survey of public willingness to pay for something that cannot be bought or sold.

Have Economists Reinvented Elections?

In order to express their support for environmental protection, many people who participate in contingent valuation surveys either refuse to answer, or give responses that the survey researchers view as unrealistically large.[12] Economists derisively dismiss very large valuations as reflecting merely the "warm glow" of altruism rather than a more sober and rational assessment of the specific survey questions. One much-discussed study found that people were willing to pay about the same amount for saving 2,000 birds, as for 20,000, or 200,000; the standard explanation is that these survey respondents were simply expressing a general willingness to make a donation to a good cause, such as saving birds. (Practitioners of contingent valuation view this as a problem to be avoided by more elaborate survey design—overlooking the possibility that people quite rationally believe in saving birds, but cannot and need not convert that belief into a dollar price per saved bird.) Other results also support the interpretation of survey responses as expressing general beliefs rather than specific values. For instance, even when surveys do not ask for round numbers, responses about willingness to pay for environmental benefits are often clustered at round numbers such as $20 or $50—like charitable donations, but unlike, say, supermarket expenditures.[13]

When survey respondents refuse to answer the questions posed to them, or when they give answers that, to the survey managers, appear to reflect unrealistically high valuations of natural resources, their responses are simply not counted. Economists dismiss such responses as "protest votes." When the data are analyzed, extreme values and other seemingly illogical responses are normally screened out; estimated environmental valuations are based only on those responses that appear well-behaved to the investigator. The standards for a well-behaved or logical response thus become of central importance: only those that meet the standards will be counted. Fully one-third of the responses to the bronchitis survey were rejected by the investigators, but this is not even close to setting a record. In contingent valuation surveys that put the valuation question in the "willingness to accept" format— that is, ask how much money respondents would demand in order to allow the relevant natural resource to be despoiled— protest rates of 50 percent or more are common.[14] Dismissing these responses creates a danger that valuations of health and nature will reflect an ad hoc process of censorship by economists, not a true cross-section of popular attitudes.

In essence, the economists' position is that everything has a price, and that the price can be discovered by careful questioning. But for most people, there are matters of rights and principles that are beyond economic calculation. Setting the boundaries of the market helps to define who we are, how we want to live, and what we believe in. There are many activities that are not allowed at any price. Some businesses would undoubtedly profit from employing child labor, killing whales, or openly bribing public officials. As filmmaker Michael Moore asked, in a question that only appears to be flippant, if General Motors was trying to maximize profits, why didn't it switch to selling cocaine when its cars sold poorly in the

1980s?[15] The magnitude of the profits that could be gained from such activities is not, for most people, an argument for changing our principles about what we do and don't allow.

Some activities are not only unpriced, but would be fundamentally changed if they become part of the market economy.[16] Sex and voting are two classic examples: doing it in exchange for cash, which is not unknown in either case, inherently degrades the sexual or electoral experience. The legal scholar Cass Sunstein makes a similar point with a simpler example: suppose that at the last minute you are forced to cancel a lunch date with an old friend whom you haven't seen in some time. Your friend has suffered a loss of your companionship, but it would be strange, even insulting, to offer to pay your friend for that loss.[17] Nature may resemble friendship, as well as sex and voting, in being changed and cheapened as soon as it is priced.

Insistence on economic analysis of the environment requires that one forget all such fundmantal problems and stubbornly assign a price to everything of value, in order to complete the numerical comparison of costs and benefits. By using public opinion surveys to calculate some of the most important values, economists have reinvented elections, holding mock referendum ballots on major questions of public policy. By narrowly constraining the conditions under which responses in contingent valuation surveys will be counted, the researchers have imposed a new literacy test for participation, demanding that voters who want their votes to be counted frame their answers in an artificially quantified vocabulary.

Natural Capitalists

An alternative approach to economics also tries to measure the role and the value of nature, with greater, though not total, success. As Herman Daly and other ecological economists have pointed out, the economy is embedded in the natural world and constantly relies on nature to provide essential inputs such as clean air, clean water, food, fiber, and other raw materials. Since the earth and its resources are finite, there is a limit to the possible expansion of production; after a certain point, economic growth must become resource-conserving rather than resource-intensive.[18]

Ecological economists have introduced the concept of "natural capital" to emphasize the role of nature in the economy. Fishermen use their boats and nets to catch fish; but they also use the population of uncaught fish in the sea, whose reproduction creates the possibility of each year's new catch. All economists recognize the boats and nets as capital equipment; ecological economists point out that the fish in the sea are playing the same role, as an essential input that is used, again and again, in production. The fish in the sea, the trees in the forest, and other natural resources can all be described as natural capital, without which production would be impossible.

Thinking about the role of nature in production also highlights the interactions of species within a habitat, which are much like the interactions of producers and suppliers within the economy. Value is produced by the system as a whole, not by the single firm (or species) that attracts the most attention. Focusing on habitats as a whole thus also helps to correct the common overemphasis on the biggest and most eye-catching species. The celebrity status of "charismatic megafauna," as they are sometimes called, threatens to obscure the value of other parts of the same ecosystems. According to contingent valuation surveys, whales have a huge existence value; it seems likely that similar surveys would find much lower existence values for the plankton, krill, and other small, drab, essential parts of the ecosystem that supports whales. A consistent set of prices for nature—if they really were prices—should include values for the inputs nature uses to make whales, reflecting the contribution that the bottom of the food chain makes to the species at the top.[19]

Ecological economics, with its analysis of natural capital and ecological constraints, is an advance over standard economics in many respects. It extends the concept of the use value of the environment to encompass uses in production as well as consumption. But ecological economics offers no new solution to the existence value problem. Many aspects of the natural world about which people care deeply, such as remote ecosystems and endangered species, are not currently used for human purposes, either as natural capital or as consumer goods; they have no discernible use value, yet they are valuable. Existence values are central to the way people think about nature, and they are not the same as natural capital.

The Newest Deal

Another style of well-intentioned economic analysis has sought, with little success, to use the conventional techniques of valuation to demonstrate the huge value of protecting nature, and thereby win adoption of protective regulation. The 1990s appear to have been the high-water mark of this type of environmental economics in practice. The endorsement of contingent valuation by the courts, and the establishment of standards by the NOAA panel, led to a proliferation of empirical studies of environmental values throughout the decade— and to a growing hope that these values would be reflected in laws and regulations.

At the same time, however, conservatives in Congress pushed for narrow cost-benefit tests for new policies, a trend that the Clinton administration sometimes embraced. For example, the Safe Drinking Water Act (SDWA) was amended in 1996 to call for cost-benefit analysis of future regulations— unlike earlier environmental laws, including the original SDWA. The revised standards for arsenic in drinking water, proposed in the year 2000, fell under the SDWA amendments, explaining why EPA performed the controversial cost-benefit analysis described in Chapter 5. It was one of the first times that cost-benefit calculations were used as the basis for setting environmental regulation.

This trend accelerated with the regime change in Washington in 2001. The incoming Bush team made no secret of its hostility to environmental protection, on high-profile issues ranging from climate change to arsenic standards to national park and forest policies. A less visible change was at least equally important: the Office of Management and Budget took on a much more active role in reviewing, and often enough rejecting, regulations adopted by the EPA and other agencies. OMB has had since the 1980s the authority to review and reject regulations, but has only occasionally rejected agency rules in the past; during the Clinton years this option was all but forgotten. But John Graham, the head of the crucial office within the OMB in the Bush administration, has been extremely active, rejecting dozens of regulations each year.

Graham has also "invited" agencies such as EPA to work closely with OMB before adopting new regulations, in order to ensure that their proposals meet OMB's standards. In this process, OMB is essentially dictating not only the use of cost-benefit analysis, but also a new, sharply limited understanding of the environmental values that will be considered in public policy. The result, needless to say, is to weaken health and environmental protection. A look at one regulatory battle shows just how narrow the approved interpretation of benefits has become.

A Fish Story: The Ones That Didn't Get Away

Cost-benefit analysis often requires numbers for such imponderables as the value of a human life, or the value of the pain and suffering associated with a severe illness. The intricately detailed disputes about these numbers, inaccessible to everyone but experts in the field, allow businesses and business-oriented public officials to hide their financial and political interests behind the technical face of economics. Much the same is true in the debates about more humble-sounding numbers, such as the dollar value of not killing a fish. Estimating this number has become surprisingly important to the protection of fish and underwater ecosystems threatened by industrial processes. Consider the sad saga of cooling towers, and the value of the fish that didn't get away.[20]

Power plants generate electricity by boiling water and using the steam pressure to make large turbines spin. A huge coal-, oil-, or gas-burning furnace, or a nuclear reactor, is used to boil the water. The plant requires a vast, continual flow of cooling water to condense the steam back into water so it can be boiled again.

Cooling water is taken from rivers, lakes, and oceans—and often contains fish. One power plant alone, the Salem nuclear plant in New Jersey, withdraws more than 3 billion gallons of water every day from the estuary of the Delaware River. A staggering number of fish get killed at Salem: small ones are sucked into the plant, and larger ones are trapped against the in-take grate, held there by the massive water flow. The abrupt temperature change—the cooling water is much warmer when it comes out of the plant than when it goes in—does further damage to the aquatic ecosystem.

This underwater massacre could be almost entirely elimi-nated with well-known, proven technologies—in particular, with the use of cooling towers. (In older facilities this is the tall structure, pinched in the middle, that defines the classic power-plant silhouette; newer cooling towers are much smaller.) With a cooling tower, water, once heated, can be cooled down and then recirculated through the plant. A cool-ing tower reduces a power plant's water needs by more than 90 percent, and as a result saves more than 90 percent of the fish.

Salem has no cooling tower, and instead relies on a "once-through" cooling water system. Salem is not unique in this re-gard. More than 500 existing power plants nationwide, producing about half of our electricity, have once-through cooling systems. They collectively use almost 300 billion gal-lons of cooling water every day, and kill many millions of fish per year. Should all of the existing plants—or any of them—be required to build cooling towers?

The EPA struggled with this question for some time. Faced with a lawsuit demanding regulation of cooling water intake structures, the agency initially analyzed the issues much as it had similar questions that arose under the Clean Water Act. As called for by the language of the act, EPA tried to identify the best technology available for mitigating the harms caused by cooling systems, without attempting to assign dollar values to the fish that would be saved by the new technology.

However, OMB rejected EPA's original approach, and instead demanded that power plants be allowed to avoid regulation entirely unless it could be proved that the dollar value of the protected fish was as high as the cost of the technology that would protect them. Thus EPA's role under the Clean Water Act has been converted from identifying the best ways to avoid environmental harm to embarking on a lengthy and obscure inquiry into the monetary value of not killing fish. Far from clarifying society's values, the resulting cost-benefit analysis represents only a temporary truce in the skirmishes between EPA's attempts to protect more fish, and OMB's insistence on doing less.

What is it worth to avoid killing a fish? The easiest fish to value are the ones that would have been caught for commercial or recreational purposes if they had not been killed by a power plant instead. For commercially valuable fish species there is an obvious market value. For recreationally desirable fish, EPA's economists have developed elaborate models of recreational anglers' willingness to pay for the enjoyment of the catch.

Yet no more than 10 to 20 percent (and often even less) of even the most valuable species of fish in the water are typically caught by commercial and recreational fishing in any one year. The remaining fish represent the "natural capital" that survives to produce next year's catch. So the fish killed by a power plant can be divided into the small minority, say 10 to 20 percent, that would have been caught, and the great majority that would have gotten away, in the absence of the power plant. The ones that would have been caught are readily assigned a commercial or recreational value.

What is the value of the natural capital, the ones that would have gotten away? Zero, according to EPA's cost-benefit analysis (or perhaps according to OMB's marching orders to the agency). One must wonder where they think next year's fish dinners will come from.

EPA did, in the face of OMB's hostility, valiantly attempt to assemble enough different values for fish to justify some cooling towers. Revisions of the analysis, in response to public comments, led to more and more elaborate calculations of fish values, leaving all but the most determined experts unable to decipher the analytical basis for the timid regulatory proposal that emerged from EPA. This escalating complexity is unnecessary, though, if all one is interested in determining is society's willingness to pay for the regulation of cooling systems. In that case, one could begin simply by asking: are people willing to pay a small increase in their electric bills to cover the cost of cooling towers?

Although, as industry and its advocates point out, cooling towers are expensive, the plants that use them generate huge amounts of electricity. As a result, the cost per kilowatt hour, and the cost per monthly electric bill, are quite modest. Requiring cooling towers on all existing power plants, the strictest regulation that EPA considered, would add $0.28 to a typical household's monthly electric bill, or $3.36 per year—in round numbers, a penny a day.[21] If, as we suspect, most households are willing to pay a penny a day to save millions of fish every year, then there is no need for the endless debates about the many ways to value a fish. On the other hand, if most households are not willing to spend a penny a day, they will not be tricked into it by a complex, statistical fish story.

In this general sense, "willingness to pay" is a part of democratic decision making. Someone has to pay the costs of building cooling towers; electric companies will undoubtedly strive to pass the costs on to their customers, who will then be forced to pay, albeit only at the penny-a-day rate. However, the supposed evaluation of public willingness to pay through hypertechnical analysis has grown so opaque and contentious that it offers no help at all. It might be better just to ask a simple, referendum-style question about the bottom line: here's what it costs, and here's what it protects—do you want it? But then, ordinary people might actually understand the issues, and clamor for other, comparably cheap protective regulations; we suspect that this, and not substandard economic analysis, is what OMB actually fears most.

Getting What You Pay For

In the cooling water analysis, even with its stingy approach to valuation, EPA initially concluded that monetized benefits exceeded costs for a regulation requiring cooling towers at about sixty of the biggest power plants. OMB economists immediately went to work attacking EPA's analysis, trying to show that technical errors in the modeling of fish populations and in assigning values to dead fish had led EPA to overestimate the benefits of cooling towers.

Perhaps the most striking criticism of EPA's analysis came from Robert Stavins, a well-known environmental economist at Harvard's Kennedy School of Government, and a frequent adviser to EPA. His comments to EPA reflected a dramatic reversal of his past views: in 1984, while working for the Environmental Defense Fund, Stavins conducted a cost-benefit analysis that contributed to the defeat of a proposed hydroelectric development on the Tuolumne River in California. At that time, he estimated there was a substantial nonuse value to the river in its natural state. As a result, he found there were greater net benefits to keeping the river undeveloped and available for recreation. His conclusion depended entirely on the nonuse value of the wild river; based on use value alone, Stavins's analysis would have favored development. Moreover, he was well aware of the limitations of cost-benefit analysis, repeatedly cautioning against overreliance on such methods:

> When particular categories of benefits and/or costs are systematically excluded from an economic assessment, benefit-cost analysis loses its value as an aid to societal decision making. . . . The B/C [benefit-cost] criterion is neither a necessary nor a sufficient condition for project investment. . . . What is crucial to keep in mind is that the benefit-cost criterion should not be used as an absolute decision rule. . . . Public-policy decisions regarding the use of the nation's scarce natural resources are ultimately political decisions, and should remain so.[22]

By 2002, the analysis of the Tuolumne River was out of print, and Stavins was consulting for Pacific Gas & Electric, the giant California energy company that starred opposite Julia Roberts in the movie *Erin Brockovich*. His cautions from the 1980s about the limits of cost-benefit analysis were long since forgotten; for the twenty-first century, Stavins offered his judgment that it is "universally accepted in economics" that "the option with the greatest (positive) difference between benefits and costs [positive net benefits] is the best option."[23] The great danger now is apparently that fuzzy thinking will lead to overstating the benefits of environmental protection, thereby burdening electric companies with the excessive costs of not killing all those fish. On behalf of PG&E, Stavins argued that EPA's cost-benefit analysis wildly exaggerates the benefits of protecting fish. There are, as far as Stavins and PG&E can see today, no grounds for assigning existence values to most of the fish killed by power plants, and indeed precious little grounds for assigning them any value at all.

This is not a sensible way to make decisions about the protection of fish and underwater ecosystems. Any hope of transparency and objectivity is long since lost, as monied interests find "experts" to pick apart the smallest details of the analysis.

Shopping for Social Value

Economic analysis of health and the environment often produces impressively large numbers for the existence value of nature. If these numbers are accepted at face value, places and things that are assigned existence values are uniquely blessed.

But there is a discriminatory pattern to these blessings: for economists, nature generally has an existence value, whereas human life and health do not.

Existence values are based on a different logic than ordinary prices. In a market economy, prices are based on what individuals are willing to pay for goods and services. Valuation of human life and health, despite its numerous logical problems, attempts to follow the same pattern: the estimated values are based on economists' (often tortured) interpretations of what individuals are willing to pay to protect themselves from harm.

Nature is unable to tell us about its own values and needs for protection. There is no Lorax[24] who speaks for the trees; all we can do is ask about society's valuation of the existence of forests. If whales were consumers, swimming up to the market with cash held in their fins, economists could interview them about their willingness to pay for not being harpooned. Instead, we are left with contingent valuation of the existence of whales as our only option for assigning a number to their lives.

This is, in a sense, an advance over the individualism of the market economy. Calculation of existence values recognizes the role of social decision making; it asks, as market economics usually does not, what the population as a whole thinks about a topic. But at the same time, the expression of social priorities through existence values asks us to view ourselves only as consumers; it attempts to replace voting with shopping.

If we all agreed to go shopping for social values, what else might we want to "buy"? Whales and wildernesses have existence values, but so do safe jobs for workers thousands of miles away, and protection from toxic chemicals for everyone's children. Most of us value the working and living conditions of people we may never meet, just as we value the natural environment of places we may never visit, like Prince William Sound. Traditionally, society would express its concern for health and safety by passing laws on the subject, based on simple, nonquantitative ideas such as, "workplaces should be as safe as possible," and "children should be protected from toxic chemicals." But if that seems passé, too twentieth-century in its approach, economists could conduct surveys to find the existence value of other people's health and safety. It is likely that the resulting numbers would be quite substantial.

Assigning monetary values to everything we care about is not a practical plan for government. Voting by shopping—using existence values to measure society's preferences in general—would bury us in a blizzard of hypothetical valuations, obscuring rather than clarifying our collective priorities. It would also raise the impossible problem of numerically "valuing" things about which people disagree. Is the "existence value" of abortion clinics a positive or negative number? It depends who you ask. It is likely that no one would be happy about making a decision based on society's average monetary valuation of the right to choose abortion.

Something large and ill-defined can be seen through the dark glass of contingent valuation: the huge estimated existence values for nature suggest that the environment matters a great deal to a great many people. Nevertheless, it is difficult to maintain the fiction that surrogate prices are being calculated, suitable for use in incorporating the environment into the market economy. The problem is not the lack of coherent judgments about big or remote environmental questions. The problem is that incoherence is introduced when environmental judgments are turned into numbers.

Follow-up interviews with respondents to contingent valuation surveys elicit comments such as, "I struggled with this money business"; "I found the money question impossible to answer"; and "I would pay the earth if I could afford to. But you can't really value it, can you?"[25] People who feel equally passionately about preserving a local environmental resource can make arbitrarily different decisions about how to turn that passion into a number. Similarly, legal research has found that jurors' judgments about the outrageousness of an injury and the appropriate punishment are relatively uniform in qualitative terms—but become erratic and unpredictable when jurors translate those judgments into monetary damages.[26]

It is not the people in these studies who are confused; it is instead the analysts who insist that every value can be fit into the market paradigm who are misguided. Existence values are real, but they are not really numbers. The passion that surrounds the preservation of whales and wild places reflects both their fragility and their meaning to posterity. Once a species or wilderness is gone, there is no way to bring it back. Yet these are part of the natural world that many of us hope to leave intact for future generations. The problem of valuing the future presents a final challenge to cost-benefit analysis and market-based policies, as we explain in Chapter 8.

8

Honey, I Shrunk the Future

In the 1989 comedy film *Honey, I Shrunk the Kids,* a bumbling, absentminded inventor accidentally shrinks his and his neighbor's children down to a height of a quarter inch. The miniaturized children are no longer readily visible, and are constantly on the verge of being crushed by ordinary household objects. Lawn mowers, cats, and bowls of cereal are all potentially fatal hazards to those who are vertically challenged to such an extreme.

In the world of public policy, much the same thing is happening to concerns about the future. A mathematical device called discounting was, like the "electromagnetic shrinking machine" of the Disney fantasy, invented for other purposes. Economic analysts then, perhaps accidentally, used discounting to render concerns about the future all but invisible. As long as the needs of the future are caught in the mathematical shrinking machine, they are at risk of being crushed by the casual desires of the present.

Many of the most urgent environmental concerns involve events that will occur decades or centuries from now. Climate change, which is already beginning to be felt, will have an enormously greater impact one hundred years or more from now. Today's high-level radioactive waste will pose severe dangers to anyone exposed to it for millennia to come. Diseases such as cancer, with long latency periods, may not be visible for decades after the fateful exposure to hazardous substances.

One of the great policy successes of the late twentieth century was the recognition of the prevention of chronic and latent disease as a legitimate and important job for government. Another was the acceptance of the need for public initiatives to protect the environment for future generations. Both of these accomplishments depended on the premise that the future—for those of us living today, and for those who come after us—is important. Indeed, one of the explicit and primary objectives of the National Environmental Policy Act, which has been called our basic charter of environmental protection, is to "fulfill the responsibilities of each generation as trustee of the environment for succeeding generations."[1]

It is not just environmental laws that talk about the future. The classic United Nations–sponsored report that first drew widespread attention to the idea of sustainable development was called "Our Common Future." Societies, like families, act as if the future matters, as if providing for generations to come is one of their highest goals and proudest accomplishments. Few political campaigns succeed by proclaiming that the present is all and the future is unimportant. Few government programs win followers by announcing that their goal is to deplete all of their resources within the short term so that nothing is left for later. As Fleetwood Mac told the world, in a song that became a favorite anthem of the Clinton White House, "Don't stop thinking about tomorrow."

Is all this future-oriented talk based on an arithmetic mistake? Economists do not begin by telling everyone to forget about tomorrow. Instead, they reasonably insist that dollars received next year are worth less than the same number of dollars received today—even in the absence of inflation. This could be just because you'd rather not have to wait for your money, or because you could invest it for the year and earn a little interest. The discounting formula has been developed to express exactly *how much less* next year's dollars are worth. It shrinks, by a little bit, the "present value" of a payment that you will receive next year—and if left running, it shrinks the far future down to insignificance.

Simple Arithmetic

Suppose that your bank account earns 3 percent interest. In that case, if you deposited $100 today, you would earn $3 in interest, giving you a total of $103 next year. Likewise, in order to get $100 next year, you need to deposit only $97 today.[2] So, at a 3 percent *discount rate,* economists would say that $100 next year has a *present value* of $97 in today's dollars.

For longer periods of time, the effect is magnified: the longer you are planning to wait, the less you need to deposit today to have $100 show up in your bank account in the future. That is to say, the present value of a sum farther in the future is smaller. At a 3 percent discount rate, $100 twenty years from now has a present value of $55. At a greater discount rate, the present value is smaller: at a 7 percent discount rate, for example, $100 twenty years from now has a present value of only $26.

Cost-benefit analysis routinely uses the present value of future benefits.[3] In other words, it compares current costs, not to the actual dollar value of future benefits but to the smaller amount you would have to put into a hypothetical savings account today to obtain those benefits in the future. This application of discounting is essential for many practical financial decisions. If offered a choice of investment opportunities with payoffs at different times in the future, you can (and should) discount the future payoffs to the present in order to compare them with one another. The important issue for environmental policy, as we shall see, is whether this logic also applies to outcomes far in the future, and to opportunities—like long life and good health—that are not naturally stated in dollar terms.

The Formula Revealed

For those who are fluent in algebra (others may safely skip this box, as it is not essential to the text), the discounting formula is as follows: If you know that something will have an *ActualValue* at a future time, *years* from now, and you know the appropriate *DiscountRate,* then the *PresentValue* today is

$$Present\,Value = \frac{Actual\,Value}{(1 + DiscountRate)^{years}}$$

For example, the present value of $100 to be received 20 years from now, at a discount rate of 7 percent, is

$$\frac{\$100}{(1.07)^{20}} = \frac{\$100}{3.87}$$

Was Manhattan a Bargain?

Discounting is just compound interest in reverse. And compound interest makes things grow bigger—slowly at first, but impressively in the end. Put even a small amount of money in a savings account and leave it there for long enough, and it will indeed grow into an enormous sum. And the longer the time period, the greater the importance of the exact rate of interest.

Everyone "knows" the story of Native Americans selling the island of Manhattan to Dutch colonists for $24 in 1626, although the historical accuracy of the tale is subject to debate. If the sale did happen at that price, was it a bargain or a swindle? Suppose that the Native Americans had immediately put their $24 in a bank in 1626 and left it there until the year 2000. At 3 percent interest they would have entered the new millennium with $1.5 million, barely enough to buy a condo in some parts of the land they once owned. But at 7 percent interest they would have had a whopping $2.3 trillion, enough to buy the entire island back many times over. (A trillion has twelve zeros; it is a million millions.)

Economic analysis of environmental problems often seems to imagine that society actually faces the Native Americans' fictitious "choice" of putting money in the bank for centuries to watch it grow. Take the problem of climate change. The impact of climate change is beginning to be felt today, but the real threat is that our descendants will face enormous environmental damages a century or more from now. Is it better to spend money now on energy conservation and renewable sources of energy to reduce the future damages from climate change? Or is it wiser to put the same amount of money in the bank for centuries, so that our descendants will have trillions of dollars to use when the time comes? The latter course of action, absurd as it sounds, is what some economic theories suggest. Sell our environmental common sense now, and the magic of compound interest will eventually allow us to buy it back, like Manhattan, with money left over.

In the fable of repurchasing Manhattan, the former owners of the island make out quite nicely if they got 7 percent for all those years, but rather less well if they got 3 percent. Likewise, the strategy of investing money now so that our descendants will be rich enough to solve their environmental problems for themselves looks more sensible (or rather, marginally less senseless) at a higher interest rate. Imagine our descendants' plight if they end up with only millions instead of trillions with which to tackle the problems we have bequeathed to them. In general, the higher the discount rate, the smaller the present value of costs and benefits in years to come—and hence the weaker the argument appears to be for acting now to protect our common future.

An additional economic argument for delay in tackling long-run problems is that technology is constantly improving. If we invest the money and wait, not only will our money grow through compound interest, the technologies for solving environmental problems will get better in the meantime. Our descendants, to whom we will pass on the mess we have made, will have more cash to clean up with, and will get more bang for each buck, too.

This way of thinking makes sense under certain circumstances, if applied to things that really have prices. You can buy a new computer now or later—and if you don't need it this year, you probably should put the money in a savings account and wait. The technology will undoubtedly keep improving, so next year's models will do more, yet cost less. In the market paradigm, buying environmental protection is just like buying a computer or any other commodity: if we don't buy it until we need it, we'll presumably get a better deal.

If environmental protection were mass-produced by the computer industry, and if environmental problems would agree to stand still indefinitely and wait for us to respond, this might be a reasonable approach. In the real world, however, it is a ludicrous and dangerous strategy. Too many years of delay may mean that the polar ice cap melts, the spent uranium leaks out of the containment ponds, the hazardous waste seeps into groundwater and basements and backyards—at which point we can't put the genie back in the bottle at any reasonable cost (or perhaps not at all).

Environmentalists often talk of potential "crises," of threats that problems will become suddenly and irreversibly worse. It is hard to imagine a price for an irreversible loss. What is the cash value of the damage done when a species is driven into extinction? No amount of money will bring it back to life. One of the ominous threats of climate change is that rapid melting of arctic ice could disrupt Atlantic Ocean currents, abruptly blocking the Gulf Stream that now warms Europe. If this switch is "turned off," there is no way to turn it back on; the affected areas would become suddenly much colder. What is the dollar price on inching ever closer to the uncertain point at which climate change might turn off the Gulf Stream? In response to such threats, environmentalists and some governments advocate the precautionary principle, calling upon regulators to err on the side of caution and protection when risks are uncertain.

Conventional economics, for the most part, does not assume the possibility of crisis. The worldview of market economics typically assumes stable problems, with control costs that are stable or declining over time, and thus finds precautionary investment in environmental protection to be a needless expense. Discounting is part of this noncrisis perspective. By implying that the present value of future environmental harms declines, steadily and predictably, with every year that we look ahead, discounting ignores the possibility of catastrophic and irreversible harms. As a prominent economist, William Baumol, wrote in an important early article on discounting the benefits of public projects:

> There are important externalities and investments of the public-goods variety which cry for special attention. Irreversibilities constitute a prime example. If we poison our soil so that never again will it be the same, if we destroy the Grand Canyon and turn it into a hydroelectric plant, we give up assets which like Goldsmith's bold peasantry, ". . . their country's pride, when once destroy'd can never be supplied." All the wealth and resources of future generations will not suffice to restore them.[4]

Although the future shrinks much more slowly at a 3 percent discount rate than at 7 percent, it eventually vanishes at any positive discount rate. Do the math, and almost nothing looks worth spending money on today if the payoff comes a century or more from now. There are two principal objections to this short-sighted conclusion.[5] One is the idea just mentioned: some problems, like climate change, could become much worse, perhaps reaching a point of irreversible catastrophe, if we do not act now.

A second objection is that discounting does not, strictly speaking, apply across time spans of more than one generation. The story that justifies discounting involves a single individual comparing costs and benefits today and in the near future. That individual can reasonably be expected to evaluate her own trade-offs between the present and the near future. The logic of discounting for financial decisions within a single lifetime is entirely sensible: people do compare interest rates when thinking about investing or borrowing money, and the discounting formula is a useful guide to the process. On the day you sign a mortgage, the present value of all your future mortgage payments, discounted at the mortgage interest rate, is exactly equal to the amount you are borrowing.

This logic breaks down when costs or benefits spread over a century and longer. No one individual will experience both the beginning and the end of the transaction; no one is able to make the personal judgment that the trade-off is, or is not, worthwhile. If we spend money on energy conservation today, reducing the carbon dioxide buildup in the atmosphere, the greatest benefits of our expenditure will be experienced after the present generation is long gone. If instead we mortgage the future in order to enjoy driving enormous cars fueled with enormous quantities of petroleum today, the most expensive mortgage payments will come due after we have turned to compost, and our cars to rust.

No matter what discounting formula we use, the market cannot tell us how to make the trade-off between the present and the world of our descendants many generations from now. The future, like life, health, and nature, is priceless. A different style of decision making is required, explicitly based on our value judgments about equity between ourselves and the future.

Accounting for Discounting

Discounting is not just used for issues that span centuries. It has become pervasive in analysis of all manner of health and environmental regulations. Frequently it has the effect of shrinking the benefits of avoiding cancer or other diseases with long latency periods. Discounting over the latency period of twenty to forty years that often separates exposure to carcinogens and the resulting appearance of disease does not quite make the future impacts disappear—but it does make them smaller, less threatening, easier to dismiss. The problems with discounting in this context are similar, but not identical, to the problems that arise with discounting in the intergenerational context.

Recall that $100 to be received twenty years from now has a present value of $55 at a 3 percent discount rate, or $26 at 7 percent. If cancer were the same as money, one could equally say that one hundred cancer cases expected twenty years from now have a present value of only fifty-five cancers today at a 3 percent discount rate, or only twenty-six cancers today at 7 percent. Don't laugh yet: this is exactly what is done in contemporary cost-benefit analyses. The economists at OMB have been outspoken in defense of this approach, insisting on it as a standard for evaluating the benefits of public policy—and most other economists have not disagreed.

Although contentious debates remain over what discount rate should be used to evaluate public policies, few mainstream economists today question the value and legitimacy of discounting future regulatory benefits, including human lives and health. What lies behind this remarkable consensus?

Three ideas are commonly cited in defense of discounting for regulatory analyses:

• Lives are just like money.
• People themselves treat the future as less important than the present.
• If we don't discount, we'll never help a single person but will instead keep our money in the bank forever (a puzzling notion which we'll explain in a moment).

As for the first idea: economists have defended discounting in the context of life-saving regulation by invoking the "time value of money," which implies that "[b]enefits and costs are worth more if they are experienced sooner."[6] This rationale has led to OMB's embrace of a 7 percent discount rate, calculated by estimating an average rate of return on a range of private financial investments.[7] The alternative rate of 3 percent reflects estimates of the trade-off between present and future for society as a whole, rather than for private investors. Some EPA studies have included parallel calculations at 3 percent and 7 percent; OMB favors the higher rate.

This would be all well and good if lives were just like money. And, in fact, OMB believes that the difference between monetized and nonmonetized goods—the difference between money and, say, lives—has been exaggerated. "[A]ll goods of finite value," OMB has insisted, are "amenable to monetization": "Individuals behave in accordance with real prices where prices exist, and *as if* prices exist in areas where they do not."[8] OMB has claimed that empirical research shows that "individuals behave as if they discount future effects that do not carry explicit prices."[9] On this line of reasoning, one would discount lives saved in the future for the same reason one would attach a monetary value to life: lives and money are not fundamentally different from each other.

A second, related justification for discounting cited by OMB and others is that individuals themselves, in their own lives, discount future events that might be harmful to them. OMB, for example, has cited studies estimating that workers discount future health effects from workplace hazards by 10 to 12 percent per year.[10] Likewise, the Environmental Protection Agency—which long resisted discounting—has, in coming around to the view that discounting is sometimes appropriate, cited surveys finding that people apply a positive discount rate to nonmonetized future effects. As EPA puts it, people "prefer projects that save lives in the near term over equivalent-cost projects that save lives in the future."[11]

A third justification for discounting is the idea that terrible consequences will flow from a refusal to discount. It is ironically the exact opposite of the problem encountered in the discussion of climate change, where discounting could lead to ignoring future benefits and postponing action. In regulatory debates involving shorter-term problems, it has been claimed that *failure to discount* could lead to indefinite delay in needed expenditures. As OMB has explained:

> To argue that a nonmonetized benefit should not be discounted implies that its value is the same whether it occurs today or at any time in the future. . . . By forgoing the expense [needed to achieve the benefit] this year and investing the resources at the discount rate, society could spend more next year (by a proportion equal to the discount rate) and achieve a higher level of welfare. As long as society places the

same value on a unit of future benefits as a unit of current benefits (i.e., it does not discount), it will be better off by delaying the action ad infinitum.[12]

This argument from unintended consequences is known as the Keeler–Cretin Paradox, after the authors who first elaborated it.[13]

The first argument—equating lives and money—was addressed in Chapter 4. Since lives are not money, and do not have a meaningful price, they are not eligible for discounting. As we have seen, discounting is just compound interest in reverse, and there is no way to put lives saved today in the bank and earn 7 percent more lives next year (or any other rate of return). The other two claims—that people care less about the future than about the present, and that we will never spend a penny to help anyone unless we engage in discounting—require more detailed responses.

Citizens, Consumers, and Future Generations

Discounting is said to reflect people's preferences, as expressed in market decisions concerning risk. However, using private market behavior as a standard for public policy overlooks the possibility that people will have different preferences when they take on different roles. The future seems to matter much more to American citizens than to American consumers, even though they are, of course, the same people.

For example, Americans are notoriously bad at saving money on their own, apparently expressing a disinterest in the future. But Social Security is arguably the most popular entitlement program in the United States. The tension between

Americans' personal saving habits and their enthusiasm for
Social Security implies a sharp divergence between the tem-
poral preferences of people as consumers and as citizens. Likewise, the very premise of many of our health and
environmental laws is that humans and the environment
should be protected from the chronic, insidious, persistent effect of workplace hazards and environmental toxins. This
premise is undermined, if not obliterated, when lives saved in
the future are shrunk to insignificance through discounting.
Private preferences for current over future consumption
should not be used to subvert public judgments that future
harms are as important as immediate ones.

Yet another problem with the argument for discounting
based on individual impatience is that it assumes that *the same
person* is deciding between spending money, or enjoying good
health, now or later. As we have seen, the argument for discounting collapses in the numerous cases where environmental programs provide benefits to future people, but impose
costs on the present.

Faced with these objections, the current advocates of discounting increasingly point to the Keeler-Cretin Paradox as
their last best defense. It is time to return this contorted notion to the obscurity it deserves.

Wait, It Gets Better

The "paradox" was described by Keeler and Cretin in a management journal in 1983, and has become important only
through its current popularity at OMB and in conservative
think-tank circles. The paradox can be summarized as follows: Suppose that monetary costs are discounted, but health

and environmental benefits are not. Suppose, also, that any number of human lives can be saved at a fixed cost per life at any time. Then, at a discount rate of 7 percent, we could either save 100 lives now, or put the money in the bank and have enough to save 107 lives next year. Since the saved lives are not discounted, this delay increases the value of the benefits to society by 7 percent, and should be preferred over the immediate life-saving expenditure. But the same logic shows that it is even better to leave the money in the bank for two years and then save 114 lives, and so on; it will always be better to wait another year.

Arguments like this generally err in their assumptions, not in their arithmetic—as a little exploration of the underlying story will reveal. Suppose that regulation of workplace exposure to a toxic chemical would save twenty lives per year. The costs of the regulation would probably be borne by the employers who would be required to maintain safer workplaces. The Keeler-Cretin Paradox requires us to assume that the employers could equally well let the twenty workers per year die for nine years, and then make an alternative expenditure, perhaps for a new traffic safety program, for instance, that saves more than two hundred lives in the tenth year, at the same cost per life. Or they could allow ninety-nine years of deaths and save more than two thousand lives in the hundredth year, for that matter.

The error here is that the imagined trade-off—allowing deaths now and saving other lives later—is both politically implausible, and is based on a hidden assumption of economic inefficiency. As a matter of practical politics, why would anyone allow employers to let twenty of their workers die each year, once the opportunity to save them has been identified?

The assumed indifference about saving lives now is utterly unfeasible in political terms.

The trade-off in this fable is also evidence of inefficiency, of the sort that cost-benefit analysis is supposed to eliminate. If a workplace safety program is required by regulation, and a traffic safety measure would save lives at the same cost, why isn't the traffic safety measure also required by regulation? If two measures, such as traffic safety and workplace safety, offer opportunities for saving lives at the same cost, then the efficiency criterion, as applied by OMB and conservative economists, implies that both measures are equally worthy of regulation. Regulating one but not the other would be inefficient; if either of the two makes sense, an efficient government will adopt both. And if the traffic safety program is required by regulation, it will already be under way, and will not be available to be introduced as a future substitute for workplace safety. In other words, the "paradox" rests on the inefficient assumption that there is a large supply of unregulated life-saving opportunities available at the same cost as the ones currently regulated.

It is hardly necessary to mention other aspects of reality that might intrude on this academic fantasy. The costs of saving lives might increase over time. Environmental problems might get worse, implying that there will be more deaths and other costs if we wait. As in the case of climate change, waiting is not a good strategy for problems that could lead to irreversible losses at some point in the future.

Fractured Lives

So far we have seen that discounting has a dramatic shrinking effect on the perceived benefits of regulations that save lives in, or protect the environment for, the future. We have also seen that the arguments in favor of discounting are very weak. It is surprising, then, to see discounting enjoying a period of unprecedented support in the federal government and to see it, moreover, mutating into an even more bizarre practice than the one we have described.

OMB has, in the Bush administration, taken an extremely aggressive posture toward the administrative agencies, in particular the Environmental Protection Agency. One way it has done this is to quarrel with the EPA's economic analyses of rules, as we saw in the last chapter with respect to the rule governing cooling water intakes that kill fish. And one key part of the quarrel about economic analyses is OMB's insistence upon discounting. Not only that, but OMB has lately invented a form of discounting so peculiar, one would think it was a vast typographical error if it hadn't appeared in OMB's handiwork more than once.

As we saw in Chapter 4, some economists now propose to evaluate life-saving regulation by considering the number of saved life-years, rather than lives. Under this approach, saving the life of a sixty-five-year-old would generally be viewed as less worthwhile than saving the life of a twenty-year-old. (If it so happened that the twenty-year-old had a disease that made her have only a ten-year life expectancy, then saving her life would be viewed as unfavorably as saving the sixty-five-year-old's life. Thus does the life-years approach partially escape the charge of age discrimination, only by adding discrimination based on health status to its list of sins.)[14]

In his work with Tammy Tengs, John Graham combined the estimation of life-years saved with the technique of discounting to produce an astonishing result. In their analysis, Tengs and Graham estimated the number of life-years that would be saved by a given policy intervention, and then discounted each life-year over the time that would pass before that year would be lived. Suppose an intervention was expected to save a five-year-old child who was expected to live to age seventy-five. Each of the seventy life-years saved in this example would, in Tengs and Graham's analysis, be discounted from the year in which it would be lived. Thus, the seventieth life-year saved would be discounted over seventy years; at a 7 percent discount rate, that year has a present value of less than 0.9 percent of a year, or about three days. The sixty-ninth year saved would be discounted over sixty-nine years; and so on. With this kind of analysis, it turns out, no one ever loses a whole life. Through the wonders of discounting, the five-year-old in our example goes from losing seventy years of her life to losing a present value of only fourteen years! Even a newborn who had eighty years to lose could not lose more than a present value of just over fourteen years. Tengs and Graham have, indeed, shrunk the kids.

Graham brought this kind of creative accounting with him to the White House. In one analysis, OMB calculated the benefits of tougher federal requirements for child restraints in cars. Here, OMB discounted the benefits of child restraints not once, but twice. First, OMB discounted the lives saved from the future date on which it thought the children would have been killed in the absence of better child restraints. This brought the estimate of the number of lives saved per year down from a range of 36 to 50 to a present value of 25 to 35. OMB next assumed that the average person saved by better child restraints was three years old and that this three-year-old had a remaining life expectancy of seventy-five years. OMB then discounted each of these remaining years by 7 percent per year, over the interval that would pass between now and the time each year would be lived. As in our last example, therefore, the child's last year of life was discounted over more than seven decades, and was "worth" just a couple of days of the current year.

This whole process resulted in a conclusion that a regulation saving 36 to 50 three-year-olds would actually save a present value of only 25 to 35 children, each with a present value life expectancy of only about fourteen years.[15] The combined effect of OMB's "double discounting" was to slash the estimated benefits of tighter restrictions on child restraints by over 85 percent. In a cost-benefit world, cutting benefits by such a large amount drastically weakens the case for government intervention.

Humpty Dumpty explained to Alice that words meant whatever he chose them to mean, and when a word worked hard for him, he always paid it extra. Perhaps John Graham has paid the words "present value" well for their efforts. The trouble is, if thirty-six children die, then thirty-six children really die, even if they die five or ten or more years from now. What is more, if a three-year-old who would have lived to seventy-eight dies, she really loses seventy-five years, not fourteen years. Human lives do not come in fractions; they do not compound like bank accounts. No amount of statistical manipulation can change these facts.

Unfortunately, the White House's quantitative sleights of hand have only become more eccentric as time goes on. Another adventure in discounting suggests that words such as "efficiency" and "life-years" are also on the payroll, working hard and meaning just what they are told to mean.

Smoke and Mirrors

By now, most of us are aware of the link between cars and trucks and air pollution. Many are less familiar with the role of boats, snowmobiles, all-terrain vehicles, forklifts, and the like. As it turns out, however, these so-called "nonroad engines" are responsible for an astonishing proportion of the harmful air pollution in the United States, because they have until recently been quite untouched by modern regulation.

In 2001, the Environmental Protection Agency finally got around to proposing standards for nonroad engines using conventional fuels (that is, not diesel fuel). In its economic analysis of its proposed rule, the agency happily presented a result not often seen in regulatory settings: the rule would not only save lives, it would save money, too! Because the rule would clean up nonroad engines primarily by pushing engine manufacturers toward different, more efficient engines, the rule would have the effect of saving consumers fuel costs. These costs, EPA estimated, would more than outweigh the costs of the rule to manufacturers that would have to retool operations to meet the new standards.

Seen in this light, one might have expected even the efficiency hawks at OMB to love this rule. They didn't. On the contrary, OMB's John Graham promptly fired a letter back to EPA, expressing skepticism that a regulation could really save money where the market hadn't done so. He also wanted to know more about the precise benefits of the rule beyond fuel-cost savings: how many lives would be saved, how many illnesses would be averted, and so on. He also worried that even if consumers would save in fuel costs as a result of the rule, maybe they would be left worse off in other ways by the move to more efficient engines.

Standing alone, this letter is striking enough. It reveals, for one thing, the deep-seated faith in the market that we saw in Chapter 2: a kind of pre-analytical view that the market always does a better job than the government. It also reflects an intense desire to collect as many numbers as possible—even when we already know enough to know the rule makes sense—to quantify, analyze, monetize a rule within an inch of its life, even when there is evidence that the rule will pay for itself based on the quantification of only one benefit (here, fuel-cost savings). But what happened in the wake of OMB's letter is even more telling.

EPA went back to the drawing board, and a year later emerged with a new, 600-page analysis. In its primary analysis, the agency concluded once again that the rule would pay for itself because it would save consumers fuel costs. The second time around, this proved enough for the OMB, and a rule finally regulating nonroad engines was published.

In this case, the real story isn't in the outcome, but in the process, because of what it may portend for future rules. In an analysis reportedly included at OMB's insistence,[16] EPA also included an alternative calculation of the benefits of the rule. In this calculation, EPA first assumed—against the advice of its own air-quality experts—that the air pollution put out by nonroad engines does not cause chronic life-threatening ill-

ness. (That is, this analysis assumed that the air pollution from
nonroad engines either kills you right away, in one blow, so to
speak, or not at all.)

Next, EPA monetized the lives saved by the rule, explicitly
assigning (for the first time in the agency's history, so far as we
know) a lower value to the lives of the elderly than to those of
younger people. Without discussion, the agency adopted the
lower values obtained by contingent valuation surveys, dis-
carding the higher values reflected in the wage premium
studies we discussed in Chapter 4. This led to an average value
per life of $3.7 million, as opposed to $6.1 million (in 1999
dollars).[17] Citing one study on the subject, the agency then
slashed that value by almost one-third for people over age
seventy[18]—even though the author of the study has stated
that his work cannot support that result, and more recent research indicates that the elderly do not, in fact, value their
lives less than younger people do.[19]

All this is disturbing enough. What EPA then did—again,
reportedly under OMB's direction—was add life-years and
discounting to the mix. The agency first converted the value
of a statistical life into the value of a lost life-year, using separate figures for people under seventy and over seventy. Then,
using its new value of a statistical life-year, they "built up" the
value of a statistical life from the value per year. Marching the
value of life up and down these steps resulted in a further
reduction—a seventy-year-old dropped to being worth only
$1.25 million. In fact, OMB's statistical shenanigans led to
some lives being valued at a mere $790,000, a new low for re-
cent studies.[20]

Thus we have come to the point where cost-benefit analysis no longer even possesses an internal logic. A valuation

method (willingness to pay) is used to assign a lower value to the lives of the elderly even though they don't think they're worth less. A new, unfamiliar concept (life-years) is introduced, thereby "proving" that if one accepts discounting of future life-years, no one ever loses more than fourteen years of life. If benefit estimates are not low enough, analysts reserve the option of switching back and forth between methodologies until the target can be hit. The only logic that remains is the credo of the antiregulatory crowd we met in the opening pages of this book: anything that makes regulatory benefits disappear will do.

When OMB's contorted new analysis made its way into the public domain, senior citizens were outraged. Coincidentally, the "senior death discount," as it came to be known, became news in the very same month then–EPA administrator Christine Todd Whitman was touring the country, conducting "listening sessions" on environmental problems as they relate to an aging population. She got an earful. By the end of her tour, she had announced that EPA would stop relying on the "senior discount" in future regulatory decisions. John Graham, for his part, demurred, acknowledging only that the specific form of the senior discount favored by his office was out of date. He continued to embrace, in principle, the idea of using age as a basis for valuing life; he stated that he was merely awaiting better "scientific" data to use for this purpose. In the meantime, he said, his office would continue to push for information concerning the number of life-years saved by regulation.

Kicking the Habit

Benjamin Franklin once described the process he used to make important decisions as a "prudential moral algebra," in which he listed the advantages of a possible action in one column on a piece of paper, and the disadvantages in another column, and then compared the two in figuring out what to do. Judge Stephen Williams, a prominent federal appeals court judge in Washington, D.C., who is known for his anti-regulatory views, quoted Franklin's description of this approach in a case suggesting that cost-benefit analysis was necessary before workplace safety measures could be required.[21] Other adherents of cost-benefit analysis have also invoked Franklin in defending their views.[22]

Ben Franklin's modest weighing of pros and cons has little in common with modern cost-benefit analysis, with its precise numerical inputs, reductive assessment of what's relevant and what's not, and its equation of money with all good things. Cost-benefit analysis is also very different from Franklin's larger ideas about how to live a good life; it is worth considering how Franklin's homespun values collide with discounting and other precepts of cost-benefit analysis.

Ben Franklin was a person who believed in sensible habits, in frugality, in moderation, in discipline. Sometimes he has been mocked for his attitudes, but on the whole we think it is fair to say that his mindset was one that many people, at least in principle, would still find admirable today. Yet discounting discourages all of the habits of mind and behavior that Franklin embraced. Planning for the future, disciplining yourself to adopt habits that require short-term sacrifice for long-term gain, doing with less—all of these attitudes are undermined, if not scorned, by the premises of discounting. People are impatient, the discounters say, and we should embrace that impatience in public policy.

Discounting society's most profound values endorses profligacy and shuns discipline. It is therefore all the more amazing that it is the Office of Management and Budget—the office created to instill fiscal discipline in the federal government—that has enshrined this practice in public life. The kids have been shrunk, to be sure, as a year at the end of a toddler's expected life is worth just days today. The notion that adults should teach children to understand and plan for the future is lost in the new mathematics of impatience. And not only the kids are diminished by discounting: the world they will inherit is scarcely worth taking seriously, its present value too small to outweigh a minor change in consumption today. Diseases that will affect us decades from now, environmental crises that will eventually change the earth's climate for the worse, nuclear and toxic wastes that will be unsafe for human contact for centuries—all these and more can be made to disappear with the flick of an equation.

In *Honey, I Shrunk the Kids,* the crazed inventor finally realizes the error of his ways and, through some combination of love, courage, ingenuity, and luck, rescues the children and restores them to full size. Can life imitate bad art? In our concluding chapter we turn to the challenge of unshrinking the future, and undoing the myriad damages done by pricing the priceless values of life, health, and nature.

9

Values Without Prices

The Clean Air Act should have been a disaster. By today's standards, the members of Congress who drafted it and voted for it, back in 1970, did everything wrong. They showed little concern for economic efficiency; they did not worry much about how affordable the rules adopted under the new law would be. Nor did they design flexible, market-based regulatory mechanisms intended to provide industry with opportunities for cost reduction and incentives for compliance. They did not quantify the effect of the Act on human life, health, and the environment, much less assign dollar values to the expected benefits; they did not conduct a formal cost-benefit analysis of the landmark law they were enacting.

Indeed, these representatives invented a whole new strategy—"technology forcing"—which was designed to pressure companies into developing new ways of controlling pollution that were not yet on the horizon when Congress acted. The authors of the Clean Air Act decreed, in traditional "command and control" fashion, that polluters would have to adopt the best emission-control technologies and meet strict performance standards. A massive new bureaucracy, the Environmental Protection Agency, was charged with enforcing the Act. A president who appeared quite conservative by the standards of the day, Richard Nixon, was persuaded to sign it all into law.

The modern economic critique of traditional regulation suggests that the Clean Air Act should have been massively inefficient.[1] Given the lack of attention to economic efficiency in the Act, one might think that cost-benefit analysis could easily demonstrate its failings. In fact, EPA's retrospective cost-benefit analysis—a giant six-year, peer-reviewed study—found that the Clean Air Act was overwhelmingly beneficial to society. EPA's best estimate of the cumulative value, from 1970 through 1990, of the most easily quantified benefits was more than $20 *trillion*—or more than forty times the total costs imposed on society.[2] As intended, the Clean Air Act made the nation's air dramatically cleaner, with emission reductions as of 1990 ranging from 30 percent for nitrogen oxides, up to nearly 100 percent for lead. As a result, people were dramatically healthier. Most of the benefits of the Act that were quantified in EPA's analysis consisted of avoided deaths attributable to the reduced air pollution.

This success story is no small exception to a rule about regulatory inefficiency. The Clean Air Act is one of the defining initiatives of the command-and-control era of regulation, with pervasive effects that continue to this day. Of course one example, no matter how big, does not prove that command-and-control regulation is always a success. What it does prove is that it is sometimes possible to make very good decisions without benefit of intricate economic analysis, and even without noticeable attention to market mechanisms.

It is fortunate that good choices can be made without prices—because it is so often necessary. We have argued throughout this book that many of the most important values protected by health, safety, and environmental laws are priceless. The imperatives of protecting human life, health, and the natural world around us, and ensuring equitable treatment of rich and poor, and of present and future generations, are not sold in markets and cannot be assigned meaningful prices. The point is not that *everything* of value is priceless; some of the benefits of protecting life, health, and nature can and should be priced. The fish we eat, the hospital beds we need when we're sick, even the experience we enjoy when visiting natural wonders, do have monetary values. Cost-benefit analysis incorporating these partial values will lean slightly toward protecting health and the environment. It will not, however, go nearly far enough; it will never reflect the full strength of our impulse to protect life, health, and nature.

Because important categories of benefits are priceless, cost-benefit analysis in practice frequently turns out to be "complete cost–incomplete benefit analysis." Cost estimates are typically relatively complete, while benefit estimates are substantially incomplete and thus guaranteed to understate true benefits. No theoretical construct or practical necessity justifies relying on such an unbalanced comparison.

Our view is sharply at odds with the contemporary style of cost-benefit analysis in Washington. The new conventional wisdom assumes that the priceless is worthless: today's decisions require calculations and bottom-line balances, and only numbers can be counted. The frequent, heavy-handed intervention in regulatory matters by the Office of Management and Budget treats monetized benefit estimates as absolute upper limits, and gives the back of the hand to unquantified values. The partisan nature of the process is clear, as OMB and

other critics of regulation also repeatedly insist on using lower
estimates of benefits than EPA and other agencies have proposed. Even when benefits at first appear to exceed costs, as in
OSHA's ergonomics standard or EPA's nonroad engine standard, spurious economic arguments are raised to imply that
regulation is now and forever inefficient.

An alternative method of decision making is badly needed.
In this final chapter we explore the options for setting policies
that reflect values without prices. We do not offer a new, mag-
ical formula that will solve all of our problems without the
messy intervention of human reason and emotion. But we do
offer a set of principles for guiding public policy on life, health,
and nature—principles that point toward a richer and more
thoughtful way of making public policy in the new century.

Precision or Participation?

The alternative is not a different formula. The multitude of
priceless values that we have identified cannot be measured
on a single scale, no matter what the units of measurement
may be. Alternative formulas for environmental evaluation,
while sometimes recognizing the need for multiple standards
of measurement, have failed to overcome the underlying limits of quantification.

One popular method—life-cycle analysis—compares a
range of technologies or policies on several different criteria.
Other techniques with names like "multiple criterion analysis" and "multi-attribute trade-off" offer new ways of combining different environmental standards into a single
judgment. At best, such methods can provide useful back-
ground information on multiple environmental impacts. At

worst, when they offer their own bottom-line evaluations, they make hidden judgments about the relative importance of different impacts—judgments that can be every bit as arbitrary and indefensible as the process of monetization. Suppose that two policies are being compared on standards including avoided deaths, carbon dioxide emissions, and loss of wetlands. How many acres of wetlands or tons of carbon dioxide are worth a human life? The question is no easier to answer than one regarding the dollar value of a life.

The development of a sound alternative approach begins with the recognition that *there is no formula*. For good decisions, public debate and participation are essential. T.S. Eliot wrote of "dreaming of systems so perfect that no one will need to be good";[3] in the same spirit, economists dream of decision rules so precise that no one will need to participate. But a classic work in economic theory demonstrates the impossibility of that dream. In 1951, Kenneth Arrow proved that the results of democratic decision making cannot be reproduced by a mathematical formula.[4] This crucial result, known as Arrow's Impossibility Theorem, derailed earlier attempts by economists to represent society's choices by a "social welfare function"—a quantitative description of what society supposedly prefers. Arrow's proof has not been refuted, though it may have been forgotten, in the rush to apply cost-benefit analysis.

Public participation is an important part of the alternative, but it is no panacea. The notion of everyone participating in everything is, of course, impossible; the "threat" of excessive participation is what led to the saying (often attributed to Oscar Wilde) that the problem with socialism is that it takes up too many evenings. The natural solution to this problem is a system with most decisions made by elected representatives, or agencies responsible to those representatives—though with active popular engagement in communicating with, pressuring, and voting for or against representatives on the basis of their stands on these issues.

Within this formal structure, what is the content of the alternative approach? What, in other words, should people push their representatives to do about health and environmental protection, in place of reliance on cost-benefit analysis? We propose four principles, elaborated in the next four sections:

- Use holistic, rather than atomistic, methods of evaluating costs and benefits.
- Learn from the military: moral imperatives are more powerful than cost comparisons.
- Adopt a precautionary approach to uncertain, potentially dangerous risks.
- Promote fairness—toward the poor and powerless today, and toward future generations.

Holistic Evaluation of Costs and Benefits

The difficulty in imagining an alternative approach to decision making comes in part from the reasonableness of the language of the conventional approach. Analysis of costs and benefits sounds objective and uncontroversial; making judgments based on willingness to pay sounds logical and democratic. How could anyone be opposed to such sensible procedures? Unfortunately, these reasonable-sounding terms are not reasonable in practice; the broadly appealing language has come to justify a narrow, controversial set of techniques.

Similar problems of double meanings occur elsewhere: "Democratic politics" means something different if it starts with a capital letter, as does a "Republican government." With lowercase letters the terms refer to important general concepts; with capital D's and R's they bespeak partisan debate. Likewise, analysis of costs and benefits, in lowercase letters, is an essential part of any systematic thought about public policy, and has always been involved in government decision making.[5] Our criticism concerns the much narrower doctrine of Cost-Benefit Analysis, which calls for a specific, controversial way of expressing and thinking about costs and benefits. The public's willingness to pay for health and environmental protection is a crucial factor in any democratic (with a small d) decision-making process. But under the banner of Willingness To Pay, an esoteric methodology marches forth to ask strange questions of strangers in shopping malls.

The source of the problem is the atomistic and reductionist approach adopted in the dominant style of Cost-Benefit Analysis. In this approach, once the basic information about monetary costs and health and environmental benefits has been assembled, the experts in effect say to the public, "We will analyze this complex situation for you. We will break down the benefits into their component particles—so many avoided deaths, so many cases of bronchitis or bladder cancer prevented, so many acres of wilderness saved—and provide an objective analysis of the monetary worth of each 'particle' of benefits. We will then be able to tell you, scientifically, whether you are willing to pay for environmental protection."

Too much is lost in the atomistic approach; the results do not necessarily agree with the public's actual desires. Indeed, the results often defy common sense, suggesting the public is willing to pay for almost nothing. Despite the evident, massive consumer spending for bottled water, inspired in part by the wish to avoid the perceived health risks of tap water, EPA's economic analysis of the arsenic rule concluded that people would not be willing to pay the modest additional amount for the strictest possible level of arsenic regulation. Likewise, under pressure from OMB, EPA rejected a proposal that would have saved millions of fish killed by power plants, because intricate research indirectly "proved" that the public would not accept increases of about a penny a day in household electric bills to pay for the proposal.

Much of the information used in an atomistic analysis would also be relevant in what we call the holistic approach, where costs as a whole (usually monetary) and benefits as a whole (often largely nonmonetary) are considered together— but are not forced to be expressed in the same units. Scientific information on risks to life, health, and the environment, and economic data on the likely effects of regulation on businesses and individuals, are of obvious importance to decisions about public policy. It is of course helpful, when evaluating broad public policies, to quantify everything that is measurable, to price everything that can be priced—while remembering how many essential values are not illuminated by these narrow-beam numerical spotlights. The evaluation of benefits and costs often means weighing deaths against dollars, ecosystems against economics. There is no need to act as if saving every human life, or every acre of wetlands, has an identical value; there is no prize for achieving an artificial consistency between losses in widely differing contexts. The nature of the risks involved, the questions of fairness and distribution of burdens, and the importance of providing for the future, all affect the policies that should be adopted to protect health and the environment. A deliberative process can acknowledge these and other factors, and adopt precautionary policies toward the uncertain dangers facing us.[6]

There are also aspects of current cost-benefit practices that we would exclude. Asking people in a shopping mall about hypothetical scenarios involving bronchitis, or talking to people who answer the phone about how much they would pay to protect the bald eagle, amounts to elevating the consumer over the citizen. It also turns the very idea of republican government on its head, suggesting that elected representatives should no longer try, through deliberation, reasoning, and debate, to shape the mass of public opinion into a sensible and lasting set of ideas, but should instead take their marching orders from a small sample of nameless individuals who answer a survey.

To those who respond that we are lost without a formula, we would point out, first, that many important decisions are made on the basis of rights and principles, not costs and benefits; as we will discuss in a moment, major resource allocation decisions are repeatedly made, in the area of military spending and national security, with little or no concern for costs. Second, in the cases where costs and benefits are the basis for decisions, something like what we are calling holistic evaluation occurs all the time in the market itself. Businesses and individuals continually make decisions that depend on multiple quantitative and qualitative factors, frequently based on the bottom-line impact of a choice, rather than on a detailed exploration of its disaggregated components. In short, a holistic assessment of one's options in the market leads to an either-or choice: to buy or not to buy.

Nothing more than that is required, from society as a whole, for evaluation of policies: assessment of overall impacts, not warring over minutiae, is what is needed to make a decision to "buy" or not to "buy" a proposed regulation. A holistic approach to the arsenic problem, for example, encourages us to ask whether it is worth the price of one or two bottles of water per person per year to ensure that everyone has tap water with the lowest possible level of arsenic. The atomistic approach sends us back to the mall to ask people about the monetary value of avoiding a nonfatal case of bladder cancer. For regulations to protect fish from power plants, the holistic approach makes us think about our willingness to pay a penny a day to avoid an underwater massacre, while the atomistic approach leads to unending technical disputes about the many ways of valuing a dead fish.

If the atomistic approach, valuing individual deaths, diseases, and environmental impacts, correctly analyzed the complete range of benefits, and if accurate, meaningful prices were available for all benefits, then the two methods would produce the same answer. However, this is clearly not the case. The monetized values of the individual components of benefits are often incomplete and incoherent, for the variety of reasons explained in earlier chapters; and the reduction of a complex scenario into individual health and environmental outcomes loses crucial information about the context in which benefits occur. Thus there is no reason to trust the atomistic estimates of willingness to pay, when they conflict with common sense and holistic evaluations of society's actual willingness to spend money on health and environmental protection.

The holistic approach to costs and benefits does not offer a purely quantitative decision; it cannot calculate for us whether our thumbs should point up or down. It can, though, take most of the information that goes into a cost-benefit analysis—everything up to the point of the attempted monetization of priceless benefits—and present it as a subject for public debate. The frequent claims that cost-benefit analysis would provide objectivity and transparency in decision making have the story backward: a holistic evaluation is desirable precisely because it is more transparent and accessible to participation, because it avoids the opaque technicalities that characterize cost-benefit studies in practice.

In advocating a holistic approach to weighing costs and benefits, we have been talking about how elected representatives and the public should think about health and environmental problems—not about how broad policies should be implemented. Most important decisions about health and the environment are filtered through administrative agencies like EPA before they can take effect; general instructions from Congress are refined and operationalized by the agencies. Once a higher-level decision has been made, the agencies should carry it out, not reopen the debate. At this stage, broad-ranging analysis can be a disaster.

The few health and environmental laws that require agencies to engage in an open-ended weighing of costs and benefits before proceeding with regulation have been failures. The broadest provision of the Toxic Substances Control Act, for example, allows EPA to regulate toxic substances, even to the point of banning them, based on a wide-ranging inquiry into costs and benefits. Yet despite its apparent breadth, this provision has been moribund ever since a court overturned EPA's ban on asbestos. The very open-endedness of the cost-benefit inquiry mandated by the statute, ironically enough, gave the court numerous opportunities to poke holes in the agency's analysis and thus justify invalidating EPA's asbestos rule. In contrast, statutory directives that provide more precise and well-defined instruction to agencies have been much more successful. Laws requiring agencies to identify the best technologies to address pollution, for example, do not allow administrative agencies (and reviewing courts) to reopen the basic debate about pollution and public policy.

Moral Imperatives and Top-Tier Issues

Reliance on cost-benefit analysis characterizes decision making in only some areas of public life. Compare the current treatment of health and the environment to a top priority issue like military spending. A passing grade in economics isn't required for the military. Even a program like national missile defense, one with only a tenuous, hypothetical link to terrorism and the foreign policy crises of the day, isn't subject to cost-benefit analysis. If it were, it too might fail the test.

Suppose that an antimissile defense system is designed to block an attack that would kill 10 million people, whose lives can be valued at $6 million each, roughly the number used in some EPA cost-benefit analyses. Avoiding such an attack appears to be a benefit worth 10 million × $6 million = $60 trillion, a truly enormous number. But that's just the beginning of a cost-benefit analysis.

How likely is the attack that the system would block? Events have tragically shown that cheaper, lower-technology methods of attack can do enormous damage; an enemy with limited resources might not bother with the expense of developing and building missiles. Suppose, then, that there is only a 1 percent chance of a missile attack being launched against the United States.

How likely is it that the missile defense system will actually work as planned and intercept the incoming missiles, in the event that it is needed? After years of research and development, tests of the system still have a very high failure rate; and none of the tests have included the full range of evasive countermeasures—e.g., numerous look-alike decoys—that could easily accompany a real attack. So suppose there is a 1 percent chance of the missile defense actually working, if it is ever used. (Does this sound unrealistically low? Read on; we'll address that question in a moment.)

When will the attack occur? If it is equally likely at any point in the system's lifetime of, say, forty years, then, statistically speaking, one could say that it is expected, on average, to be twenty years from now.

Combining all these assumptions, the expected benefit of the missile defense system is 10 million × $6 million × .01 × .01 = $6 billion, to be experienced twenty years from now. Discounting $6 billion over twenty years, even at a modest 3 percent rate, reduces the benefit to a present value of $3.3 billion. Since the system will cost far more than $3.3 billion, this cost-benefit analysis implies that the missile defense system should be canceled on grounds of extreme economic inefficiency. However, no one will be surprised at OMB's failure to call for the program's cancellation.

This contrived example contains several of the characteristic elements of real cost-benefit analysis as applied to environmental protection:

- the obvious undertone of hostility to the program being evaluated;
- the use of obscure, unintuitive valuations for the benefits ($6 million per life);
- the low estimate of the probability of actually achieving the program's intended benefits;
- the capricious use of discounting to lower the present value of benefits; and
- the smoke screen of technical arguments concealing the real value judgments in the analysis.

In particular, the two assumed probabilities of 1 percent are crucial to the outcome. Repeat the calculation with both probabilities set at 50 percent, and the answer would be entirely different. But we, after all, are professional analysts; never mind that we have no particular expertise in *military* analysis. Are you sure that you know enough to question our professional judgment about such arcane, technical matters? Meanwhile, we can circulate the story and soundbite to our friends in the media: "New study finds missile defense worth only $3.3 billion."

Our point is not, of course, to defend the specifics of this "analysis" of missile defense. Rather, we aim to draw an analogy to many well-publicized conservative analyses of health and environmental protection. With no more expertise on the environment than we possess on military technology, Washington think-tankers render precise, hostile, quantitative judgments which—like our 1 percent probabilities—guarantee that environmental policies and regulations will fail cost-benefit tests.

Military spending is not typically justified by doing calculations like ours with more favorable numbers. None of the responses to terrorism after September 11 were based on cost-benefit analysis (although OMB announced, in 2003, its interest in developing such analyses for new terrorism-related initiatives). Instead, advocates of military spending appeal to beliefs about threats to our way of life, offering broad strategies for response and, in classic "command and control" mode, proposing major weapon systems on the basis of their expected technical performance. Questions of cost minimization and budget constraints enter only at a much later stage, in the details of implementation. Those who complain about excessive costs are suspected, often correctly, of harboring deeper objections to the weapons programs under discussion.

All the same points apply equally well to the environment. The argument for health and environmental protection is a claim about threats to our way of life. People are dying from air and water pollution, from dangerous working conditions, from toxic chemicals used in industry and agriculture. Indeed, these deaths are more certain and more continual than the deaths that military spending seeks to prevent. Technologies offering protection from most environmental threats are available and proven to work. Those who complain most vociferously about the costs frequently do oppose environmental programs on other grounds. The parallel between environmental and military forms of defense seems complete—except for the level of funding and political support that they receive at the top levels of government.

In short, the most fundamental problem is not in the details of any particular cost-benefit analysis, but rather in the framing decision about which policies are and which are not subject to such analyses. The supposed urgency of detailed cost-benefit analysis reflects the assumption that there is only a fixed (and apparently quite small) amount of money to spend, so that it is important to set priorities for that money wisely. But what sum of money is it? It is not a number that can be found anywhere in the federal budget; most of the costs identified in cost-benefit analyses are the costs to business of compliance with regulations, not expenditures by government agencies. Why, then, do we imagine that there is a stingy, fixed total of resources available for defending ourselves, our children, and our surroundings against environmental and occupational harm? No one ever imagines that when it comes to defending ourselves against military threats.

In many situations, the zero-sum image is appropriate; tight budget constraints often do force painful trade-offs between desirable expenditures. Government agencies, nonprofit organizations, municipal governments, and countless other institutions have little or no control over their total funding. They do, therefore, continually have to worry about whether one good program is crowding out another, better one. Economics offers analytical tools designed for exactly this problem; some introductory textbooks even define economics as the study of choices under constraints.

But it is also important to recognize the limits of the zero-sum image. It can be applied quite inappropriately to situations that are not characterized by scarcity and trade-offs. Advocates of recycling often encounter the perverse criticism that they are diverting energy into a low-priority activity and letting people too easily feel that they have already done their part for the environment, thereby weakening campaigns around more urgent issues. It is as if there was a fixed time budget for environmentalism, so that every minute spent on recycling means one less minute spent on stopping global warming and cleaning up toxic waste.

Survey data tell a different story, showing that those who recycle are motivated by broad environmental concerns, and are more, not less, likely to work for other environmental goals as well.[7] Recycling is the gateway drug of the environmental movement: get the kids hooked on sorting their trash, and soon they'll be addicted to harder stuff. Cost-benefit analysis of time spent on recycling versus other environmental efforts would miss the all-important synergy between these closely related activities.

Are there other cases where synergy between related activities is more important than trade-offs and competition for resources? At the national level, government resources are not fixed; changes in tax rates and in the extent of government borrowing happen all the time. Moreover, the total allocations to broad areas, such as the military or environmental protection, can change rapidly in response to changing circumstances. Federal budget allocation is not a zero-sum game. Effective advocacy for a particular issue can easily lead to greater total resources for a broad area, rather than to painful trade-offs with other, closely related issues.

In the area of medical research, single-issue activists successfully politicized the issues of funding for AIDS and breast cancer in the late 1980s and early 1990s. At the time, many observers worried about whether the activists were diverting limited funds away from research on other diseases. The growth in funding for the "politicized" diseases was impressive: from 1990 to 1995, peak years of activist success, funding for breast cancer research rose from $90 million to $465 million, while AIDS research funding, already over $700 million in 1990, climbed to more than $1.3 billion five years later.[8] Yet, in the same years, funding for all other medical research grew slightly faster than either the total federal government budget or gross domestic product (GDP), a common measure of national income. Funding for medical research, exclusive of AIDS and breast cancer, grew by 5.2 percent annually, while GDP grew by 5 percent and the federal budget by 5.1 percent per year.[9]

Was there a trade-off between funding for different diseases in the early 1990s? It seems at least as believable that the advocates drew attention to the urgency of medical research, thereby winning increased total research funding. In the absence of noisy and successful advocacy for some diseases, total medical research funding might have grown much more slowly, leaving no more for other diseases, or even less, than they actually received during the early 1990s.

A cost-benefit analysis of priorities for an assumed, fixed total of research funds might well have shown, for instance, that more should have gone to heart disease and less to breast cancer and/or AIDS. But that analysis would have missed the intriguing possibility that single-issue advocacy increased awareness and funding for medical research in general. The happy outcome in this case, with strident single-issue advocacy promoting the common good, is not guaranteed to occur every time; but it is significant to realize that it does happen sometimes. Trade-offs in the context of limited resources are not the only kinds of decisions that we have to make.

At a national level, particularly in a society as wealthy as ours, resource allocation is not a zero-sum game. Successful advocacy is couched, not in intricate analysis of economic trade-offs, but in sweeping moral imperatives—as proponents of military spending have long known, as the environmental advocates of the 1970s realized, and as breast cancer and AIDS activists have more recently demonstrated. The health and environmental threats discussed in this book are urgent because people are dying from preventable causes, and because shortsighted choices made today are threatening to destroy the environment we will leave to our descendants. How can bizarre, hypothetical calculations about tiny sums of money stand in the way of using our knowledge and resources to do the right thing?

The principle at stake here is not simply that a different problem needs a little more money or attention. Rather, the question is about society's priorities, about which are the top-tier issues that deserve priority treatment. A large, and growing, chunk of our collective resources is already allocated to the military on the basis of passionate claims about moral imperatives. Those who care about civilian objectives have to answer in kind, not imagine that they can win the debate with careful spreadsheets and subtle trade-offs alone.

The Importance of Precaution

I'm not saying it's safe for humans. I'm not saying it's unsafe for humans. All I'm saying is that it makes hermaphrodites of frogs.
—Tyrone B. Hayes, Associate Professor of Integrative Biology, University of California at Berkeley, on his discovery that male frogs exposed to low doses of the weed killer atrazine developed multiple sex organs.[10]

One of the fundamental assumptions of the conventional economic analysis of health and environmental hazards is that every risk can be represented by a number: this many deaths, or that much loss of habitat, or an increase of a certain number of degrees in average global temperatures. Yet often enough, the most serious hazards have impacts so uncertain that they cannot be quantified. No one knows exactly how much of the earth's climate will change as a result of carbon dioxide emissions, or how rapidly the change will occur. Some of the most ominous toxic chemicals have not been fully researched. As we saw in Chapter 5, debate has raged for decades about exactly how much of a danger to human health is posed by dioxin, and a century of research has not resolved the ongoing disagreements about the effects of low-level radiation.

A cost-benefit analysis requires a number for each cost and benefit, no matter what the level of uncertainty may be. There is enormous pressure, in effect, to ignore all uncertainty and develop a single best estimate based on what is known today. If researchers offer high and low estimates to reflect uncertainty, there is a strong tendency to use the average and ignore the extremes. If some researchers believe there is a problem but others disagree, then skeptical economic analysts may seize on the disagreement as grounds for ignoring the problem altogether until scientists can reach a consensus.

A better answer is the precautionary principle, calling for action on serious threats even before there is a scientific consensus. If atrazine causes reproductive abnormality in frogs, should we use it until it is proved to harm humans, or stop using it until it is proved to be safe? Many lives have been needlessly lost waiting for more research, even after hazards have been clearly identified. The terrible impact of asbestos on workers' lungs was convincingly described in a British government inspector's report nearly a century before the adoption of asbestos regulations in Europe. And asbestos is unfortunately not alone in this regard.

Science is never finished, and consensus is never absolute. A few scientists still doubt the ever-growing international consensus about the seriousness of climate change. The writings of these "climate skeptics" have been widely distributed (and often financed) by energy companies seeking to undermine the notion that everyone agrees about the climate problem. There is even a handful of scientists willing to claim, in exchange for tobacco industry funding, that smoking is not nearly as hazardous as most people believe.

The general idea of the precautionary principle is easy enough to describe: we should pay attention to early warnings of serious hazards, rather than wait for final proof and precise quantification of the expected impacts. The difficulty comes in implementation. How can this idea be turned into practical guidance for public policy?

The beginnings of an approach are suggested by a little-known result in economic theory, again based on work done by Kenneth Arrow, in this case jointly with Leonid Hurwicz; its relevance to the precautionary principle was pointed out by Richard Woodward and Richard Bishop.[11] Arrow and Hurwicz considered a situation in which there are several forecasts of future outcomes, all of which are known to be possible; but nothing is known about the relative probabilities of the different forecasts—a reasonable description of many dilemmas involving health and environmental hazards. In such situations, the best public policy depends only on the *extremes* of the range of possible outcomes. If decision makers know the extremes of the range of possibilities, nothing is added by any estimate or guess about the single most likely outcome.

This theory calls for a more tolerant approach to uncertainty, acknowledging and exploring the differences of opinion rather than battling over the best available single estimate of impacts. The low case, arguing that health and environmental risks will turn out to be minimal, has often been elaborated in loving detail by Washington's conservative think-tank community, or by OMB itself. Those who are more concerned about the risks should explore the other extreme, spelling out the credible high case: what if Chicken Little was at least partly right after all? In the worst case, how much of the sky really might be falling? How bad could the effects of dioxin, climate change, low-level radiation, and other controversial hazards turn out to be?

Once the extremes of the possible have been identified, the right approach is *not* to take the average and treat it as the consensus forecast. Rather, both extremes deserve serious consideration. Indeed, careful assessment of fundamental alternatives is often taken as one of the hallmarks of a precautionary approach.[12] It may be helpful to consider the question: if one side of the debate later turns out to be right, what are the costs of accepting the other side's forecast? If the low case is right, and the uncertain risks are in fact minimal, then acting on the high case will mean that society has substantially overinvested in health and environmental protection, spending much more on emission controls, cleanup, and clean technologies than was required. If the high case is right, and the uncertain risks are in fact very serious, acting on the low case will mean that society has failed to defend the present and future generations from substantial, preventable harms.

These are not symmetrical errors, offering equal dangers on both sides. Our preference is to tilt toward overinvestment in protecting ourselves and our descendants. The likely rejoinder is that this is prohibitively expensive. As we saw in Chapters 2 and 3, claims about regulatory costs have been greatly exaggerated; actual compliance costs tend to decline over time after regulations are in place. But even if the costs of health and environmental protection are very high, once again military spending provides an instructive counterexample.

In retrospect, it seems likely that the United States significantly overinvested in military protection throughout the Cold War years. The Soviet economy was weak, technologically far behind and, in its later years, stagnating while the U.S. economy was growing. The United States maintained an overwhelming lead in military spending and many types of weaponry throughout the period. The sum total of Soviet attempts at military expansion after the 1940s consisted of one disastrous intervention in Afghanistan. It seems likely that any threat from such a weak opponent could have been blocked at significantly lower cost.

Assuming that Cold War military spending was, in hindsight, much more than was needed, how should the economic experience of those years be interpreted? (We are ignoring, for the moment, the ominous military climate of the Cold War, and focusing solely on its domestic economic impacts.) Was the inefficiency, excessive public spending, and huge military bureaucracy a disastrous drain on the private sector? Would everyone be wealthier and happier today if more economically efficient, leaner military budgets had been adopted? With perfect hindsight, a much better economic growth strategy for those years could be described. But at the time, military spending was one of the foundations of U.S. economic growth, providing jobs and incomes to millions of Americans. The computer industry and modern microelectronics in general, now seen as premier success stories of private enterprise, largely began as spin-offs from decades of massive military investments in research and development.

Advocates of Cold War military spending could have seen the situation in terms much like our interpretation of the precautionary principle. The actual military risk was uncertain, and the danger of being exposed to attack in the high-risk case seemed much greater than the danger of spending too much in the low-risk case. Preparing for the high-risk case did not bankrupt the nation, but created jobs and industries that sustained economic growth.

The same is true for the health and environmental risks we face today. The high case involves dangers of irreversible climate change, of mounting levels of carcinogens in our air, food, and water, of increasingly unsafe workplaces and highways, of destruction of wilderness and extinction of species. The low case involves the economic dangers of spending too much on clean energy, on elimination of toxins, on safety precautions, on preservation of nature. The process of spending "too much" on defense against health and environmental threats might create new industries, just as the Cold War did, offering jobs to millions and spawning new technologies that will transform the future as radically as the computer industry has transformed the present.

Despite numerous parallels with military spending, there is one big difference: investing in health and environmental protection does not involve developing technologies designed to kill human beings, let alone contemplating the total nuclear destruction of life on earth. After two generations of the Cold War economy, our culture is saturated with the glorification of violence and military conflict. After two generations of war on health and environmental hazards, what other ethos might infuse the movies, the games, and the dreams of patriotic Americans?

Fairness and the Future

Health and environmental protection ultimately involve our values about other people—those living today, and those who will live in future generations. Here, the analytical apparatus of economics stands mute: the market cannot tell us the worth of, or the rights of, other people. Determination of our obligations to others alive today, and to future generations, is an ethical question that must be answered prior to detailed decision making. It is not a question of efficiency, and is not a matter to be settled by cost-benefit analysis and consumer willingness to pay.

The problems of environmental justice, touched on in Chapter 6, have become well-known. "Not in my backyard" protests against local hazards work well for the wealthy, but not so well when the backyard belongs to the poor or powerless. Questions of equity are inescapable—and often lead to deeper questions of whether cleaner alternatives can be found, so that the hazards do not end up in anyone's backyard.

The logic of the market does not address distributional questions. As economists are fond of pointing out, efficiency and equity are two separate goals; most economic analysis deals with efficiency. Some writers have even suggested that equity and income distribution are not even part of economics; apparently these topics have been deported, perhaps to the sociology or political science department. In the extreme, a competitive market can be perfectly efficient, even if some participants literally starve while others stuff themselves. Remarkably, economists have proved that there is no reason in theory to assume that all participants in an efficient market are able to survive from one period to the next.[13] There is equally no reason in theory to oppose the provision of adequate minimum standards of living for all; many European countries have gone much further in this direction than the U.S., without bankrupting or destroying their economies. Our preference is for a much more equal world—not because it is more, or less, efficient, but because it is the right way to live.

The relationship between wealth, poverty, and environmental protection is different in industrial and developing countries. In the wealthiest parts of the world, the greatest threat to the environment may arise from the high and growing levels of consumption of energy and materials by the affluent. Regulation is often needed to protect the natural world from the encroachment of human activity, as well as to protect the poor from becoming the dumping ground for the rich.

In developing countries, on the other hand, there are serious environmental threats that arise from poverty. The pervasive problem of tropical deforestation is sometimes driven by the desperate search for fuelwood and farmland by the poor. In such cases, more economic security for the poor will lead directly to reduced environmental destruction. Biodiversity in fields and forests often is protected in practice by the people who live and work there. For instance, in southern Mexico, the region from which corn originated, traditional farming practices rely on the cultivation of numerous native varieties of corn—many found nowhere else, and providing the genetic reservoir from which new varieties can be developed. Today, this living biodiversity is threatened by cheap U.S. exports of subsidized, chemical-intensive hybrid corn, including genetically modified varieties.[14] The challenge of creating a sustainable way of life in southern Mexico that includes preservation of the ancestral biodiversity of corn blends the concerns of environmental protection, economic justice, and national development in ways that reach far beyond conventional market analysis.

Equally complex questions arise in regard to future generations. This topic rests on a leap of faith: we do not know for a fact that there will be future generations, and we will not live to see that fact confirmed, beyond the few generations immediately following our own. If one believed that the end times are upon us, or that divine intervention is going to bring life as we know it to a close in a final rapture at a date certain, there would be no point in preserving resources, a livable climate, or anything else for the future. The long-term survival of humanity and the earth's ecosystems is only a guess. No one reading this book will be around to find out if we guessed correctly.

Since there is no way to know in advance, we advocate acting as if our descendants will prosper—and therefore acting concerned about the nature of the world they will inherit. How should we allocate resources between the present and the future? Economic theory has struggled with this question, as noted in Chapter 8, but without impressive success. The discount rate paradoxes, discussed there, are inescapable: any positive discount rate writes off the far future, while a zero discount rate seems senseless for short-run financial decisions. The only sensible strategy is to recognize that, in talking about human lives and the far future, we are in the grip of a moral dilemma, in which interest rates and rates of return on financial investments are of no help.

The problem of coordination between the present and future cannot be solved by the market. Future generations do not yet exist; their needs and wants are unknown in any detail. Since their preferences will depend in part on what we leave to them, it is mathematically circular to try to deduce what we should leave to them from hypotheses about their preferences.[15] The market is speechless on the question of intergenerational resource allocation, until given its cue by the earlier generation's nonmarket decision about what to leave for its descendants.

The problem is more than a mathematical one. The choices we make today will determine what kind of life exists for future generations. People are remarkably adaptable, and within very broad ranges will grow up accepting their surroundings as normal. As the philosopher Mark Sagoff has observed, this means that we have to choose what kind of future we want to create. People brought up in an asphalt junkyard will develop an aesthetic based on those surroundings. People brought up in a natural world in all its wild diversity will develop a different aesthetic.[16]

Thus the decisions about the needs of future generations are in the end reflections of our own values about the present. We will create a future at least partly in our own image; what do we want that image to look like? Many environmental advocates have suggested an image of stewardship, in which we are not owners of nature but rather its temporary caretakers.

Perhaps each generation should act like a guardian, empowered only to take care of the earth and its environment until the next generation comes of age.[17]

A common objection to this concern for the future is the claim that it ignores the needs of the present. How can we worry about future generations, or give up any opportunities for immediate economic growth, when so many people around the world are trapped in poverty today? It is a good question that too often leads to a bad answer. The same market forces that threaten our environmental future are also the cause of inequality today. Frequently, as we have seen, the two problems are combined: the worst effects of pollution often fall on the poorest and least powerful members of society. Unregulated economic growth does not automatically eliminate either pollution or poverty; the market economy must be restrained and channeled in the direction of sustainable development in order to meet the needs of both the present generation and those who will follow us.

And that is why it is so important to restore the legitimacy of regulation, to stop the wholesale dismissal and repeal of past successes that is under way in Washington, to remember the great things that we as a nation have done—and will do again.

To Be Continued

Thirty years ago, Congress passed sweeping laws to protect human health and the environment. While the details always can be improved upon, the underlying impulse, and the broad outlines of the laws, were not wrong. In some ways, these laws were thoroughly modern: they created a massive new federal bureaucracy, demanded the best science the nation could offer, and invented whole new regulatory concepts such as technology forcing. At their core, however, the new laws were conservative in the oldest and best sense of the term: they restored old-fashioned values like humility, fairness, and a sense of moral urgency to a central place in our relationships with one another and with the environment.

These are the fundamental values at stake—and at risk—in the debates over economic analysis of health and environmental protection. Cost-benefit analysis of health and environmental policies trivializes the very values that gave rise to those policies in the first place. Moreover, through opaque and intimidating concepts like willingness to pay, quality-adjusted life-years, and discounting, economic analysts have managed to hide the moral and political questions lying just under the surface of their precise and scientific-looking numbers. It is time to blow their cover.

It is also time to get back to the basics—to remember the simple insights that inspired citizens and their representatives, a generation ago, to demand and produce legal protections for health and the environment. To do so, we must give up the idea, reassuring to many, that there is, somewhere, a precise mathematical formula waiting to solve our problems for us. In its place, we offer an attitude rather than an algorithm: one that trusts collective, commonsense judgments, and is humble in the face of uncertainty, steadfast in confronting urgent problems, and committed to fairness within and beyond this generation.

The benefit of our approach? Priceless.

Notes

CHAPTER 1: PRICES WITHOUT VALUES

1. Donald A. Redelmeier and Robert J. Tibshirani, "Association Between Cellular Telephone Calls and Motor Vehicle Collisions," *New England Journal of Medicine* 336 (1997), 453–58.

2. Michael Specter, "The Phone Guy," *The New Yorker,* November 26, 2001, 62, 67.

3. Dennis Utter, "Passenger Vehicle Driver Cell Phone Use: Results from the Fall 2000 Occupant Protection Use Survey," National Highway Traffic Safety Administration Research Note (July 2001).

4. Robert W. Hahn, Paul C. Tetlock, and Jason K. Burnett, "Should You Be Allowed to Use Your Cellular Phone While Driving?" *Regulation,* 23, 46; Robert W. Hahn and Paul C. Tetlock, *The Economics of Regulating Cellular Phones in Vehicles,* AEI-Brookings Joint Center for Regulatory Studies, Working Paper 99–9 (October 1999); Donald A. Redelmeier and Milton C. Weinstein, "Cost-Effectiveness of Regulations against Using a Cellular Telephone while Driving," *Med. Decision Making,* 19, no. 1, 1 (January–March 1999); Joshua Cohen et al., Harvard Center for Risk Analysis, "Cellular Phones and Driving: Weighing the Risks and Benefits," *Risk in Perspective* 8 (July 2000), 1–6 (funded with $300,000 grant from AT&T Wireless Communications).

5. For more details, see Jamie L. Kitman, "The Secret History of Lead," *The Nation,* March 20, 2000, 11.

6. The $8,346 value is developed in EPA, *Economic Analysis of Toxic Substances Control Act Section 403: Lead-Based Paint Hazard Standards,* December 2000, Chapter 6, available at http://www.epa.gov/lead/403_ea_d21.pdf.

7. Adrienne S. Ettinger, *Chelation Therapy for Childhood Lead Poisoning: Does Excretion Equal Efficacy?,* available at http://www.hsph.harvard.edu/Organizations/DDIL/chelation.htm.therapy.

8. Randall Lutter, *Valuing Children's Health: A Reassessment of the Benefits of Lower Lead Levels,* AEI-Brookings Joint Center for Regulatory Studies, Working Paper 00–02 (2000), available at http://www.aei.brookings.org/publications/working/working_00_02.pdf.

9. Office of Management and Budget, Office of Information and Regulatory Affairs, *Stimulating Smarter Regulation: 2001 Report to Congress on the Costs and Benefits of Regulations and Unfunded Mandates on State, Local, and Tribal Entities* (2002), 110.

10. Office of Management and Budget, Office of Information and Regulatory Affairs, *Making Sense of Regulation: 2001 Report to Congress on the Costs and Benefits of Regulations and Unfunded Mandates on State, Local, and Tribal Entities* (2001), 63, Table 7.

11. Eban Goodstein, *The Trade-Off Myth: Fact and Fiction About Jobs and the Environment* (Washington, DC: Island Press, 1999).

12. Calculated from Bureau of Labor Statistics data, in Frank Ackerman and Rachel Massey, "Prospering with Precaution" (Tufts University, 2002), available at http://www.ase.tufts.edu/gdae/policy_research/Precaution AHTAug02.pdf.

CHAPTER 2: MYTHS AND MARKETS

1. Terry L. Anderson, Vernon L. Smith, and Emily Simmons, *How and Why to Privatize Federal Lands,* Cato Institute, December 1999.

2. *Ibid.*

3. Eric Pianin, "Free-Market Environmentalists Gaining Stature: Group No Longer on Fringes as Bush Incorporates Proposals in Land Policies," *Washington Post,* June 4, 2001, A4.

4. Terry L. Anderson and Donald R. Leal, *Free Market Environmentalism* (New York: Palgrave, 2001), 25.

5. *Ibid.,* 45, 47.

6. *Ibid.,* 125.

7. *Ibid.,* 159–60.

8. Jake Tapper, "Retiring, Not Shy," *New York Times Magazine,* September 1, 2002 (quoting one of "Armey's axioms").

9. Elliot D. Sclar, *You Don't Always Get What You Pay For: The Economics of Privatization* (Ithaca, NY: Cornell University Press, 2000).

10. One of us (Ackerman) worked extensively as a consultant to state agencies that regulated electric utilities in the 1980s.

11. This account draws heavily on "Causes and Lessons of the California Electricity Crisis," Congressional Budget Office (2001), available at http://www.cbo.gov.

12. Richard Rosen, "Regulating Power: An Idea Whose Time is Back," *The American Prospect,* March 25, 2002.

13. Benito Mussolini, *My Autobiography* (New York: Charles Scribner & Sons, 1928), 14.

14. For an excellent discussion of the tendency to exaggerate costs in advance of regulation, see Thomas O. McGarity and Ruth Ruttenberg, "Counting the Cost of Health, Safety, and Environmental Regulation," *Texas Law Review* 80 (2002), 1197.

15. See, among many other publications, Nicholas A. Ashford and Charles C. Caldart, *Technology, Law, and the Working Environment* (Washington, DC: Island Press, 1996), 251.

16. U.S. Congress, Office of Technology Assessment, *Gauging Control Technology and Regulatory Impacts in Occupational Safety and Health—An Appraisal of OSHA's Analytic Approach,* OTA–ENV–635 (Washington, DC: U.S. Government Printing Office, 1995).

17. Eban Goodstein, "Polluted Data," *American Prospect,* November–December 1997, available at http://www.prospect.org; Hart Hodges, "Falling Prices: Cost of Complying with Environmental Regulations Almost Always Less Than Advertised," *Economic Policy Institute* (1997), available at http://epinet.org. Both publications report on the same study.

18. Winston Harrington, Richard D. Morgenstern, and Peter Nelson, "On the Accuracy of Regulatory Cost Estimates," *Journal of Policy Analysis and Management* 19, no. 2 (Spring 2000), 297–322.

19. See Paul Hawken, Amory Lovins, and L. Hunter Lovins, *Natural Capitalism* (New York: Little, Brown, 1999) for examples and discussion of this trend.

20. There is an extensive, ongoing academic discussion of this idea, the so-called "Porter Hypothesis." See, for example, Michael E. Porter and Class van der Linde, "Toward a New Conception of the Environment-Competitiveness Relationship," *Journal of Economic Perspectives* 9, no. 4 (Fall 1995), 97–118.

21. Robert W. Hahn, "Regulatory Reform: What Do the Government's Numbers Tell Us?," in *Risks, Costs, and Lives Saved: Getting Better Results from Regulation* (New York: Oxford University Press and AEI Press, 1996), 226.

CHAPTER 3: THE UNICORNS OF DEREGULATION

1. John F. Morrall III, "A Review of the Record," *Regulation,* November/December 1986, 25, 30, Table 4.

2. John D. Graham, *How to Save 60,000 Lives,* Edison Electric Institute (1995), available at www.eei.org.

3. Testimony of John D. Graham, Ph.D., Director, Center for Risk Analysis, Harvard School of Public Health, Before the Committee on Governmental Affairs, U.S. Senate (April 21, 1999) (testimony on S. 746, the Regulatory Improvement Act of 1999).

4. Brief of Respondents Appalachian Power Co., *American Trucking Ass'ns v. Browner,* No. 99–1426 (U.S. Supreme Court 2000 Term), 18 (citing Ralph L. Keeney and Kenneth Green, "Estimating Fatalities Induced by Economic Impacts of EPA's Ozone and Particulate Standards," available on Web page of Reason Public Policy Institute, http://www.rppi.org/environment/ps225.html).

5. For a critical review of Lomborg's book, see Frank Ackerman, "Tree-Huggers No Longer!," *The Nation,* March 25, 2002, avail-

able at http://www.ase.tufts.edu/gdae/publications/AckermanNation LomborgReview.PDF.

6. We have published detailed rebuttals to these antiregulatory myths elsewhere. Lisa Heinzerling, "Regulatory Costs of Mythic Proportions," *Yale Law Journal* 107 (1998); Lisa Heinzerling and Frank Ackerman, "The Humbugs of the Anti-Regulatory Movement" *Cornell Law Review* 87 (2002), 648–70; Lisa Heinzerling, "Five-Hundred Life-Saving Interventions and Their Misuse in the Debate Over Regulatory Reform," *Risk: Health, Safety & Environment* 13 (Spring 2002), 151.

7. Tammy O. Tengs, Miriam E. Adams, Joseph S. Pliskin, Dana Gelb Safran, Joanna E. Siegel, Milton C. Weinstein, and John D. Graham, "Five-Hundred Life-Saving Interventions and Their Cost-Effectiveness," *Risk Analysis* 15 (1995), 369.

8. Testimony of John D. Graham.

9. As Tengs and Graham themselves acknowledge. Tengs et al., "Five-Hundred Life-Saving Interventions," 372.

10. In 1992 OSHA estimated that the reduction in the permissible exposure level for formaldehyde in the workplace from a daily average of 1 part per million (ppm) to 0.75 ppm prevents 3 cases of cancer and 21,568 cases of respiratory distress annually. "Occupational Exposure to Formaldehyde," OSHA Fact Sheet 92-27, U.S. Department of Labor, available at http://www.pp.okstate.edu/ehs/training/oshafhyd.htm.

11. Morrall, "A Review of the Record," 28–29.

12. However, Tengs and Graham's unusual approach to discounting (revealed only by digging deep into their equations, not by reading their text) means that their bias toward the young is not as pronounced in practice as one might expect. They discount future life-years saved, making them less valuable if they occur farther in the future. We discuss their peculiar methodology in more detail in Chapter 8.

13. Tammy O. Tengs and John D. Graham, "The Opportunity Costs of Haphazard Social Investments in Life-Saving," in *Risks, Costs, and Lives Saved: Getting Better Results from Regulation,* ed. Robert W. Hahn (New York: Oxford University Press and AEI Press, 1996), 167, 168 [hereinafter "Opportunity Costs"].

14. *Ibid.,* 169.

15. We obtained a complete list of the interventions considered in this study from Tammy Tengs. (Personal communication from Tammy Tengs to Lisa Heinzerling, April 2001.) This list indicates that ninety of the interventions were environmental measures. See also Tengs, "Optimizing Societal Investments in Prevention of Premature Death," Appendix Q, 150 (1994) (unpublished Sc.D. dissertation, Harvard University) (indicating that ninety interventions based on "EPA Regulation" were considered in the dissertation that formed the basis of Tengs and Graham's "Opportunity Costs" study).

16. See, e.g., Hearing on S. 981, the Regulatory Improvement Act of 1998, Before the U.S. Senate Committee on Governmental Affairs 105th Congress 4 (February 24, 1998) (Joint Testimony of Robert W. Hahn and Robert E. Litan, the American Enterprise Institute and the Brookings Institution).

17. Testimony of John D. Graham.

18. Brief of Amici Curiae AEI-Brookings Joint Center for Regulatory Studies et al., *American Trucking Ass'ns. v. Whitman* (U.S. Supreme Court 2000, No. 99–1426), 1–2 (citing Tengs and Graham, "Opportunity Costs").

19. For example, ten of the ninety environmental measures included in the study are bans on certain asbestos products. As the study on which Tengs and Graham relied for their data on the costs and effectiveness of these measures clearly states, however, these products were never banned by EPA. See George L. Van Houtven and Maureen L. Cropper, *When Is a Life Too Costly to Save?*, Policy Research Working Paper 1260, Table 1 (Environment, Infrastructure, and Agriculture Division, Policy Research Department, World Bank, March 1994).

20. Keeney and Green, "Estimating Fatalities Induced by Economic Impacts of EPA's Ozone and Particulate Standards."

21. For the seminal statement of this hypothesis, see Aaron Wildavsky, "Richer Is Safer," *Public Interest* 60 (1980), 23, 27–29. For the most extensive critique of the "richer is safer" thesis in the legal literature, see Thomas O. McGarity, "A Cost-Benefit State," *Administrative Law Review*

50 (1998), 7, 40–49; see also Adam Finkel, "A Second Opinion on an Environmental Misdiagnosis: The Risky Prescriptions of Breaking the Vicious Circle," *New York University Environmental Law Journal* 3 (1995), 295, 324–27.

22. For the original study, see Ralph L. Keeney, "Mortality Risks Induced by Economic Expenditures," *Risk Analysis* 10 (1990), 147. For a critique of a proposed use of Keeney's work in evaluating regulations, see GAO, Report to the Chairman, Committee on Governmental Affairs, U.S. Senate, "Risk-Risk Analysis: OMB's Review of Proposed OSHA Rule" (July 1992).

23. See W. Kip Viscusi, "Risk-Risk Analysis," in *The Mortality Costs of Regulatory Expenditures* (Boston: Kluwer Academic, 1994), 9–12.

24. Randall Lutter, John F. Morrall, III, and W. Kip Viscusi, "The Cost-Per-Life-Saved Cutoff for Safety-Enhancing Regulations," *Economic Inquiry* 37 (1999), 599.

25. Health may create wealth, rather than vice versa. See, e.g., C.P. Wen et al., "Anatomy of the Healthy Worker Effect: A Critical Review," *Journal of Occupational Medicine* 25 (1983), 283 (discussing studies suggesting that "healthy worker effect" is a result of selection for employability, meaning that healthy people are the ones who get jobs). Moreover, the correlation between health and wealth may not connect health directly to income itself, but rather to factors correlated with income, such as education or social class, which may not change with small variations in income. See, e.g., Eric Brunner, "The Social and Biological Basis of Cardiovascular Disease in Office Workers," in *Health and Social Organisation: Towards a Health Policy for the Twenty-First Century,* ed. David Blane, Eric Brunner, and Richard Wilkinson (London: Routledge, 1996).

CHAPTER 4: THE $6.1 MILLION QUESTION

1. Calculated from EPA, *The Benefits and Costs of the Clean Air Act, 1970 to 1990,* October 1997 and EPA, *Arsenic in Drinking Water Rule: Economic Analysis,* December 2000 (EPA 815-R-00-026).

2. We first encountered Aethelbert's role in the valuation of life in Adam

Davidson, "Working Stiffs: The Necessary Parasites of Capitalism," *Harper's,* August 2001, 48–54.

3. Thanks to Steven Marrone for helpful insights into medieval church history.

4. For example, a 1705 Virginia statute allowed killing a slave in the course of disciplining him. A. Leon Higginbotham, Jr. and F. Michael Higginbotham, " 'Yearning to Breathe Free': Legal Barriers Against and Options in Favor of Liberty in Antebellum Virginia," *New York University Law Review* 68 (1993), 1213, 1223.

5. Davidson, "Working Stiffs."

6. Justice Department Web site, http://www.usdoj.gov/victimcompensation/.

7. As quoted in Lisa Belkin, "Just Money," *New York Times Magazine,* December 8, 2002, 96.

8. *Ibid.,* 122.

9. A number of the issues raised here are presented in more formal, mathematical language in Peter Dorman, *Markets and Mortality: Economics, Dangerous Work, and the Value of Human Life* (Cambridge: Cambridge University Press, 1996).

10. For an argument against valuation on grounds like these, see Elizabeth Anderson, *Value in Ethics and Economics* (Cambridge, MA: Harvard University Press, 1993). For an extended exploration of issues of incommensurability, see Cass Sunstein, "Incommensurability and Valuation in Law," *Michigan Law Review* 92, no. 4 (1994), 779–861, reprinted in Sunstein, *Free Markets and Social Justice* (New York: Oxford University Press, 1997).

11. For further elaboration, see Lisa Heinzerling, "The Rights of Statistical People," *Harvard Environmental Law Review* 24 (2000), 189, 203–6.

12. The probability of surviving each event is 0.99, so the probability of surviving 100 independent events is $0.99^{100} = 0.366$. This is very close to $\frac{4}{11} = 0.364$.

13. John Broome, "Trying to Value a Life," *Journal of Public Economics* 9 (1978), 91, 92.

14. Skiing: in 1999 there were 30 fatalities and 52.2 million skier/snowboarder visits to ski slopes, for a death rate of 0.57 per million skier-days (National Ski Areas Association, http://www.nsaa.org).

Construction: in 1997 there were 14.1 fatal injuries per 100,000 full-time construction workers; assuming 250 days per full-time year, the death rate was 0.56 per million days of work (NIOSH, *Worker Health Chartbook 2000*, 36.)

Arsenic (extrapolating from limited available data): male lifetime cancer rates per ppb of arsenic are 2.53×10^{-5} for bladder cancer and 2.75×10^{-5} for lung cancer (EPA, *Arsenic in Drinking Water Rule: Economic Analysis*, December 2000 [EPA 815-R-00-026], Exhibit B-2, B-8). (Female cancer rates are higher.) Death rates are 26 percent for bladder cancer and 88 percent for lung cancer, for a combined male mortality rate of 3.08×10^{-5} per lifetime ppb of arsenic.

The EPA analysis is based on a person who drinks 2 liters of water per day. So lifetime consumption over 70 years is $2 \times 70 \times 365 = 5.11 \times 10^{4}$ liters. If risk is proportional to arsenic consumption, the risk per ppb per liter = $(3.08 \times 10^{-5}) / (5.11 \times 10^{4}) = 6.03 \times 10^{-10}$ per ppb per liter, or 3.01×10^{-8} per liter of 50 ppb water. At that rate, the risk from 19 liters of 50 ppb water equals the risk from a day of skiing.

15. For an effort to quantify the additional value of avoiding involuntary risks, see Richard L. Revesz, "Environmental Regulation, Cost-Benefit Analysis, and the Discounting of Human Lives," *Columbia Law Review* 99 (1999), 941, 968–71.

16. E. J. Mishan, *Cost-Benefit Analysis: An Informal Introduction,* 4th ed. (London: Routledge, 1988).

17. W. Kip Viscusi, "Cigarette Taxation and the Social Consequences of Smoking," National Bureau of Economic Research Working Paper 4891 (October 1994), 33; published in *Tax Policy and the Economy* 9 (ed. James M. Poterba, MIT Press, 1995).

18. See, among many sources, Gordon Fairclough, "Smoking Can Help Czech Economy, Philip Morris–Little Report Says," *Wall Street Journal,* July 16, 2001. The original report, *Public Finance Balance of Smoking in the Czech Republic,* is available at http://www.nosmoke.org/images/pmczechstudy.pdf.

19. James P. Bruce, Hoesung Lee, and Erik F. Haites, ed., *Climate Change 1995: Economic and Social Dimensions of Climate Change* (New York: Cam-

bridge University Press, 1995), Chapter 6, especially 196–97. The differing values of life are presented explicitly in one of the principal sources for the IPCC report: Samuel Fankhauser, *Valuing Climate Change: The Economics of the Greenhouse* (London: Earthscan, 1995), 47–48. Fankhauser based his estimates on willingness to pay for risk reduction, and described the middle and low-income estimates as "arbitrary" (*Ibid.*, 47). The first prominent critics of the IPCC valuations were the Global Commons Institute; the issue is discussed on their website, http://www.gci.org.uk. Our description of the controversy also relies on personal communication from William Moomaw, one of the lead authors of the IPCC reports in 1995 and in 2001.

20. Bruce et al., *Climate Change 1995;* Bert Metz, Ogunlade Davidson, Rob Swart, and Jiahua Pan, ed., *Climate Change 2001: Mitigation* (Cambridge: Cambridge University Press, 2001), available at http://www.ipcc.ch. In the 2001 report, discussion of the value-of-life controversy appears in Section 7.4.4.2.

21. OMB, *Analytical Perspectives on Federal Budget for Fiscal Year 2003,* 421, available at http://www.whitehouse.gov/omb/budget/fy2003/pdf/spec.pdf.

22. EPA Office of Air and Radiation, *Final Regulatory Support Document: Control of Emissions from Unregulated Nonroad Engines,* September 2002, (EPA 420-R-02-022), Chapter 10, 24.

23. Steven Greenhouse, "Hispanic Workers Die at Higher Rate," *New York Times,* July 16, 2001, A11.

24. National Institute for Occupational Safety and Health, *Worker Health Chartbook 2000,* 39.

25. See, for instance, Thomas DeLeire and Helen Levy, "Gender, Occupation Choice and the Risk of Death at Work," National Bureau of Economic Research Working Paper 8574 (November 2001).

26. John D. Leeth and John Ruser, "Compensating Wage Differentials for Fatal and Nonfatal Injury Risk by Gender and Race," Bentley College Department of Economics, June 2002. Dollar figures from this study are in 1998 dollars.

27. Average risk premium is based on the mean fatal risk for blue-collar and service workers by gender, for all workers and for union members (Leeth

and Ruser, Table 6), multiplied by each group's value of life, divided by an assumed 2,000 hours per full-time year. Estimates of wage premium for higher risk occupations are based on applying the same data to the rates of occupational fatalities in dangerous occupations, in our Table 4.2.

28. Alan Krupnick, Anna Alberini, Maureen Cropper, Nathalie Simon, Bernie O'Brien, Ron Goeree, and Martin Heintzelman, "Age, Health, and the Willingness to Pay for Mortality Risk Reductions: A Contingent Valuation Survey of Ontario Residents," Resources for the Future Discussion Paper 00-37 (2000), available at http://www.rff.org.

29. EPA Office of Air and Radiation, *Final Regulatory Support Document*.

30. Matthew D. Adler and Eric A. Posner, "Implementing Cost-Benefit Analysis When Preferences Are Distorted," *Journal of Legal Studies* 29, no. 2, part 2 (June 2000).

31. His surveys include W. Kip Viscusi, *Fatal Tradeoffs: Public and Private Responsibilities for Risk* (New York: Oxford University Press, 1992); "The Value of Risks to Life and Health," *Journal of Economic Literature* 31, no. 4 (December 1993), 1912–1946; *Rational Risk Policy* (Oxford: Clarendon Press-Oxford University Press, 1998).

32. The original calculation can be found in EPA, *The Benefits and Costs of the Clean Air Act, 1970 to 1990,* Appendix I. For an example of a subsequent analysis citing the Clean Air Act analysis and adjusting only for inflation, see EPA, *Arsenic in Drinking Water Rule: Economic Analysis,* December 2000, (EPA 815-R-00-026), 5–23.

33. Viscusi's figures are most often expressed in 1990 dollars; these are equivalents in 2001 dollars.

34. W. Kip Viscusi and Joseph E. Aldy, "The Value of a Statistical Life: A Critical Review of Labor Market Estimates Throughout the World," National Bureau of Economic Research Working Paper 9487 (February 2003), available at http://papers.nber.org/papers/w9487.pdf. The $7 million estimate, described as the median of the most credible U.S. labor market studies reviewed by Viscusi and Aldy, is in 2000 dollars.

35. *Ibid.,* Table 2.

36. Viscusi himself has argued in the past that the value of risk should be proportional to income; see W. Kip Viscusi and W. Evans, "Utility Functions

That Depend on Health Status: Estimates and Economic Implications,"
American Economic Review 80, no. 3 (June 1990), 353–74. However, his
most recent work (*Ibid.*) suggests that the value of a statistical life rises
more slowly than income. A recent literature review, Ted R. Miller,
"Variations Between Countries in Values of Statistical Life," *Journal of
Transport Economics and Policy* 34, part 2 (May 2000), 169–88, estimates an
income elasticity of close to 1.0, implying that the value of a statistical life
is proportional to income. Research on valuation of risk in Taiwan, during a period of rapid growth, suggests that the value of a life may rise
much faster than income: James K. Hammitt, Jin-Tan Liu, and Jin-Long
Liu, "Survival Is a Luxury Good: The Increasing Value of a Statistical
Life," NBER Summer Institute Workshop on Public Policy and the Environment, Cambridge, MA, August 2000.

37. Dora L. Costa and Matthew E. Kahn, "Changes in the Value of Life,
1940–1980," December 2002 (unpublished).

38. For recent literature reviews, see Janusz R. Mrozek and Laura O. Taylor,
"What Determines the Value of Life? A Meta-Analysis," Georgia State
University Department of Economics, August 2001, and Miller, "Varia-
tions between Countries in Values of Statistical Life."

39. Calculated from National Safety Council data. NSC has the only contin-
uous data series on occupational fatalities extending back to the 1970s; its
data are not strictly comparable to government data cited elsewhere in
this chapter.

40. For a review of some of the extensive literature on this subject see Frank
Ackerman, Neva R. Goodwin, Laurie Dougherty, and Kevin Gallagher,
ed., *The Changing Nature of Work* (Washington, DC: Island Press, 1998).

41. Michael H. Belzer, *Sweatshops on Wheels: Winners and Losers in Trucking
Deregulation* (New York: Oxford University Press, 2000), 21.

42. Douglas Birsch, "Product Safety, Cost-Benefit Analysis, and the Ford
Pinto Case," in *The Ford Pinto Case: A Study in Applied Ethics, Business, and
Technology*, ed. Douglas Birsch and John H. Fielder (Albany, NY: SUNY
Press, 1994).

43. The original Ford memo is E.S. Grush and C.S. Saunby, "Fatalities Asso-

ciated with Crash-Induced Fuel Leakages and Fires," reprinted in Birsch and Fielder, *The Ford Pinto Case.*

CHAPTER 5: AN OUNCE OF PREVENTION

1. There are other available methods. For example, EPA's *Handbook for Non-Cancer Health Effects Valuation* (available at http://www.epa.gov/osp/spc/), Chapter 3, contrasts eight different methods of valuation. See also Patrick Hofstetter and James K. Hammitt, EPA Office of Research and Development, *Human Health Metrics for Environmental Decision Support Tools: Lessons from Health Economics and Decision Analysis,* 2001 (EPA 600/R–01/104), especially 2–6.

2. W. Kip Viscusi, Wesley A. Magat, and Joel Huber, "Pricing Environmental Health Risks: Survey Assessments of Risk-Risk and Risk-Dollar Trade-offs for Chronic Bronchitis," *Journal of Environmental Economics and Management* 21 (1991), 41. The article does not report the date of the interviews. However, monetary amounts mentioned in the interviews are all reported in 1987 dollars. The article was submitted for publication in 1989.

3. *Ibid.,* 46.

4. EPA, Office of Air and Radiation, *The Benefits and Costs of the Clean Air Act, 1970 to 1990,* October 1997, I-4–I-5.

5. *Ibid.,* I-5.

6. Thomas McGarity, "Professor Sunstein's Fuzzy Math," *Georgetown Law Journal* 90 (2002), 2341.

7. Virginia Morell, "Oregon Puts Bold Health Plan on Ice," *Science* 149 (August 3, 1990), 468.

8. "[The Oregon Health Plan] has not operated as the scientific vessel of rationing that it was advertised to be. Although initial rankings were based in large part on mathematical values, controversies around the list forced administrators to make political concessions and move medical services 'by hand' to satisfy constituency pressures and the federal government. Analyses of the original list have shown that subjective judgments, not the

initial formula, are the primary influence on service rankings." Jonathan Oberlander, Theodore Marmor, and Lawrence Jacobs, "Rationing Medical Care: Rhetoric and Reality in the Oregon Health Plan," *Canadian Medical Association Journal* 164 (May 29, 2001), 1586. See also Tammy Tengs et al., "Oregon's Medicaid Ranking and Cost-Effectiveness: Is There Any Relationship?," *Medical Decision Making* 16 (1996), 99–107.

9. Oberlander et al., "Rationing Medical Care," 1585–6.

10. Erik Nord, *Cost-Value Analysis in Health Care: Making Sense out of QALYs* (New York: Cambridge University Press, 1999).

11. Patrick Hofstetter and James K. Hammitt, *Human Health Metrics for Environmental Decision Support Tools: Lessons from Health Economics and Decision Analysis* (EPA Office of Research and Development, 2001, 22EPA/600/R-01/104), Table III, 36, and related discussion.

12. Tengs et al., "Oregon's Medicaid Ranking," 103.

13. In addition to Nord's discussion of the issue, see Anna Alberini et al., "Does the Value of a Statistical Life Vary with Age and Health Status? Evidence from the United States and Canada," Resources for the Future Discussion Paper 02-19 (April 2002), available at http://www.rff.org/disc_papers/PDF_files/0219.pdf.

14. *Congressional Record* 147, daily ed. (March 6, 2001), S1842 (statement of Senator Paul Wellstone).

15. Robert W. Hahn, "Bad Economics, Not Good Ergonomics," *Wall Street Journal,* November 24, 1999, A18.

16. 15 U.S.C. § 651(b).

17. Office of Technology Assessment, *Gauging Control Technology and Regulatory Impacts in Occupational Safety and Health: An Appraisal of OSHA's Analytic Approach,* OTA-ENV-635 (September 1995). See also the discussion of the overstatement of regulatory costs in Chapter 2.

18. *OSHA Ergonomics Standards: Hearing Before the Senate Subcommittee on Labor, Health and Human Services, Education, and Related Agencies of the Senate Committee on Appropriations,* 107th Cong. (2001) (statement of Baruch Fellner) (March 6, 2001).

19. Eugene Scalia, "OSHA's Ergonomics Litigation Record: Three Strikes and It's Out," CATO Institute Policy Analysis No. 370 (May 15, 2000).

20. *Ibid.*, 3–4.

21. A well-known example of potential over-response is the aggressive treatment of slow-growing prostate cancers in older men, since many but not all of these men will die of something else long before the prostate cancer affects them.

22. The Business Roundtable, "Blueprint 2001: Drafting Environmental Policy for the Future," available at http://www.brtable. org/pdf/496b.pdf, 6.

23. *Ibid.*, 7.

24. Jason K. Burnett and Robert W. Hahn, "EPA's Arsenic Rule: The Benefits of the Standard Do Not Justify the Costs," AEI-Brookings Joint Center for Regulatory Studies, Regulatory Analysis 01-02 (January 2001).

25. For instance, the linear no-threshold model implies that the death rate from 20 ppb of arsenic is exactly half the death rate from 40 ppb. But if there is a threshold at 20 ppb then the death rate from 20 ppb is zero, much lower than the linear no-threshold model predicts. The higher the threshold, the greater the deviation will be from the no-threshold relationship.

26. E.g., Cass Sunstein, "The Arithmetic of Arsenic," *Georgetown Law Journal* 90 (2002), 2255.

27. Gina Kolata, "For Radiation, How Much Is Too Much?," *New York Times*, November 27, 2001, F1.

28. Barrie Lambert, "Radiation: Early Warnings; Late Effects," in European Environment Agency, *Late Lessons from Early Warnings: The Precautionary Principle 1896–2000* (London: Earthscan, 2002).

29. Kolata, "For Radiation, How Much Is Too Much?"

30. Jeff Bailey, "Dueling Studies: How Two Industries Created a Fresh Spin on the Dioxin Debate," *Wall Street Journal,* February 20, 1992, A1.

31. Linda Greer and Rena Steinzor, "Bad Science," *Environmental Forum* 19 (January/February 2002), 28, 38–40.

32. EPA, *Exposure and Human Health Reassessment of 2,3,7,8-Tetrachlorodibenzo-p-Dioxin (TCDD) and Related Compounds,* Draft (EPA 600/P-00/001), available at http://www.epa.gov/ncea.

33. EPA Office of Research and Development, "Information Sheet 1— Dioxin: Summary of the Dioxin Reassessment Science," May 25, 2001,

available at http://www.epa.gov/ncea/pdfs/dioxin/factsheets/dioxin_ short2.pdf.

34. "OMB Split Over Whether Dioxin Should Undergo NAS Review," *Inside EPA's Environmental Policy Alert,* August 7, 2002, 13–14.

35. As quoted in Joel Tickner with Carolyn Raffensperger, "The American View on the Precautionary Principle," in *Reinterpreting the Precautionary Principle,* ed. Tim O'Riordan, James Cameron, and Andrew Jordan (London: Cameron and May, 2001).

36. David Kriebel et al., "The Precautionary Principle in Environmental Science," *Environmental Health Perspectives* 109, no. 9 (September 2001), 873, 875.

37. This issue is discussed further in Chapter 9. The few available academic sources on the economics of precaution include J. Barkley Rosser, Jr., "Complex Ecological-Economic Dynamics and Environmental Policy," *Ecological Economics* 37 (2001), 23–37; Richard T. Woodward and Richard C. Bishop, "How To Decide When Experts Disagree: Uncertainty-Based Choice Rules in Environmental Policy," *Land Economics* 73 (November 1997), 492–507; and Christian Golier, Bruno Julien, and Nicolas Treich, "Scientific Progress and Irreversibility: An Economic Interpretation of the 'Precautionary Principle,' " *Journal of Public Economics* 75 (2000), 229–53. See also Ann Maria Bell, "Taking Externalities Seriously: An Economic Analysis of the Precautionary Principle," forthcoming from Redefining Progress (San Francisco); and Frank Ackerman and Rachel Massey, "Prospering with Precaution: Employment, Economics, and the Precautionary Principle," (Tufts University, 2002), available at http://ase.tufts.edu/gdae/policy_research/PrecautionAHTAug 02.pdf.

38. Bell, "Taking Externalities Seriously."

39. European Environment Agency, *Late Lessons from Early Warnings.*

40. David Gee and Morris Greenberg, "Asbestos: From 'Magic' to Malevolent Material," in *Late Lessons from Early Warnings,* 52–63.

41. The decision overturning EPA's asbestos ban is *Corrosion Proof Fittings v. EPA,* 947 F.2d 1201 (5th Cir. 1991). For a powerful critique of the decision, see Thomas O. McGarity, "The Courts and the Ossification of

Rulemaking: A Response to Professor Seidenfeld," *Texas Law Review* 75 (1997), 525, 541–49.

CHAPTER 6: DREADFUL EVENTS

1. All of the annual U.S. mortality statistics in this paragraph refer to 1998, and are from *Statistical Abstract of the United States, 2001* (United States Census Bureau, 2002), 79, Table 105.
2. Timur Kuran and Cass R. Sunstein, "Availability Cascades and Risk Regulation," *Stanford Law Review* 51 (1999), 683, 718.
3. Stephen Breyer, *Breaking the Vicious Circle: Toward Effective Risk Regulation* (Cambridge, MA: Harvard University Press, 1993), 4–5, Fig. 1.
4. Paul Slovic, "The Perception of Risk," *Science* 236 (April 17, 1987), 280.
5. Neil D. Weinstein, "Optimistic Biases About Personal Risks," *Science* 246 (December 8, 1989), 1232.
6. John D. Graham, "Making Sense of Risk: An Agenda for Congress," in *Risks, Costs, and Lives Saved,* ed. Robert W. Hahn (New York: Oxford University Press and AEI Press, 1996), 183–207.
7. Cass R. Sunstein, "The Arithmetic of Arsenic," *Georgetown Law Journal* 90 (2002), 2255.
8. Breyer, *Breaking the Vicious Circle,* 61–64.
9. *Ibid.,* 67. Breyer nowhere comes to terms with the fact that funding is already generously provided for some of his pet projects, such as vaccination programs. Like banning lead in gasoline (recall our discussion of Graham's and Tengs's research in Chapter 3), we cannot vaccinate the same people over and over again, saving additional lives each time.
10. *Ibid.,* 62.
11. See, e.g., Lisa Heinzerling, "Political Science," *University of Chicago Law Review* 62 (1995), 449.
12. John D. Graham, "Presidential Management of Regulatory Policy: A Stronger Role for Science, Engineering, and Economics" (speech given before the National Academy of Engineering, February 20, 2002), available at http://www.whitehouse.gov/omb/inforeg/regpol-admin_speeches.html.

13. Letter from John D. Graham to David L. Greenberg, Vice President, Government Affairs, Philip Morris Cos. (October 21, 1991), available at http://www.citizen.org/congress/regulations/graham/tobacco/2023545705_5706.pdf.

14. Centers for Disease Control and Prevention, *TIPS: Tobacco Information and Prevention Source,* available at http://www.cdc.gov/tobacco/research_data/economics/mmwr5114.highlights.htm.

15. Tammy O. Tengs et al., "Five-Hundred Life-Saving Interventions and Their Cost-Effectiveness," *Risk Analysis* 15 (1995), 369.

16. Ultimately, HCRA was forced to return the check to Philip Morris when the dean of the Harvard School of Public Health (HCRA's institutional home) reminded Dr. Graham that the school had a policy of not accepting donations from tobacco companies. No matter: Graham simply obtained funding from Kraft, Philip Morris's parent corporation, instead. Letter from Enrique Guardia, Vice President, Scientific Relations, Kraft General Foods to John D. Graham (August 12, 1992), available at http://www.citizen.org/congress/regulations/graham/tobacco/kraft/20000kraftcheck.PDF. ("[Kraft is] delighted to have you and your group as . . . unbiased participants in the debate.")

17. Slovic, "The Perception of Risk," 284.

18. *Ibid.,* 282–83.

19. The individual and social consequences of citizens' risk perceptions are discussed in more detail in Lisa Heinzerling, "Environmental Law and the Present Future," *Georgetown Law Journal* 87 (1999), 2025.

20. Michael Edelstein, *Contaminated Communities: The Social and Psychological Impacts of Residential Toxic Exposure* (Boulder: Westview Press, 1988).

21. Henry M. Vyner, *Invisible Trauma: The Psychological Effects of Invisible Environmental Contaminants* (Lexington, MA: Lexington Books, 1988), 57.

22. Kai Erikson, "Toxic Reckoning: Business Faces a New Kind of Fear," *Harvard Business Review* (January–February 1990), 121.

23. Kai Erikson, *A New Species of Trouble: Explorations in Disaster, Trauma and Community* (New York: W.W. Norton, 1994), 21–22.

24. Erikson, "Toxic Reckoning," 122.

25. *Ibid.,* 124.

26. See, e.g., Edelstein, *Contaminated Communities,* 70–82; Erikson, *A New Species of Trouble,* 129–33 (leaking underground gas tank in East Swallow, Colorado); Martha R. Fowlkes and Patricia Y. Miller, *Love Canal: The Social Construction of Disaster* (United States Federal Emergency Management Agency, U.S. Docs. FEM 1/2:L 94, 1982), 117–33; Kenneth M. Bachrach and Alex J. Zautra, "Assessing the Impact of Hazardous Waste Facilities: Psychology, Politics, and Environmental Impact Statements," in *Advances in Environmental Psychology* (Hillsdale, NJ: L. Erlbaum Associates, 1986), 71, 84 (describing hazardous waste facility in Arizona); Bruce P. Dohrenwend, "Psychological Implications of Nuclear Accidents: The Case of Three Mile Island," *Bulletin of the New York Academy of Medicine* 59 (1983), 1071–72; Paul Slovic et al., "Perceived Risk, Trust, and the Politics of Nuclear Waste," *Science* 254 (1991), 1603, 1606.

27. Paul Slovic, "Perceived Risk, Trust, and Democracy," *Risk Analysis* 13 (1993), 675, 677.

28. Edelstein, *Contaminated Communities,* 76.

29. B.P. Dohrenwend et al., "Stress in the Community: A Report to the President's Commission on the Accident at Three Mile Island," *Annals of the New York Academy of Science* 365 (1981), 159. Dohrenwend attributes the term "demoralization" to Jerome Frank. See Dohrenwend, "Psychological Implications of Nuclear Accidents," 1065 (citing J.D. Frank, *Persuasion and Healing* [Baltimore: Johns Hopkins University Press, 1973]). Bruce Dohrenwend led the task force on behavioral and mental health effects convened as part of the President's Commission on the Accident at Three Mile Island.

30. See Clayton P. Gillette and James E. Krier, "Risks, Courts, and Agencies," *University of Pennsylvania Law Review* 138 (1990), 1027, 1073.

31. Compare, e.g., *Palmer v. Liggett Group, Inc.,* 825 F.2d 620, 627 (1st Cir. 1987) ("Cigarette smoking, at least initially, is a voluntary activity") with *Carlisle v. Philip Morris, Inc.,* 805 S.W.2d 498, 516 (Tex. App. 1991) ("Failure to warn of cigarettes' addictive nature could be the essence of a plaintiff's complaint. In such a case, the fact that the plaintiff's smoking may have been 'initially' voluntary would be immaterial.").

32. On the influence of scientific evidence of the harmfulness of secondhand

tobacco smoke on regulation of smoking in public places, see *Flue-Cured Tobacco Cooperative Stabilization Corp. v. United States,* 857 F.Supp. 1137 (Middle Dist. N. Car. 1994). On the influence of evidence of manipulation of nicotine levels on the Food and Drug Administration's first-ever (and ultimately invalidated) effort to regulate smoking, see *Food and Drug Administration v. Brown & Williamson Tobacco Corp.,* 529 U.S. 120 (2000).

33. The phrase is from the title of an important book on environmental justice, Robert D. Bullard, ed., *Unequal Protection: Environmental Justice and Communities of Color* (New York: Random House, 1994).

34. For a detailed discussion of the movement, see Luke W. Cole and Sheila R. Foster, *From the Ground Up: Environmental Racism and the Rise of the Environmental Justice Movement* (New York: NYU Press, 2001).

35. For a detailed critique of this program, see Richard Toshiyuku Drury et al., "Pollution Trading and Environmental Injustice: Los Angeles' Failed Experiment in Air Quality Policy," *Duke Environmental Law & Policy Forum* 9 (Spring 1999), 231.

36. J.H. Dales, *Pollution, Property and Prices: An Essay in Policy-Making and Economics* (Toronto: University of Toronto Press, 1968), 89 (emphasis in original).

37. *Ibid.,* 91–92.

38. Richard L. Revesz, "Environmental Regulation, Cost-Benefit Analysis, and the Discounting of Human Lives," *Columbia Law Review* 99 (1999), 941, 968–71.

39. University of Chicago legal scholar Cass Sunstein has argued that the distinction between voluntary and involuntary risks has been overdrawn, and that often the only difference between supposedly voluntary and involuntary risks is the magnitude of the cost of avoiding them. Cass R. Sunstein, "A Note on 'Voluntary' Versus 'Involuntary' Risks," *Duke Environmental Law & Policy Forum* 8 (Fall 1997), 173.

40. Available at http://www.whirledbank.org/ourwords/summers.html.

41. *Ibid.*

CHAPTER 7: UNNATURAL MARKETS

1. The jury also granted the local community the largest punitive damages award in the nation's history, $5 billion. After years of legal battles, the $5 billion award was reversed by a federal appeals court in 2001, and sent back to a lower court for further consideration in light of a recent Supreme Court case restricting punitive damage awards on constitutional grounds. *In re* Exxon Valdez, 270 F.3d 1215 (9th Cir. 2001).

   The punitive damages captured an important component of the dispute: the anger and outrage that followed this avoidable accident. Punitive damages, unlike compensatory damages, do not purport to reflect objective and measurable harm; instead, they are designed to punish wrongdoers like Exxon, to send a message that the conduct in question should not happen again. Thus punitive damages are closely related to the issues of fairness discussed in Chapter 6, and fit awkwardly if at all into conventional economic analysis: they are neither measures of use value, nor of the most common categories of nonuse value.

2. Richard T. Carson et al., *Contingent Valuation and Lost Passive Use: Damages from the* Exxon Valdez, Report Submitted to the Alaska Attorney General (November 1992).

3. Robb Mandelbaum, "Consumer Confidence," *New York Times,* October 28, 2001. The quote refers to statistical measures of consumer confidence.

4. John B. Loomis and Douglas S. White, "Economic Benefits of Rare and Endangered Species: Summary and Meta-analysis," *Ecological Economics* 18 (1996), 197–206; values, in 1993 dollars, from 199, Table 1.

5. *Ibid.*

6. V. Kerry Smith and Laura L. Osborne, "Do Contingent Valuation Estimates Pass a 'Scope' Test? A Meta-analysis," *Journal of Environmental Economics and Management* 31 (1996), 287–301; amounts in 1990 dollars.

7. Paul R. Portney, "The Contingent Valuation Debate: Why Economists Should Care," *Journal of Economic Perspectives* 8, no. 4 (Fall 1994), 3–17; Robin Grove-White, "The Environmental 'Valuation' Controversy: Observations on Its Recent History and Significance," in *Valuing Nature?*

Economics, Ethics and Environment, ed. John Foster (London: Routledge, 1997), 21–31.

8. *State of Ohio v. Department of the Interior,* 880 F.2d 432 (D.C. Cir. 1989). Among many other sources, see Brian R. Binger, Robert F. Copple, and Elizabeth Hoffman, "The Use of Contingent Valuation Methodology in Natural Resource Damage Assessments: Legal Fact and Economic Fiction," *Northwestern University Law Review* 89, no. 3 (1995), 1029–1116.

9. For a review of the economics literature on nonmarket valuation (whose coincidentally similar title we were not aware of when we began our work), see V. Kerry Smith, "Pricing What Is Priceless: A Status Report on Non-Market Valuation of Environmental Resources," in *International Yearbook of Environmental and Resources Economics, 1997/1998: A Survey of Current Issues,* ed. Hank Folmer and Tom Tietenberg (Cheltenham: Edward Elgar, 1997), 156.

10. Similar calculations show that the removal of the elevated highway will create an additional $750 million of property value. Kayo Tajima, "On Top of the Big Dig: Economic Analysis of the Urban Parks Created by the Boston Central Artery/Tunnel Project," masters thesis, Department of Urban and Environmental Policy and Planning, Tufts University, 2002; Kayo Tajima and Frank Ackerman, "The Billion-Dollar Bonus," *Boston Globe,* July 1, 2002, A11.

11. Peter Hoyt, "Whale Watching 2001: Worldwide Tourism Numbers, Expenditures, and Expanding Socioeconomic Benefits" (Yarmouth Port, MA: International Fund for Animal Welfare, 2001), 15. The $160 million figure is for U.S. whale-watch revenues alone. If indirect expenditures such as food, travel, accommodations, and souvenirs associated with whale watching are included, the total reaches $330 million. The same source reports that world totals are about three times as large as the U.S. figures.

12. B.S. Jorgensen, et al. "Protest Responses in Contingent Valuation," *Environmental and Resource Economics* 14 (1999), 131–150.

13. On the importance of "noneconomic" influences on willingness to pay for environmental protection, see C.L. Spash, "Ethical Motives and Charitable Contributions in Contingent Valuation: Empirical Evidence from

Social Psychology and Economics," *Environmental Values* 9 (2000), 453–79.

14. Robert C. Mitchell and R.T. Carson, *Using Surveys to Value Public Goods* (Washington, DC: Resources for the Future, 1989), 34, as quoted in Daniel Kahneman, Jack L. Knetsch, and Richard H. Thaler, "Anomalies: The Endowment Effect, Loss Aversion, and Status Quo Bias," *Journal of Economic Perspectives* 5, no. 1 (Winter 1991), 193–206.

15. Michael Moore, *Downsize This! Random Threats from an Unarmed American* (New York: Crown Publishers, 1996), 253–57.

16. Arild Vatn and David W. Bromley, "Choices Without Prices Without Apologies," *Journal of Environmental Economics and Management* 26 (1994), 129–48.

17. Cass R. Sunstein, *Free Markets and Social Justice* (New York: Oxford University Press, 1997), 73–74.

18. One of the most accessible, nontechnical introductions to this perspective is Herman E. Daly and John B. Cobb Jr., *For the Common Good* (Boston: Beacon Press, 1989). The International Society for Ecological Economics and its journal, *Ecological Economics,* provide numerous other sources.

19. See the interesting proposal for a consistent set of ecological prices in Bruce Hannon, "Ecological Pricing and Economic Efficiency," *Ecological Economics* 36 (2001), 19–30. Hannon proposes to extend the input-output economic model to encompass ecological services, and then use the model to impute prices to inputs. This would produce a consistent set of use values, improving on available ad hoc estimates; however, it would not include prices for existence values.

20. This account draws on comments on the proposed regulation by Frank Ackerman, prepared for Riverkeeper, an environmental group committed to protection of the Hudson River ecosystem. The comments are available at http://riverkeeper.org/document.php/114/Dr_Frank_Ackerm.doc.

21. Synapse Energy Economics Comments on EPA's Proposed Phase II Regulation (August 2002), available at http://riverkeeper.org/campaign. php/fishkills.

22. "The Tuolomne River: Preservation or Development? An Economic

Assessment" (Berkeley, CA: Environmental Defense Fund, 1984; principal author Robert Stavins), 16, 31, 32, 101.

23. Robert Stavin's Final Comments on Proposed 316(b) Rule (July 19,
2002), 8.

24. In a Dr. Seuss children's classic, *The Lorax* (New York: Random House,
1971), the fictional title character "speaks for the trees" and protests the
destruction of forest ecosystems for short-run commercial gain.

25. Judy Clark, Jacquelin Burgess, and Carolyn M. Harrison, "'I Struggled
with This Money Business': Respondents' Perspectives on Contingent
Valuation," *Ecological Economics* 33 (2000), 45–62.

26. Cass R. Sunstein, Daniel Kahneman, and David Schkade, "Assessing
Punitive Damages (with Notes on Cognition and Valuation in Law),"
Yale Law Journal 107 (1998), 2071–2153.

CHAPTER 8: HONEY, I SHRUNK THE FUTURE

1. 42 U.S.C. 4331(b)(1).

2. The examples in the text are rounded off to the nearest dollar.

3. *Cost-effectiveness analysis*—such as the cost-per-life-saved analysis of Morrall, Graham, and Tengs—also calculates the net present value of future
benefits such as human lives, but does not translate lives into monetary
terms. In this kind of analysis, the lives themselves are discounted, rather
than the monetary value of a life being discounted.

4. William J. Baumol, "On the Social Rate of Discount," *American Economic
Review* 58 (1968), 788, 801.

5. On a more technical level, there is an interesting alternative known as hyperbolic discounting. Under the standard approach to discounting, postponing a benefit from 2 years in the future to 4 years has the same effect
as postponing it from 20 years from now to 22, or from 100 years to 102.
Some psychological research, however, suggests that people do not actually think this way about the future. Postponing an event from 2 years to
4 years from now could also be interpreted as doubling the delay—in
which case it should be considered comparable to postponing from 20
years to 40, or from 100 years to 200. The more complicated mathemat-

ics for this alternative ends up implying that the annual discount rate is not constant, but steadily declines, coming closer and closer to zero as we look farther and farther into the future. This does not eliminate, but substantially slows down, the paradoxical shrinking of the future. While theoretically appealing for its gentler treatment of the future, hyperbolic discounting has not yet been applied in actual decisions about public policy.

6. "Benefit-Cost Analysis of Federal Programs; Guidelines and Discounts," 57 *Fed. Reg.* 53,519, 53,522 (1992) (known as "OMB Circular A-94").

7. *Ibid.*

8. Office of Management and Budget, Regulatory Program of the United States Government, April 1, 1990–March 31, 1991, 39–40.

9. *Ibid.,* 40.

10. *Ibid.*

11. EPA, *Guidelines for Preparing Cost-Benefit Analysis,* September 2000 (EPA 240-R-00-003), 54.

12. OMB, Regulatory Program 1990–91, 40.

13. Emmett B. Keeler and Shan Cretin, "Discounting of Life-Saving and Other Nonmonetary Effects," *Management Science* 29 (1983), 300.

14. Tammy O. Tengs, "A Response to Lisa Heinzerling, Five-Hundred Life-Saving Interventions and Their Misuse in the Debate Over Regulatory Reform" *Pierce Law Review* 1 (Fall 2002), 115, 118.

15. Ranking Regulatory Investments in Public Health, FY 2003 Budget-Analytical Perspectives Section 24, and the Technical Appendix (February 4, 2002), Appendix, A-2 available at http://www.whitehouse.gov/omb.

16. Seth Borenstein, "Elderly Less Valuable in Cost-Benefit Analysis," *Miami Herald,* December 18, 2002 (reporting that OIRA insisted on analysis differentiating between lives of elderly and of younger people).

17. EPA, *Final Regulatory Support Document: Control of Emissions from Unregulated Nonroad Engines,* September 2002 (EPA 420-R-02-022), 10–29.

18. *Ibid.,* 10–30. We note that EPA's analysis leaves some ambiguity as to whether people become worth less in dollar terms at age sixty-five, or at age seventy.

19. Borenstein, "Life of Elderly Less Valuable in White House Cost-Benefit Analysis."

20. Perversely, the lowest value of life occurred for middle-aged, not elderly, people. In practice, OIRA found the age-differentiated value of a life-year by starting with the value of a life and dividing it among the remaining expected life-years; this boosted the value of older people's life-years, since they have, on average, fewer years left. Then, after discounting and reassembling the life-years into (lowered) values per life, it turned out that a forty-year-old was "worth" much less than a seventy-year old. This unexplained reversal of fortune should have made it clear that something was fundamentally wrong with OIRA's technique.

21. *Int'l Union, United Automobile, Aerospace and Agricultural Implement Workers of America, UAW v. Occupational Safety and Health Administration,* 938 F.2d 1310, 1321 (D.C. Cir. 1991).

22. See, e.g., John O. McGinnis, "Presidential Review as Constitutional Restoration," *Duke Law Journal* 51 (2001), 901, 940, n. 177.

CHAPTER 9: VALUE WITHOUT PRICES

1. Daniel H. Cole and Peter Z. Grossman, "When Is Command-and-Control Efficient? Institutions, Technology, and the Comparative Efficiency of Alternative Regulatory Regimes for Environmental Protection," *Wisconsin Law Review* (1999), 887–938. For another discussion of the potential efficiency of command and control, see N.T. Yap, "Who Says Command-and-Control Doesn't Work?," *Policy Options* 21 (April 2000), 65–70 (examining Taiwan's experience with environmental programs).

2. EPA, *The Benefits and Costs of the Clean Air Act, 1970 to 1990,* October 1997.

3. T.S. Eliot, "Choruses from 'The Rock,'" in T.S. Eliot, *The Complete Poems and Plays: 1909–1950* (New York: Harcourt, Brace & World, Inc., 1962), 106.

4. A "social welfare function" is a formula that takes individual preferences as inputs and computes society's collective preferences as its output.

Arrow's result, originally called the General Possibility Theorem and often referred to as "Arrow's Impossibility Theorem," shows that any social welfare function, defined over all possible patterns of individual preferences, that satisfies minimal standards of logical consistency, must be dictatorial—that is, it always agrees with one particular individual's preferences, no matter what others want. A famous illustration of the problem is the "Condorcet paradox": with three rival policies, it is possible that a majority prefers A to B, a different majority prefers B to C, and yet another majority prefers C to A. In this case, there is no mathematical decision rule that predicts society's choice; the outcome presumably depends on the order of voting and/or the process of deliberation. See Frank Ackerman, "Utility and Welfare II: Modern Economic Alternatives," in *Human Well-Being and Economic Goals* ed. Frank Ackerman et al. (Washington, DC: Island Press, 1997), 81–92.

5. Cost-benefit analysis has occasionally been interpreted in this broader sense, as encompassing a wide range of values and a multidimensional objective function; see James T. Campen, *Benefit, Cost, and Beyond* (New York: Ballinger, 1986). Unfortunately, these broader ideas have not been able to alter the dominant meaning and practical application of cost-benefit analysis.

6. In a similar spirit, Elizabeth Anderson has called for "democratic alternatives" to cost-benefit analysis. Elizabeth Anderson, *Value in Ethics and Economics* (Cambridge, MA: Harvard University Press, 1993).

7. Jacob Hornik, Joseph Cherian, Michelle Madansky, and Chem Narayana, "Determinants of Recycling Behavior: A Synthesis of Research Results," *Journal of Socio-Economics* 24, no. 1 (1995), 105–127; Gordon Ewing, "Altruistic, Egoistic, and Normative Effects on Curbside Recycling," *Environment and Behavior* 33, no. 6 (2001), 733–64. See also Frank Ackerman, *Why Do We Recycle? Markets, Values, and Public Policy* (Washington, DC: Island Press, 1997).

8. Amy Sue Bix, "Diseases Chasing Money and Power: Breast Cancer and AIDS Activism Challenging Authority," in *Health Care Policy in Contemporary America,* ed. Alan I. Marcus and Hamilton Cravens (University Park, PA: Pennsylvania State University Press, 1997), 5. Data are from

the National Cancer Institute and the American Foundation for AIDS Research. The article first appeared in *Journal of Policy History* 9, no. 1 (1997).

9. Total medical research funding (excluding research by drug companies and other medical products manufacturers) was $12.7 billion in 1990, and $17.1 billion in 1995, according to the Center for Medicare and Medicaid Services (http://cms.hhs.gov/statistics/nhe/historical/), Table 2. AIDS plus breast cancer funding was $834 million in 1990, and $1.803 billion in 1995 (see previous note). Total federal spending was $1,229 billion in 1990 and $1,576 billion in 1995; GDP was $5,803 billion in 1990, and $7,400 billion in 1995, according to the National Income and Product Accounts from the Bureau of Economic Analysis (http://bea.gov/bea/dn1.htm). All figures are in current dollars.

10. "Weed Killer Deforms Frogs in Sex Organs, Study Finds," *New York Times* (April 17, 2002), A19.

11. Richard T. Woodward and Richard C. Bishop, "How to Decide When Experts Disagree: Uncertainty-Based Choice Rules in Environmental Policy," *Land Economics* 73 (November 1997), 492–507.

12. Alternatives assessment is emphasized in Mary O'Brien, *Making Better Environmental Decisions: An Alternative to Risk Assessment* (Cambridge, MA: MIT Press, 2000).

13. Jeffrey L. Coles and Peter Hammond, "Walrasian Equilibrium without Survival: Existence, Efficiency, and Remedial Policy," in *Choice, Welfare, and Development: Festschrift in Honor of Amartya K. Sen,* ed. K. Basu, P. Pattanaik, and K. Suzumuru (New York: Oxford University Press, 1995), 32–64.

14. Alejandro Nadal, "Zea Mays: Effects of Trade Liberalization of Mexico's Corn Sector," in *Greening the Americas: NAFTA's Lessons for Hemispheric Trade,* ed. Carolyn L. Deere and Daniel C. Esty (Cambridge, MA: MIT Press, 2002); Nadal, *The Environmental and Social Impacts of Economic Liberalization on Corn Production in Mexico* (Washington, DC: World Wildlife Fund for Nature, 2000).

15. Richard B. Howarth and Richard B. Norgaard, "Intergenerational Transfers and the Social Discount Rate," *Environmental and Resource Economics* 3

(1993), 337–58; discussed in Ackerman et al., *Human Well-Being and Economic Goals.*

16. Mark Sagoff, *The Economy of the Earth: Philosophy, Law, and the Environment* (Cambridge:Cambridge University Press, 1988).

17. For an economic analysis along these lines, see Daniel W. Bromley, "Searching for Sustainability: The Poverty of Spontaneous Order," *Ecological Economics* 24 (1998), 231–40.

Acknowledgments

We are indebted to many people for their help with this book and the work that preceded it.

In the beginning, this book was made possible by Karen Florini, senior attorney at Environmental Defense, who introduced us by sending us electronic copies of each other's work and suggesting we join forces. It was co-authorship at first sight, and even before: thanks to Karen, we started writing the book together before we ever met in person.

Diane Wachtell of The New Press wisely encouraged us to write a book that would be accessible to a broad audience, and reined in our innate tendency toward delving ever deeper into the details of the debates. She made the book better in many ways, large and small. Beth Slovic patiently shepherded the manuscript through the production process. The Bauman Foundation provided crucial financial support for the writing and marketing of the book.

At Tufts and at Georgetown, we have benefited from the many insights of students, friends, and colleagues. For comments on individual chapters, we thank Toni Amato, Les Boden, Cornelia Herzfeld, Tom Webster, and Frank's students in environmental economics. For comments on the whole manuscript, we are grateful to Kevin Gallagher, Jennifer Lappin, Rachel Massey, and Tim Wise. At Georgetown, Erin Ekeberg, Daniel Holloway, Sandra Kaczmarczyk, Adam Lazar, Marguerite McLamb, John Ritsick, and Trevor Wiessmann provided fabulous research assistance for the book and/or for academic work leading to the ideas expressed here—as did Regina Flores and Eliza Waters at Tufts. Faculty workshops at numerous law schools around the country furnished stimulating ideas and criticisms for Lisa's contributions to the book, and workshops and seminars at Tufts, the University of Massachusetts, and Georgetown did the same for Frank.

Many people have helped, more generally and over a long period, to shape the ideas presented here. Our (joint and individual) ongoing collaborations and friendships with John Echeverria, Kevin Gallagher, Steve Goldberg, Richard Lazarus, Rachel Massey, Tom McGarity, Gerry Spann, Rena Steinzor, Cass Sunstein, Robin West, and Tim Wise have enriched our thinking and our work. Parts of several chapters first emerged in work we did at the request of the Natural Resources Defense Council, Riverkeeper, and groups active in the anti-toxics movement—all of whom wanted to understand and be able to respond to the intricately technical, anti-environmental economics that has become so powerful in public life today. We hope this book helps them, and all our readers, write the next chapter in the unfinished story of health and environmental protection.

Frank Ackerman
Tufts University, Global Development and Environment Institute

Lisa Heinzerling
Georgetown University Law Center

Index